ECHOES OF
COMBAT

ANCHOR BOOKS DOUBLEDAY
NEW YORK LONDON TORONTO SYDNEY AUCKLAND

ECHOES OF
COMBAT

THE VIETNAM WAR IN
AMERICAN MEMORY

FRED TURNER

AN ANCHOR BOOK
PUBLISHED BY DOUBLEDAY
a division of Bantam Doubleday Dell Publishing Group, Inc.
1540 Broadway, New York, New York 10036

ANCHOR BOOKS, DOUBLEDAY, and the portrayal of an anchor are trademarks of
Doubleday, a division of Bantam Doubleday Dell Publishing Group, Inc.

BOOK DESIGN BY F. J. LEVINE

Excerpt from *Four Hours in My Lai* by Michael Bilton and Kevin Sim. Copyright © 1992
by Michael Bilton and Kevin Sim. Used by permission of Viking Penguin, a division of
Penguin Books USA Inc.

Excerpts from *Warrior Dreams: Violence and Manhood in Post-Vietnam America* by James
William Gibson. Copyright © 1994 by James William Gibson. Reprinted by permission
of Hill and Wang, a division of Farrar, Straus & Giroux, Inc.

Excerpts from *Close Quarters* by Larry Heinemann. Copyright © 1977 by Larry
Heinemann. Reprinted by permission of Farrar, Straus & Giroux, Inc.

Library of Congress Cataloging-in-Publication Data
Turner, Fred.
    Echoes of combat: the Vietnam war in American memory / Fred Turner.
        p.   cm.
    Includes bibliographical references and index.
    1. Vietnamese Conflict, 1963–1975—United States.   2. Vietnamese Conflict, 1963–
1975—Psychological aspects.   3. United States—Civilization—1970–   I. Title.
    DS558.T87   1996
    959.704′3373—dc20   96-20601
                                                                              CIP

ISBN 0-385-47563-2
Copyright © 1996 by Fred Turner

CONTENTS

ACKNOWLEDGMENTS

I COULD NOT HAVE WRITTEN THIS BOOK WITHOUT THE encouragement and assistance of many people. First and foremost, I'd like to thank the Vietnam veterans with whom I've worked and especially the members of the Veterans Improvement Program (VIP) of Boston, Massachusetts, for entrusting me with their recollections of combat and its aftermath. I'm also grateful to the VIP staff—Dr. Lisa Fisher, Christine Makary, Dr. Jonathan Shay, and particularly Dr. James Munroe—for helping me to understand the nature of post-traumatic stress disorder. Likewise, I'm thankful to Dr. David Lisak of the University of Massachusetts at Boston and Dr. Terence Keane, Director of the National Center for Post-Traumatic Stress Disorder, both of whom have gone out of their way to familiarize me with current research on psychological trauma.

For their attention to the book's historical and cultural dimensions, I am deeply indebted to Marilyn Young of New York University and Michael Schudson of the University of California–San Diego. Through conversation, correspondence, and generous comments on chapters, both pushed me toward a more complex understanding of the war and the processes of social memory than I could have come to on my own. I'm also grateful to Chris Appy of the Massachusetts Institute of Technology for his extensive knowledge of the war and of veterans' lives and for his willingness to share it and to Betsy Sherman for admitting me into her unique archive of postwar pop culture artifacts.

It would have been extremely difficult to find the time and resources to complete this book without the support of Suzanne Flynn and the Department of Foreign Languages and Literatures at the Massachusetts Institute of Technology. In my time as a lecturer and visiting researcher in the department, I have enjoyed not only the use of MIT's facilities, but the chance to participate in the daily life of a department permeated with a sense of intellectual adventure and camaraderie. I'd also like to thank Paul Vermouth, Michael Pavelecky, and the staff of the MIT Humanities Library for tracking down hard-to-find materials and for teaching me how to do the same. At Harvard University, I'm grateful to Jan Shubert of the John F. Kennedy School of Government for her confidence in my work, her advice, and her willingness to help me find my way into the university's extensive research facilities. I'd like to thank Lars Erickson and Judy Hung for donating the computer on which I wrote this book and for offering good company during the writing. Thanks too go to my energetic and efficient research assistant, Sarah McGrath.

I'm extremely lucky to have found my way to my editor, Charles Flowers, and my agent, Geri Thoma. Generous, gentle, and thorough, both have been a pleasure to work with.

There is a small group of people to whom I am especially indebted. When I was younger, Rebecca Busselle and Bop Sinclair each took me into their homes and gave me examples of how I might live an emotionally engaged and intellectually committed life—examples I have always tried to follow, if not always successfully. Patricia Caldwell and Michael Harper taught me to love American history and literature and trusted me to find my own voice. Some years later, when I was in danger of losing that voice, Dr. David Doolittle and Penny Locey helped me find it again.

Most of all, I'm grateful to my friend Bill Marx and to my wife, Annie Fischer. Each read every draft of this book, curbing my excesses, urging me to expand where necessary, and always encouraging me to keep writing. They were my first readers and they remain my closest companions.

ECHOES OF
COMBAT

CHAPTER ONE

PRIVATE TRAUMA
AND PUBLIC MEMORY

ON MAY 24, 1992, THE DAY BEFORE MEMORIAL DAY, SOME 25,000 motorcyclists, many of them Vietnam veterans, straddle their bikes, start their engines, and roar by the gates of Arlington National Cemetery. Two-by-two they turn out over the Potomac on their way to the Vietnam Veterans Memorial in Washington, D.C. The noise of their engines makes the pavement shake. Some fly huge American flags off the backs of their bikes; others the black-and-white banners of the POW-MIA movement. Some are fat, tattooed, long-haired, hoary; others skinny, spick-and-span in their leather jackets.

Like soldiers on parade, they ride by precisely and it's hard not to hear the echoes of combat twenty years before. From the giant engines of their Harleys comes the *whump-whump-whump* of old Huey helicopters. Riders aim video cameras at onlookers as if they were M-16 rifles. Motorcycle helmets replace boonie hats, while leather vests stand in for flack jackets. Even the name of the event, Operation Rolling Thunder, belongs to the past: In 1965 it was President Johnson's code name for America's bombing of North Vietnam. For these veterans, the long convoy into the heart of Washington, D.C., isn't just a bit of nostalgia, but a mission: a memory of combat twisted by time and reenacted.

When they reach the Mall, they leave their bikes in the grass and begin to mill. On the steps below the Lincoln Memorial, the rally's organizers exhort the crowd to remember those still missing in Southeast Asia. "American soldiers are expendable!" shouts Top Holland, a stocky POW-MIA activist in camouflage fatigues. "America doesn't care about POWs, just like they didn't care about soldiers in battle!" His audience whistles, claps, hoots.

As he speaks, veterans and others cluster on the paths that lead into and out of the Vietnam Veterans Memorial. In twos and fours they walk down the alley of souvenir stands lining the approach to the Memorial. They finger bracelets engraved with the names of soldiers still missing in action. Each bracelet comes with a typed sheet detailing what the man was doing when he was last seen: bailing out of a plane, fighting back an ambush. The veterans study these sheets, maybe buy a bracelet, and move on to look at T-shirts with the words I SURVIVED THE TET OFFENSIVE written over orange flames, or shirts with the POW-MIA logo—the silhouette of a bowed head seen against a guard tower and a strand of barbed wire—and the words YOU ARE NOT FORGOTTEN.

Down a little way from the T-shirt stands there is a tent surrounded by pamphlet tables and sign-up sheets for the In Touch program, through which the children of soldiers killed in Vietnam try to find men who knew their fathers. The names of the dead fathers are posted; men who might have known them can leave their names and addresses and the details of their wartime service. The program is sponsored by Electronic Data Systems Corporation, headed by Ross Perot. All up and down the paths to the Memorial there are signs of his presidential campaign. The front page of the *U.S. Veteran News and Report*'s April issue headlines "The Magic of H. Ross Perot." A sandwich board displaying hazy black-and-white photographs of Americans purported to still be prisoners in Hanoi offers the message WE NEED ROSS, as if Perot could bring the men in the snapshots home.

A few feet from the sign a veteran named Michael Miholics is standing behind a card table showing passersby how to play Vietnam Survival

Tour—365, a board game he's invented. The playing board consists of 365 tiny green squares (numbered for the days in a standard Army tour of duty) surrounding a large square labeled POW CAMP HANOI HILTON (after the infamous wartime prison). At the beginning of the game, each player is issued a twelve-man platoon. To win, he has to march his platoon through all 365 days of its tour, overcome obstacles such as "satchel charges" and "free-fire zones," and liberate the prisoners in the Hanoi Hilton. According to Miholics's glossy promo brochure, "the game is a history lesson and the results are both educational and lots of fun."

Listening to him make his pitch, I can't help but wonder: How could a twice-wounded infantryman like Miholics finger the game's green plastic soldiers without recalling his own suffering or that of the men around him? How could his children land on the square marked ZIPPO (as in the cigarette lighter) without wondering whether their father had himself set fire to the thatched huts of the Vietnamese? Miholics's brochure describes Vietnam Survival Tour—365 as "A game that takes your patrol on a tour of duty thru [sic] the jungles of Vietnam. Can you survive the tour? Can you survive without ordering the game that will survive?" Neither the American soldiers who are Miholics's game pieces nor the civilians who manipulate them are aggressors, but rather, survivors. Victory in the game does not mean, as it once did in Vietnam, crushing the Viet Cong. It is now enough simply to have stayed alive. And in his brochure, Miholics implies that the rest of us will not survive without "ordering the game," without literally *buying into* a certain set of rules for remembering, for *replaying* the war.

Miholics's game does contain a grain of historical truth. For many combat soldiers in Vietnam, survival really was the only form of victory. Brought into their units one at a time, made to fight for twelve or fourteen months, and sent home alone, many grunts of the Vietnam era, unlike their fathers in World War II, saw little connection between their personal tours of duty and the aims and scope of America's national commitment to the war. Against a guerrilla enemy whose soldiers could stage an ambush and then melt back into the jungle or the local civilian population, American infantrymen often were the potential victims that Miholics's game makes them out to be.

Still, watching Miholics take orders for the game, I can't help feeling like I've tumbled down the rabbit hole of history. Twenty-two years ago, from April 19 through April 23, 1971, 2,000 Vietnam veterans occupied this same spot. Led by Vietnam Veterans Against the War (VVAW), they called their demonstration Dewey Canyon III. Dewey Canyons I and II had been the names of American incursions into Laos; according to the VVAW, Dewey Canyon III would be "a limited incursion into the country of Congress." Over the course of four days, they camped on the Mall, marched across the Potomac from the Lincoln Memorial to Arlington National Cemetery, and hurled dozens of ribbons and medals, including Bronze Stars and Purple Hearts, over a wire police fence and onto the steps of the Capitol. Unlike the veterans of Operation Rolling Thunder, they were ashamed of their service and eager to find some way to turn their time in Southeast Asia to account. Their spokesman, John Kerry, a Navy veteran and now a U.S. Senator from Massachusetts, addressed the Senate Foreign Relations Committee:

> We are here to ask: Where are McNamara, Rostow, Bundy, Johnson, and so many others? Where are they now that we, the men whom they sent off to war, have returned? . . . We wish that a merciful God could wipe away our own memories of that service as easily as this Administration has wiped away their memories of us. But all that they have done and all that they can do by this denial is to make more clear than ever our own determination to undertake one last mission—to search out and destroy the last vestige of this barbaric war . . . so when thirty years from now our brothers go down the street without a leg, without an arm, or a face, and small boys ask why, we will be able to say "Vietnam" and not mean a desert, not a filthy obscene memory, but mean instead the place where America finally turned and where soldiers like us helped in the turning.

For Kerry and the men of Dewey Canyon III, Vietnam was more than a 365-day survival tour. It was a war that lopped off legs and arms and for its veterans, "a filthy obscene memory" they wished "a merciful God could wipe away." For the men of Operation Rolling Thunder, on the other hand, the Vietnam War was neither "filthy" nor "obscene," but something to take pride in having survived. Far from wishing their memories washed away, the veterans of 1992 were building whole identities around their participation in the war. They belonged to motorcycle clubs open only to Vietnam vets and wore jackets embossed with maps of Vietnam. They worked the POW information booth or boosted Ross Perot. For these men, the war was no longer the poisonous source of shame that it had been for John Kerry. On the contrary, like other, more popular wars before it, Vietnam was a source of memories to be celebrated with a parade.

After watching that parade, I wondered what had happened, how it was that a war that many Americans would have agreed by its end was a colossal mistake, if not an outright obscenity, could now spark a celebration. How was it that less than twenty years after the last Americans choppered out of Saigon, one could think of the war, as Michael Miholics did, and have "lots of fun"?

Not long after leaving Miholics, I met Roger Hulbein. A big man, Hulbein has a panther tattooed the length of one forearm; his knuckles are studded with silver rings—a skull, a Harley-Davidson eagle. His given name is Roger, but he was an Army sergeant in the war and he goes by Sarge now. As we got to talking, he explained that he had driven supply trucks in Vietnam and had seen some combat. But in the seventeen years since his discharge, he had stopped admitting he was a veteran. He had become a fireman and worked a lot of overtime. "The only socializing I ever did was in bars," he said. And when people in bars asked him if he was in the war, he said no.

Then, four years ago, a high school friend who was also a vet was helping Hulbein clean out his basement. Rummaging through some boxes, his friend found Hulbein's discharge papers and his Purple Heart. "He started telling me it was okay to be a vet," said Hulbein, "and that I had nothing to be ashamed of."

A year later his friend took Hulbein to the Vietnam Veterans Memorial. "He knew what was going to happen, but he didn't tell me," said Hulbein. "I walked by it eighteen times before I got to the wall." When Hulbein started down the flagstone path into the Memorial, he kept his eyes on his feet. "It was right there, but I couldn't look up. I remember a lot of fear. I remember feeling a lot of guilt. I tried to think about the guys who I knew who were there on the wall whose names I still can't remember."

A few weeks after he got home from that trip, his memories of combat began to visit him. "I was having dreams. I was seeing faces, names without faces, faces without names. I started waking up in the night, in fear. I would be so soaking wet the first couple of times I could have sworn I pissed the bed. The dog looked at me like I had fourteen heads."

In one memory Hulbein and a friend named Washington drove supplies to a base in the village of Lai Khe. "He was a black kid, all of four feet tall," said Hulbein. "He had, like, five presidents' names. His mother liked presidents. Any time I got terrified, I could find him and he could make me comfortable. He could make me laugh. He had this attitude: If he was gonna die, he was gonna die happy." That night he and Washington were talking to some friends out on the perimeter. They were standing around laughing when the jungle erupted: Bullets popped, mortars thumped, rockets hissed in from the tree line. "We ran for the bunkers," said Hulbein, his voice flat. "The stuff was kind of close. He went one way and I went another way. They said he went headfirst into the hole and the rocket went right in after him." After the firestorm had passed, Hulbein dug through the ruins of Washington's bunker for three hours. He sorted through arms and legs and torsos, the bones and bits of flesh of the forty men inside. He never found Washington.

For Hulbein, Vietnam really was a 365-day survival tour, and he had lived what Miholics's customers would merely play. He had also brought out with him a knowledge of combat that he was willing to share. Listening to him talk about the death of Washington, I remembered a man I knew who had been a Marine in World War II. This man had witnessed slaughter on Iwo Jima, but the most he would ever say about the fighting on the island was that it was "tough." Maybe he had his own reasons for keeping quiet, but I wonder whether he also saw that the 24,000 Marines who were killed or wounded on the island have faded from our minds. The Battle of Iwo Jima lingers in our popular memory as an image of five men struggling together to raise a flag. What veteran would stain that picture of handsome young men and their derring-do with bloody recollections of hand-to-hand combat?

But after Vietnam there was no image of victory to defend. Instead, there was the fact of defeat. More than 58,000 Americans had lost their lives. More than *three million* Vietnamese had been killed, nearly two million of whom were civilians. Americans had dropped seven million

tons of bombs and defoliated six million acres of the Vietnamese countryside and still, in April 1975, the North Vietnamese Army had swept
into Saigon. Americans had lost their first war and with it, their confidence not only in their political and military leaders, but in the moral
righteousness of their nation.

Hulbein's experience explains how what was unspeakable after
World War II might have offered Americans a way of making sense of
Vietnam. In a way, Hulbein's private loss at Lai Khe could be read as an
emblem of America's national losses in the war. As he described himself
standing in the ruins of Washington's bunker, Hulbein depicted himself
as a helpless giant, trapped in the jungles of Asia, much like the one that
many Americans once saw their country as. The bodies around him
could symbolize the thousands of American men and women who lost
their lives during the war. The randomness of their deaths—Why was
Washington's bunker blown up and not Hulbein's?—suggested itself as a
model for the pointlessness of the conflict in which they died. The
invisibility of the enemy, the way they fired from and merged back into
the jungle, illuminated the hypervisibility of the American army and its
ignorance of Vietnam's physical and social landscape. The solitude in
which Hulbein described himself digging recalled the loneliness in
which thousands of mothers and fathers, girlfriends and boyfriends,
brothers and sisters of the dead greeted the aluminum coffins that slid
down the ramps of C-130 cargo planes every day for more than ten
years.

As the years have gone by, the outline of Hulbein's story has in fact
become a common one. In memoirs and oral histories, veterans have
traced their descent from the safety and order of the pre-combat world
into the lethal chaos of battle. They have recalled seeing beliefs they
thought were secure upended and crushed and with them, their faith in
the possibility of community. Again and again, they have described
themselves as solitary men, caught like Hulbein in a universe of gore.
Their stories have also found echoes in the most popular postwar films
and novels about Vietnam. In Francis Ford Coppola's cinema epic *Apocalypse Now,* for instance, the CIA sends Willard the assassin deep into the
jungle to kill the renegade Colonel Kurtz. When Willard finds him,
Kurtz has cut himself off from everyone he knew—his family, his
friends, the Army. He now inhabits a crumbling palace, surrounded by

the bloody corpses of his enemies. Like Hulbein, Kurtz finds himself alone in a universe of carnage. And nearly ten years later, in *Rambo: First Blood Part II,* the most popular of dozens of prisoner of war rescue flicks, American soldiers are locked up in bamboo cages in the middle of the jungle, nearly mute. Kurtz might have opted to go off on his own, but these men have lost all powers of choice. Like Hulbein at the moment the rockets fell, they have been cut off by circumstance from everything they love and afflicted with a terrifying isolation.

This desperate solitude is the disease the doctors of the sitcom *M*A*S*H* have had to cure, the wound the nurses of the TV series *China Beach* have had to sew up and kiss away. Nor is it confined to the jungles of Southeast Asia. In any number of novels about the war, by veterans and civilians alike, it is a kind of psychological syphilis brought home from the front. Take the hero of veteran Larry Heinemann's *Paco's Story* (1979), a popular novel that is often assigned to college classes on the war. Paco is the sole survivor of his platoon. For two days, he lies wounded, surrounded by the bodies of his comrades and the jungle. When he eventually returns to the States, he is crippled, his skin pocked with shrapnel scars. He lives alone in a rooming house, surrounded by the ghosts of his friends and the jungle of his now strange and threatening homeland. Somehow, over the last two decades, the knowledge of helplessness, isolation, and loss in combat, a knowledge almost unspeakable for the men who fought World War II, has seeped into our culture at large. The image of a solitary soldier lost in a jungle, surrounded by death and dismemberment, an image born on an actual battlefield, has come to life as a public symbol for the entire American experience of the war.

But how did it acquire its uncanny power? During the war years, especially the years after the 1968 Tet Offensive and the disclosure of the My Lai massacre in 1969, the American soldier was often depicted as omnipotent, a Techno-God who delighted in leveling jungles and rounding up helpless peasant farmers. A 1965 photograph, for example, which was used as an antiwar poster for many years, shows fifteen or twenty Vietnamese—women with nursing babies, a toothless old man, a boy with his hands up—huddled against a crumbling stone wall. Over them looms an American GI whose huge forearms make the limbs of the

Vietnamese look birdlike. In the photo he looks back over his shoulder to the cameraman, but only for a moment. His M-16 still points at the huddle of Vietnamese as if, once the photograph has been taken, he'll return to the business of execution. In addition, many who opposed the fighting, particularly in the wake of My Lai, tended to see American GIs as atrocity-makers, even Nazis. "Most American soldiers in Viet-Nam do not question the orders that lead them to raze villages and wipe out men, women and children for the 'crime' of living in Viet Cong-controlled or -infiltrated areas," wrote Eric Norden, a reporter for the left-wing monthly *Liberation,* in 1966. "To many critics of the war this 'new breed of Americans' bears a disquieting resemblance to an old breed of Germans."

How is it then, that in little more than twenty years, the image of the American soldier as executioner should have vanished and that of the American soldier as victim should have taken its place? Why do so many Americans cling as tenaciously now to the image of the veteran-as-survivor as they once did to the notion of the GI-as-stone-cold-killer?

The questions tangle, breed, multiply. Was Vietnam something Americans did? Or was it something that happened to them? By commemorating the war, by talking about it in novels and movies and memoirs and poems, what exactly are Americans remembering? A war they launched, a horror they endured, some combination of the two? And what about the men who did the fighting? What has become of their terrible knowledge?

One thing seems clear: Soldiers in war lead double lives. On the one hand, they are private men engaged in the business of defending and attacking, killing and being killed. On the other, they represent the society that sent them into battle. As soon as they put on their uniforms, they become "our boys"—literally *and* figuratively. What they do, they do on our behalf, and in that sense, we do it too. When they kill, we kill; when they are wounded, we are wounded. Despite the insistence of many veterans on the primacy of their own experiences, Sarge Hulbein is not the only one who has to bear the horror of the attack at Lai Khe. Symbolically, at least, the memories he brought home belong to all of us. Retold in novels and films and volumes of history, these violent, private recollections have become the stuff of our collective nightmares.

They have confronted us with the fact that we too can be—and as citizens of the nation that sent Hulbein to war, collectively have been—destroyers and destroyed, victims and wreakers of havoc.

That knowledge has left a rift in both the private memories of traumatized combat veterans such as Hulbein and in our collective responses to the war as well. As psychiatrists such as Robert Jay Lifton and Judith Herman have pointed out, attacks like the one at Lai Khe are lessons to their survivors. They teach that life, order, and companionship are illusions. In the language of terror, they whisper that the *real* world is one where friends disappear for no reason, where the landscape is full of hidden killers, where no matter how deep you dig your bunker, a rocket can always find its way in. The survivor of such horror is forced to contend with two competing visions of the world: one of relative order before the attack and one of mayhem after.

If the two pictures can't be reconciled right away—and usually they can't—a new kind of memory emerges. During his first trip to the Vietnam Veterans Memorial, Sarge Hulbein "tried to think" about the men he knew on the wall. He tried to recall the past and by recalling, control it. But when he got home, his past took control of him. "Names without faces, faces without names" swam up into his mind unbidden. His body began to sweat with the terror he had known in Vietnam twenty years before. It was as if the universe of dismemberment revealed by Washington's death had hovered alongside the last two decades of Hulbein's life. Hulbein had built a marriage, had children, bought a house, gotten a good job, and made what from the outside looked like a well-ordered life. But hiding in the back of his mind, mocking his achievements, lay the knowledge that bunkers could be collapsed, companions destroyed, and bodies blown apart.

Psychiatrist Mardi Horowitz, an expert in human responses to extreme stress, has written that attacks like the one at Lai Khe present their survivors with a dilemma: If they accept the fact that they can be killed by a rocket on a moment's notice and at random, they give up their belief in their own ability to control their futures and become paralyzed. Why should they do anything if, a few seconds from now, a rocket might destroy them? On the other hand, if they cling to their original belief that the world is a reasonably predictable, well-ordered place, that bunkers provide safety and that people die in combat for reasons they can control, they will have to deny all the evidence to the contrary that they have just seen.

To resolve this dilemma, says Horowitz, most people try to set the new, disruptive information aside and cling to their original beliefs. But the traumatic event doesn't go away. Instead, it asserts itself in nightmares, daydreams, and compulsions. Hulbein finds himself waking up soaked with sweat. Other soldiers speak of walking down the street, scanning parked cars for snipers. Sometimes full-blown flashbacks occur and the soldier finds himself back in Vietnam or Korea or the Argonne Forest. The idiom in which the traumatic memory makes itself known varies, but the message remains the same: This new information somehow has to be brought together with the worldview it seems to shatter. Somehow the terrible helplessness of a man crouched in a filthy mud bunker, listening to the rockets fall, has to be woven into the life of a middle-aged father and fireman.

Until it is, Horowitz explains, the survivor of horror will endure an excruciating cycle of consciously remembering and seeming to forget. He will thrust the images that threaten him deep into his unconscious. The deeper he pushes them, the calmer he feels. Then, like sea monsters when the surface of the ocean is smooth, the images will rear up. The survivor will endure what he can, then submerge his memories once more, and the cycle will repeat itself. According to Horowitz, only when the survivor can draw new maps of the world, maps which incorporate both the horrific landscapes of the past and the comparatively well-ordered fields of the present, will the wheels of recollection and denial grind to a halt.

Looking back at the last twenty years of movies and books about the Vietnam War, I believe we can see Horowitz's cycle at work in American culture at large. By the time the last Americans had been airlifted out of Saigon, the war had posed a series of challenges to American beliefs, challenges at least as threatening to those beliefs as the rocket attack on Lai Khe was to the worldview of Sarge Hulbein. When they drove their conquering tanks onto the grounds of South Vietnam's Presidential Palace in 1975, the North Vietnamese taught Americans that they were not exceptional, that like other peoples they could be defeated in war, even by members of a race they had thought subhuman. When the Viet Cong converted C-ration cans into explosive booby traps or lined trails with pungi sticks, Americans learned that the advanced technology which made them call themselves a "superpower" could be rendered powerless. And when they committed atrocities, when they destroyed hamlets in order to save them or napalmed civilians, Americans taught themselves that they were no more humane than they had imagined their enemies to be.

The Vietnam War presented Americans with a dilemma: On the one hand, Americans could cling to the popular image of a pre-Vietnam, post–World War II America—industrial giant, loyal ally, beacon of the "free" world; on the other, they could accept the evidence of the war that for all its industrial and military might, America was no more moral than other nations—it could still start an unnecessary war, lose it, and commit numerous atrocities along the way. Nor was this simply an abstract choice. Thousands of young American men had killed and died on behalf of the first image. If it were to disintegrate, what would justify the harm they had done and the sacrifices they had made?

In the years immediately after the war, many Americans did what Sarge Hulbein did: They tried to avoid reminders of the war. Veterans, of course, were the most visible reminders of all. As their society's representatives on the field of battle, they had come to stand for all that Americans were ashamed of in the war. After the fighting ended, their presence challenged the prewar symbolic order for which many Americans longed much as Hulbein's memories of Lai Khe challenged his own assumptions about the safety and coherence of his postwar world. For that reason, established veterans organizations such as the Veterans of Foreign Wars or the American Legion often turned Vietnam veterans away from their posts and refused to support legislation on their behalf. Even the families of returning soldiers admonished their sons not to talk about where they had been. Vietnam veterans were to be neither heard nor seen, but were to blend into civilian American society as if they had never been to Southeast Asia.

Like Sarge Hulbein, many Americans hoped to hang on to a worldview that had in fact been shattered by the war. On April 23, 1975, a week before the fall of Saigon, more than a few were ready to believe President Gerald Ford when he told an audience at Tulane University:

Today America can again regain the sense of pride that existed before Vietnam. But it cannot be achieved by refighting a war that is finished—as far as America is concerned. The time has come to look forward to an agenda for the future, to unity, to binding up the nation's wounds and restoring it to health and optimistic self-confidence.

On the same day that Ford was asking his audience to stop "refighting" the war in their memories, a group of government maintenance workers back in Washington, D.C., was covering up the Tomb of the Unknown for the Vietnam War. Congress had authorized the Tomb in 1973, yet even though it had been marked by a smooth, 5,000-pound slab of white marble, it remained empty in 1975. As North Vietnamese forces pushed toward Saigon and the President asked Americans to put the war behind them, the government grounds crew removed the white marble slab and replaced it with the red granite blocks used as flooring around the Tombs of other wars. The hollow crypt remained, but was now invisible. Not until 1982 was the empty vault marked with a plaque and not until 1984 were the remains of an unknown soldier from the Vietnam War actually interred there. For many in the late 1970s, the Vietnam War was a blank, a hollow space to be hidden and ignored.

The national fog of silence and denial began to lift in 1980, when Congress authorized the construction of the Vietnam Veterans Memorial in Washington, D.C., and Ronald Reagan, in a campaign speech to the Veterans of Foreign Wars, announced that "It is time we recognized that [in Vietnam] ours, in truth, was a noble cause. We dishonor the memory of 50,000 young Americans who died in that cause when we give way to feelings of guilt. . . ." Suddenly it seemed that what had been hidden could now be dug up and brought into the light. The soil of the Mall could be scooped away to reveal a shiny black granite list of the names of the dead. Veterans could emerge from their houses and wear their uniforms without being insulted. The long night of horror seemed to be over. By 1984, Reagan was proclaiming that it was now "Morning in America."

New mornings do not make old nights go away, nor do new victories erase old defeats. On the contrary, they measure their power to haunt. For a conflict that so many once wanted to forget, the Vietnam War has spawned an astonishingly large memory industry. In the last fifteen years, more than 1,000 books about the war have been published; today there are still more than 750 in print. There have been dozens of films—prisoner of war flicks like *Rambo: First Blood Part II,* conventional men-at-arms tales like *Platoon* or *Full Metal Jacket,* homecoming sagas like *The Deer Hunter* or *Coming Home.* There have been comic books, records, posters, political speeches, newspaper articles, magazine features, photo albums, art exhibitions, collections of poetry, replica medals, T-shirts, bumper stickers, doctoral dissertations, scholarly journals, congressional inquiries, radio talk shows, weekly newsletters, and monthly magazines devoted to the war. Once repressed, memories of Vietnam have been returning in spades.

But what is it exactly that Americans are remembering? And what are they forgetting?

CHAPTER TWO

THE HORROR, THE HORROR:

THE VIETNAM WAR AS INDIVIDUAL AND CULTURAL TRAUMA

BETWEEN AUGUST 1965 AND AUGUST 1966, ROBERT MASON flew Army helicopters in South Vietnam, an experience he recounts in his memoir *Chickenhawk*. Day after day he would load his helicopter with teams of infantrymen and fly into the jungle. Often, as he tried to land, he would see Viet Cong tracer bullets seeking out his ship or hear them *tick-tick-tick* into the side of his helicopter. "I learned how to function, even though I was scared shitless," he writes. "I had become efficient, numb, or stupid." In the course of his twelve-month tour of duty, Mason survived dozens of near-death situations, witnessed the execution of unarmed Vietnamese prisoners and the mutilation of American corpses, and still kept flying. By the end of his year in the battle zone, though, the numbness had taken its toll and he had begun to hallucinate. When he got home to the United States, Mason set up housekeeping with his wife and son and enrolled in college, but his memories of combat snuck up on him anyway. In daydreams and nightmares they turned his bedroom into a jungle, refused him rest, and disrupted the life he was trying to build for himself.

Nor was Mason alone. Between 1959 and 1975, more than a million and a half Americans saw combat in Vietnam. When they came home, psychologists estimate that as many as 40 percent of them brought with them some form of post-traumatic stress disorder (PTSD). Like those afflicted with "shell shock" after World War I or with "combat fatigue" during World War II, soldiers who acquired PTSD in Vietnam suffered repeated intrusive recollections of combat. Simultaneously drawn to and repelled by situations like those that had traumatized them, they felt compelled both to reenact and to run from the mayhem they had experienced. In Vietnam, these soldiers had seen acts of extraordinary violence, acts that threatened to undermine everything they believed about the world, overwhelm their senses, and leave them psychologically paralyzed. In order to survive, these men set aside the full emotional impact of what they had seen, locked their experiences in the back rooms of their psyches, and got on with what they had to do. But when they returned to the safety of the United States, their memories haunted them. They found themselves faced with the long-delayed task of integrating a horrific past into a pacific present.

So too did the country that sent them into the fray. The Vietnam War was as damaging to the myths of American culture as the experience of combat was to the beliefs of American soldiers. Not since the Civil War had Americans seen the kind of riots and upheaval that accompanied the fighting in Southeast Asia. Beamed into millions of living rooms on the evening news, the war exploded Americans' assumptions about themselves and their society. Split into doves and hawks, hippies and hard hats, civilian Americans were caught, like combat veterans, between a knowledge of the war's horror, a horror largely brought down on Vietnam by Americans themselves, and the memory of a seemingly safe, coherent prewar world. Psychologists tell us that the foundation of psychological health is a faith, acquired in infancy, that the world makes sense, that it has an order, and preferably a benevolent order, within which an individual can take his or her place. For both combat soldiers and civilians, the Vietnam War offered a direct challenge to that faith.

For combat soldiers, the challenge could be as immediate and extreme as a land mine or an enemy ambush. For civilians, the challenge was far more subtle. The war had not—and never could—put lives at risk in America itself. For civilians, it was the *idea* of America, rather than the country's borders or the survival of their families, that came to be at stake in Vietnam. In that sense, the threat the war posed to civilian psychological security was far less extreme than the threat combat posed to soldiers.

Even so, the war had similar effects on both combatants and civilians. In the early 1960s, many Americans thought of their individual place in the world very much in terms of their nation's mythology. In his 1989 memoir *In the New World: Growing Up with America from the Sixties to the Eighties,* journalist Lawrence Wright recalls that in the wake of World War II, "America had a mission—we thought it was a divine mission— to spread freedom, and freedom meant democracy, and democracy meant capitalism, and all that meant the American way of life." For individual citizens, the "American way of life" boiled down to the daily round. Every day a man left his house to participate in capitalism, and as he did, he could believe himself to have a place in the divine order of democracy. He was an agent of the divine will, both an example of and a proselyte for the godly principle of "individual freedom." His personal happiness and success were the results and reflections of the culture's general well-being.

Against this psychological background, the war in Vietnam seemed to take shape as another in a long line of national missions. American leaders repeatedly depicted the war not merely as an abstract, political affair, but as a deeply personal struggle. What was at stake in Vietnam, they claimed, was much more than the fate of a small Asian country—it was each American's individual place in the divine drama of democracy and freedom. Speaking in February 1965, for instance, President Lyndon Johnson announced that "History and our own achievements have thrust upon us the principal responsibility for protection of freedom on earth. . . . No other people in no other time has had so great an opportunity to work and risk for the freedom of all mankind." A year later, in Honolulu, Johnson explained that "In the forties and fifties, we took our stand in Europe to protect the freedom of those threatened by aggression. . . . Now the center of attention has shifted to another part of the world where aggression is on the march and the enslavement of free men is the goal. . . . That is why it is vitally important to every American family that we stop the Communists in South Vietnam."

Of course, on the battlefield, the Viet Cong bore little resemblance to the German Army of World War II. They were not the invaders from the North that Johnson suggested they were, but often indigenous South Vietnamese. Moreover, the government of the Republic of South Vietnam was less an agency of free men than an American puppet regime. When members of the Senate Foreign Relations Committee suggested as much in February 1966, Democrat and Senate Majority Whip Russell Long of Louisiana responded by comparing the Viet Cong to Indians and Americans to Pilgrims:

> This Nation [sic] was founded because we had courageous men. We became a great nation because the people had courage. They did not give up because they had to fight Indians. If the men who came on the *Mayflower* were frightened to helplessness the first time they had to fight Indians, they would have gone back to England on the *Mayflower*. But they fought the Indians and won, meanwhile losing some fine Americans, until this Nation became great. We are upholding [in Vietnam] our commitments in the proud tradition of our fathers, grandfathers, great-grandfathers, and many other courageous Americans who fell on the field of battle.

Unfortunately, Senator Long wasn't the only one to compare the Vietnamese to Indians. All over Vietnam, American soldiers referred to enemy-held territory as "Indian Country." In 1966, Maxwell Taylor, the American Ambassador to South Vietnam, tried to explain recent troubles with the American plan to gather Vietnamese into "strategic hamlets" so as to defend them from the Viet Cong by saying, "It is very hard to plant corn outside the stockade when the Indians are still around. We have to get the Indians farther away. . . ." The *New York Daily News* headlined one battle report: "Wagon-Train GIs Drive Off Redmen."

Peopled by Indians, the landscape of Vietnam in the early years of the war was the landscape of American mythology. From a distance of thirty years, it might be tempting to see Johnson or Long simply as politicians cynically calling on old myths to justify new battles. Certainly, at times, they were that and yet, to their constituents at least, they were also mediators. In the early and mid-1960s, tales of American efficacy and moral rectitude pervaded American culture. As political leaders, men like Long and Johnson had the power to bring those tales to life in the real world. When they exercised that power by taking the country to war, they also granted Americans a renewed connection to their myths and, through them, to their history. They became living links between the America of today and the half-imagined, heavily mythologized America of the past.

In that respect, they resembled America's masculine icon, John Wayne. To moviegoers all across the country, Wayne personified a code of behavior that was simultaneously individual and national. "John Wayne," writes Lawrence Wright,

> was always setting people straight, with his fists or his gun, and he was invariably right. . . .
>
> That was my image of America's role in the world. . . . In the real world the only certainty of justice came from our power, our willingness to use violence appropriately. It seemed to me then that strength and truth were welded together and that if one exercised power, justice would naturally follow.

In the early 1960s, John Wayne served as an intermediary between private lives and national myths. Through him, individual citizens gained access to the immense emotional treasure-house of American right and might. In backyards and back alleys, Wayne's "willingness to use violence" impelled prepubescent boys to play cowboys and Indians and to attack each other with chrome-plated mock revolvers. In the political realm, it prompted their parents to support the use of violence overseas. Having seen that justice flowed in John Wayne's wake in the movies, many Americans assumed that justice must likewise naturally flow in the wake of American interventions abroad. American power was a sign of America's moral superiority over other nations and as they watched John Wayne, Americans—particularly young male Americans—could feel that power in themselves.

Until 1968, mainstream American newspapers and television shows presented relatively little information that would allow the Vietnam War to challenge civilian faith in American myths. The exceptions were notable: In August 1966, *The CBS Evening News* broadcast Morley Safer's report on American Marines burning down the village of Cam Ne. Featuring pictures of "Zippo squads" setting fire to thatched roofs, the report triggered an intense, but brief, political controversy. In October of the same year, Neil Sheehan told readers of *The New York Times* that American aircraft and artillery had leveled a series of villages in Quang Ngai Province. In 1967, Jonathan Schell described the razing of the village of Ben Suc in *The New Yorker*.

But by and large, until 1968, American journalists suggested that the American mission in Vietnam differed little from its mission in Europe twenty-five years earlier. They told stories of American boys "in action," often noting the soldiers' hometowns as Ernie Pyle had in World War II. They printed maps of Vietnam decorated with the same bold campaign arrows that had marked the maps of Europe twenty-five years before. Throughout the years of American escalation in Vietnam, American soldiers were regularly depicted, in the words of *Time* magazine, as the kind of men whose "main concern in off-duty hours is aiding Vietnamese civilians." Before 1968, American civilians who made no effort to find out more about the war than what they could learn from the evening news on TV might plausibly conclude that Vietnam was in fact the legitimate child of World War II, that America truly was the last bastion of freedom on earth, and that their country, with they themselves on board, was indeed embarked on a bold and necessary journey.

During those same years, however, soldiers in Vietnam were learning far different lessons. From the moment they arrived in-country, they faced evidence that the John Wayne wars they had seen in hometown movie houses bore little likeness to the war in Southeast Asia. In the first years of the war, soldiers arrived in Vietnam on ships, but later most GIs flew in on commercial jets. As one soldier describes it: "It didn't take long to see that something was seriously wrong. There we were, flying into Nam on a fancy commercial jet, sipping drinks like a bunch of goddamn businessmen, and as far as we knew the VC were going to start shooting us up as soon as we touched down! . . . It was crazy!" Was this a combat zone or wasn't it? "We might have been over Gary, Indiana," writes Rob Riggan in his novel *Free Fire Zone*. "Stewardesses with polished legs and miniskirts took our pillows away from us. As we trooped out the door [they] said 'Good luck! See you in 365 days!' "

When the stewardesses opened the hydraulic doors of the DC-10s, however, soldiers stepped down into a world that bore little resemblance to the world they knew. Psychologically prepared to defend the "American way of life," many were shocked to encounter the Vietnamese way of life. Fred Widmer, later a participant in the My Lai massacre, recalls his own, fairly typical arrival this way:

> We had just left Hawaii with all its hotels and nightclubs and bars and we wound up in Vietnam where people went right out and shit in the rice paddy in the morning, drop their drawers right along the trail anytime. It was hard to consider people in the modern day and age living like they did. I think it went against our value of what human life is.

A Marine who arrived in Vietnam in 1966 remembers that he and his buddies "were disgusted with the Vietnamese":

> They dress differently and the women chew betel nut and have these ugly teeth. The kids deal dope all the time and all these things which to us make them look like animals—and they wear these filthy clothes and they have all these habits we're not used to, like sleeping on dirt, picking up and spreading out manure with their hands, eating food we wouldn't be seen with, drinking terrible water, not brushing their teeth or washing. I realized the Vietnamese people were the enemy.

These were not grateful, hygienic Europeans, as the World War II movies had prepared Widmer and the Marine to expect. For the Marine, their strangeness made them the enemy; for Widmer, they were not even entirely human.

Soldiers soon learned that Vietnam did not operate according to the moral laws that governed the myths with which they had grown up. When they arrived, for instance, many soldiers hoped to help the Vietnamese. But they quickly learned that their help was not always wanted. On their way out of the airport, soldiers were herded into buses whose windows were covered with wire mesh. If the soldiers asked why, their officers told them that the citizens of the capital they had been sent to defend had a habit of throwing hand grenades at their defenders. After the GIs had been in Vietnam for a few days, they might run into packs of excited children. Raised on images of their fathers giving gum to the ragtag children of France and Italy, new arrivals in Vietnam often expected to play Santa Claus. But they were usually in for a surprise. If, for example, the children held up two fingers in what was, in World War II at least, a victory sign, they were probably pimps, announcing that the price of "boom-boom" was two dollars. As John Durant, a former helicopter crew chief, puts it, "Those kids, raised during years of killing, they'd sell their mothers and sisters for a gang rape for enough piasters. Very soon I got the message: I would rather be dead than Vietnamese."

Even as their parents settled into their armchairs and read about "Wagon-Train GIs" driving off "Red-men," combat infantrymen were discovering that Vietnam might not bear any resemblance to the Old West. As Americans, they had been raised on the faith that if they went to battle, they would, like John Wayne, acquire a muscular masculinity. War would "make them men," grant them hard bodies and the ability to control them, to make choices, to be in charge of their destinies. Yet, when they actually arrived in combat, soldiers found that they often had little control over their fates. They learned, in the words of Philip Caputo, that survival was often a matter of "Chance. Pure chance. The one true god of modern war is blind chance." As a soldier bent over to tie his shoe, a bullet might slam into a sandbag where his head had been a moment before. Or, as Robert Mason did, a pilot might land his helicopter in a mine field and somehow avoid detonating a single mine. "When you're in that setting, it's like being in an arena surrounded by death," says one former Marine. "It's hard to explain what happens once you start seeing people die. That's *something we don't do* [italics in the original]. We just don't see people die."

The men of Vietnam, of course, were not the first American soldiers to find themselves "surrounded by death." Even so, few if any of them had any sense of the randomness or carnage of combat before they arrived. The generation of men who fought in World War II and Korea were remarkably silent on such issues, and perhaps even if they had spoken, their sons might not have comprehended the true violence of combat. Moreover, the soldiers who fought in Vietnam were under a kind of attack few of their fathers had seen. Outnumbered and technologically overmatched, the Viet Cong and the North Vietnamese Army refused by and large to fight set-piece battles. Instead, they melted into the population, planted the landscape with booby traps, and bided their time.

The psychological effects of the booby traps were especially severe. As Philip Caputo explains:

> The foot soldier has a special feeling for the ground. He walks on it, fights on it, sleeps and eats on it; the ground shelters him under fire; he digs his home in it. But mines and booby traps transform that friendly, familiar earth into a thing of menace, a thing to be feared as much as machine guns or mortar shells. The infantryman knows that any moment the ground he is walking on can erupt and kill him; kill him if he's lucky. If he's unlucky, he will be turned into a blind, deaf, emasculated, legless shell. . . . Walking down the trails, waiting for those things to explode, we had begun to feel more like victims than soldiers.

In Vietnam, the earth itself could not be trusted. The dirt hid mines; the trees hid snipers. America's allies too, the people our soldiers were risking their lives to save, were also suspect. As Fred Widmer puts it:

> You couldn't pinpoint who exactly was the enemy. In the end anybody who was still in that country was the enemy. The same village you had gone in to give them medical treatment . . . you could go through that village later and get shot at on your way out by a sniper. Go back in, you wouldn't find anybody. Nobody knew anything. . . . You didn't trust them anymore. You didn't trust anybody.

Over time, many soldiers came to distrust even their own perceptions. In Vietnam, said one:

> Nothing is what it seems. That mountain there—maybe it was there yesterday, and won't be there tomorrow. You get to the point where you're not even sure it *is* a mountain.

This was not the universe of power promised them by the American myths on which they had been raised. Where they had expected to find themselves feeling capable and in charge, many soldiers found themselves feeling powerless, afraid, and alone.

Sadly, our soldiers were not only helpless before the enemy. Often, they were also powerless before their own leaders. As Jonathan Shay, a psychiatrist who works with traumatized Vietnam veterans, has written: "The dependence of a modern soldier on his army and on its civilian masters is as total as the dependence of a small child on its family." This is especially true in combat situations, where the soldier depends not only on the weapons and food that his army has supplied, but on the emotional sustenance that, like a family, the men of a fighting unit traditionally offer one another. Even as the random carnage of battle threatens the individual soldiers' faith in a benevolent moral order, the cohesion of the fighting unit works to restore it. Officers become symbolic fathers and their men, symbolic sons. As part of this symbolic arrangement, soldiers come to assume that their leaders will treat them fairly, honestly, and perhaps with affection, and that, in turn, they will offer loyal service and perhaps even give up their lives on behalf of their comrades.

In Vietnam, however, many combat soldiers found themselves treated with far less than paternal regard. Granted, a leader didn't have to be particularly corrupt to undo the emotional ties between himself and his men. The principles of American tactics in Vietnam—the search-and-destroy mission, the body count, the length of the combat tour—conspired to corrode the infantryman's trust in his officers. On a search-and-destroy mission, for example, it was often an officer's duty to order his men to bait the enemy. He would send or, if he were a captain or a lieutenant, perhaps lead them into small villages or down jungle paths in the hope that the Viet Cong or North Vietnamese Army would attack them and thus expose themselves to the retaliatory fire of American aircraft and artillery.

Many officers habitually exaggerated their battlefield accomplishments and taught their men to do the same. By and large, commissioned officers in Vietnam served only six months in combat—half the time of those of the men in their charge—and they had to make those six months count: Performance in the field was a key to advancement at home. Since a primary measure of an officer's success in Vietnam was the number of the enemy his unit killed, soldiers at every level, from grunts in the field to generals in Saigon, came to inflate enemy casualty figures. Under pressure from their leaders, combat troops became less than picky about what constituted an enemy corpse. Unarmed women and children were often added to the list, since, according to a common saying at the time, "If it's dead and Vietnamese, it's VC." As they watched their officers inflate body counts and pursue medals and promotions, soldiers began to question the rightness of their mission. Were their officers in this with them? Or were the grunts just flunkies, there to push the officers up the military's corporate ladder?

Officers also entangled their men in another damaging fiction, one designed, like the policy of body counts, to improve the efficiency of the military's combat performance, but one which, like the body counts, undercut soldiers' perceptions of moral order. As Jonathan Shay explains, officers (and, often enough, other enlisted men as well) frequently nullified the perceptions and experiences of their men. One former Airborne trooper whom Shay had treated described watching three boats pull into a harbor. "The word came down that they were unloading weapons off them," he said. He and his unit attacked, but:

> Daylight came, and we found out we killed a lot of fishermen and kids.
> . . . The fucking colonel says, "Don't worry about it. We'll take care
> of it." Y'know, uh, "We got body count! We have body count!" So it
> starts working in your head . . . you know in your heart it's wrong,
> but at the time, here's your superiors telling you that it was okay. So, I
> mean, that's *okay* then, right? This is part of war. Y'know?

In this case, the colonel had demonstrated to the soldier that whatever moral order there might be in Vietnam, it was not the one in which he had been raised. But the colonel had also taught the soldier that, questions of right and wrong aside, his perceptions were inaccurate and his emotional reactions inappropriate. In his role as symbolic father, the officer had refused to honor and accept his surrogate son's experience. On the contrary, he presented the soldier with a terrible choice: He could accept his own emotions and perceptions and give up his faith in his symbolic father, or he could deny what he knew and felt to be true and remain in his symbolic father's good graces.

Soldiers in Vietnam faced such choices every day. In combat, there was rarely time to mourn. Again and again, soldiers were forced to disregard or deny feelings of sadness, rage, and grief, and to get on with the business at hand. Nor could they always turn to their symbolic brothers, their fellow grunts, for sympathy. Despite the intense cohesion of units under fire, soldiers knew that if they weren't killed first, their buddies—and they themselves—would leave when their one-year tours of duty were up. Designed to offer combat soldiers a motivating light at the end of the tunnel, this system of troop rotation also offered men in combat a strong incentive to retain an emotional distance from one another. Even within the symbolic family of the combat unit, men could at times feel like orphans.

Their psychological isolation, in turn, compounded their sense of powerlessness. Don McCullin, a combat photographer who worked in Vietnam in 1968, could have been speaking for a great many combat troops in Vietnam when he wrote:

> In this kind of war you are on a schizophrenic trip. You cannot equate what is going on with anything else in life. If you have known white sheets, and comfort, and peace in the real world, and then you find yourself living like a sewer rat, not knowing day from night, you cannot put the two worlds together. None of the real world judgments seem to apply. What's peace, what's war, what's dead, what's living, what's right, what's wrong? You don't know the answers. You just live, if you can, from day to day.

In retrospect, those who managed to just live "from day to day" were the lucky ones. Others found themselves becoming something they hardly recognized. When he first arrived in the combat zone, says one veteran, "I couldn't believe what I was seeing. I couldn't believe Americans could do things like that to another human being . . . but then I *became* that. We went through villages and killed everything, I mean *everything,* and that was all right with me." When he went through villages and killed, this soldier suffered a gross inversion of both personal and national meaning. He was shocked not only at what he became, but at what *Americans* could become. Suddenly the people whom Lyndon Johnson had charged with "the principal responsibility for the protection of freedom on earth" had become criminals. Within the mind of this soldier, the moral order under which he had gone to war had been turned upside down: America was now the enemy and, by extension, so was he.

According to one well-known study of Vietnam veterans, nearly one in every ten combat soldiers committed an act of abusive violence, such as torturing prisoners, raping civilians, or mutilating a corpse. Approximately one in three witnessed such an act and when they did, they suffered a direct and severe blow to their assumptions about the world. Michael Bernhardt, a soldier who refused to fire during the My Lai massacre, explains:

> You know, when I think of somebody who would shoot up women and children, I think of a real nut, a real maniac, a real psycho, somebody who's just completely lost control and doesn't have any idea of what he's doing. . . . Then I found out that an act like, you know, murder for no reason could be done by just about anybody.

Knowing that "just about anybody" could commit "murder for no reason," Bernhardt could no longer believe, as he might have as a child, that the world was basically benevolent. He knew that even those he was close to could commit atrocities.

Other veterans knew not only that anyone could commit murder, but also that committing murder could get to be a pleasure. One veteran writes:

> I have to admit I enjoyed killing. . . . There was a certain joy you had in killing, an exhilaration that is hard to explain. After a fight, guys would be really wired. "Wow, man, did you see that guy get it? Holy shit. Did you see that?"
>
> During ground attacks, a guy is dead and just as he is about to fall over, the volume of outgoing fire can be so intense a couple of rounds pick him up. He starts to fall over again and—*whack*—they pick him up. We would have contests to see how long we could keep the bodies

weaving. For most people seeing this, it's a horrible, horrible sight. We were so sadistic that we were *trying* to make it happen.

Perhaps most frightening of all, acts of abusive violence seemed not only to undermine the American moral order, but to suggest the absence of any higher moral authority at all. After he and several other soldiers had raped several teenaged girls, for example, infantryman Jerry Samuels watched his buddies shoot the victims. As he did, he says:

> I felt like a big bolt of lightning was supposed to come out of the sky with Uncle Sam's name attached to it and strike me dead. But it didn't. This wasn't a conscious thought. It was just that now that I think about it later, I was hoping for some kind of reprimand, somebody to say, "You just murdered innocent people." But nobody did. . . . You know, I wanted God, somebody to show me that was wrong. This is one of the things I dwell on so damn much now—it wasn't wrong then.

"These acts," says another veteran, "make you think there is no God."

By the time they boarded the DC-10 that would fly them back to America, more than a few combat soldiers had come to know a world without God. Raised to believe that America had been given a divine mission and that in Vietnam they had been given the assignment of furthering that mission, many had discovered that there might be no mission at all. Combat in Vietnam had not given them the sense of moral and personal efficacy John Wayne had promised them. Nor had it given them a chance to share in the great power of their nation. On the contrary, it had taught them that both they and their country could be rendered powerless. Since the logic of American myth dictated that America's power was the measure of its moral rectitude, the war taught them that neither they nor their country could claim the moral superiority they had once thought was their birthright. As the stewardesses passed around the pillows, many soldiers flew home to a world which once had meaning, but in which now they would have to live, if they could, simply from day to day.

Yet the country to which they returned had also begun to change. Though fought on the other side of the earth, the Vietnam War seemed to have insinuated itself into every nook and cranny of America by the late 1960s. As the war progressed, it began to corrode many civilians' faith in the meanings of America and the meanings of their lives. The war was a sponge, sucking up issues of race and poverty, class and age, issues that had their own long and independent lives in American culture, and making of them a single challenge to American myth. For black leaders, the war pointed up gross inequalities at home: As Martin Luther King, Jr., said, by 1967, Americans had "been repeatedly faced with the cruel irony of watching Negro and white boys on TV screens as they kill and die together for a nation that has been unable to seat them together in the same schools." For young people, the war also illuminated class divisions: The draft quickly taught them that in America, all men were not created equal—those with upper- and even middle-class connections did not have to go to war. Finally, to the generation that had fought World War II, Vietnam offered the dissolution of a dream: As they watched race riots, campus takeovers, and huge antiwar marches, they also watched the sense of national unity and purpose, the vision of "one nation, under God, indivisible" that had governed their war, disappear.

The fear of national collapse peaked in 1968. In that year, more than any other, Americans at home came face-to-face with the kinds of helplessness and psychological isolation their troops confronted in Vietnam. The Tet Offensive, the assassinations of Martin Luther King and Robert Kennedy, the Democratic National Convention in Chicago—all worked together to unravel the old meanings of the phrase "the American way of life" and with them, the psychological security of many Americans.

The year began by revealing the head of American forces in Vietnam, General William Westmoreland, to be either an incompetent or a liar. Since 1964, Westmoreland had been making optimistic pronouncements on the progress of the war. On November 21, 1967, he told the National Press Club, "With 1968, a new phase is starting. . . . We have reached an important point where the end comes into view." Then, in the early morning hours of January 31, the beginning of the lunar new year known as Tet in Vietnam, a sapper team blew a hole in the outer wall of the U.S. Embassy in Saigon. For the next six hours, Americans found themselves pinned down in what they had supposed was the most secure point in all of South Vietnam. Within twenty-four hours, people all over the United States saw pictures of American MPs, crouching under fire, trying to regain the embassy. They also learned that the Communists, the same Communists whom Westmoreland and others had long told them were near the breaking point, had launched massive assaults on cities and military installations all over South Vietnam.

In the first hours of the Tet Offensive, Americans rallied to their leaders. But as the battles dragged on, day after day, week after week, Americans began to reevaluate not only their leaders, but the Vietnam War as a whole. With Tet, writes historian Richard Slotkin, "The victory that was about to complete the official narrative [of the Vietnam War] suddenly vanished." When it did, the truth of the entire national mythology, of which the Vietnam War story was but one part, was called into question. "National leaders had declared that the national fate was tied to Vietnam," writes sociologist and former antiwar activist Todd Gitlin, "little calculating that the blood tie went both ways. A nation that commits itself to myth is traumatized when reality bursts through—in living color."

For many civilians, the reality that burst through exposed the chaos of combat and the helplessness of the individual American soldier for the first time. Television networks that had formerly been reluctant to depict the carnage of the war now broadcast footage of civilian and military casualties every day. *Life* magazine ran full-page pictures of American Marines pinned down at Khe Sanh, their airplanes shot down, their ammunition dumps exploding in flames. The Marines at Khe Sanh were not "Wagon-Train GIs"; instead, wrote *Life,* they were "tethered bullocks." Later *Life* ran a photo essay on the battle to regain the city of Hué. In the pictures, what was once the ancient capital of Vietnam and one of the most beautiful cities in the country was now reduced to rubble. The Marines were terrified creatures, crawling through the ruins. They had "Eyes that speak a prayer in the midst of horror" and in one of the most famous photographs of the war, they could be seen leaving Hué as wounded bodies piled on a tank, exhausted and near death.

This carnage was not what their leaders had told Americans to expect in Vietnam. Militarily, the United States did in fact win the battles of Tet. When they brought Viet Cong cadres out into the open and exposed them to the full force of American firepower, as they did throughout the Tet Offensive, the North Vietnamese lost thousands of men and much of their guerrilla infrastructure. But in the United States, Tet tasted like defeat. Like their soldiers, Americans at home had been primed to expect a display of personal, national, and technological prowess in Vietnam. When Tet offered them images of Vietnamese military might instead, their national confidence crumbled. Writing in the aftermath of Tet, historian Arthur Schlesinger explained that:

> The failure of half a million American soldiers with nearly a million allies, employing the might of modern military technology, to defeat a few thousand guerrillas in black pajamas has shaken our faith in our power, as the destruction we have wrought in the pursuit of what we conceived as noble ends has shaken our faith in our virtue.

Suddenly Americans at home learned what many of their soldiers in Vietnam already knew: They and their country were not all-powerful.

In addition, images of what appeared to be American military helplessness suggested to the public that the cause itself might not be worthwhile. In fact, for the first time, many began to acknowledge the damage Americans were doing in Vietnam. Surveying the ruins left by the fighting in Hué during Tet, the editors of *Life* wrote that "the fate of Hué demonstrated the sickening irony into which the war has fallen—the destruction of the very things the U.S. is here to save." These were the same editors who had almost certainly watched Morley Safer's 1965 report on the burning of Cam Ne. They knew full well that Americans had been destroying the homes of those they had been sent to defend for more than three years. Yet, now that the Tet Offensive had suggested that the notion that America was winning the war was a fiction, they suddenly felt free to stop promoting the glories of American might and to focus instead on its destructive force.

Many Americans took the challenge the Tet Offensive offered to American myth very personally. When America's military and political leaders told them they were winning the war, Americans took heart not only in the progress of the war, but in the rightness of the cultural assumptions with which they were winning it. To millions of Americans, men like William Westmoreland and Lyndon Johnson embodied the qualities of competence, efficiency, and honesty that were the personal

expressions of American national myths. When Tet showed Westmoreland and Johnson to be ineffective at best and at worst dishonest, it
undermined not only their personal credibility, but that of the values for
which they stood. Writing several years after Tet, essayist Benjamin De-
Mott explains the problem:

> A powerful lesson taught by the Vietnam war from the mid-sixties
> onward . . . was that bureaucrats, diplomats, generals and presidents
> who allow themselves to be locked into orthodox, culturally sanc-
> tioned patterns of thought and assumption make fearful mistakes. . . .
> No event in American history cast sterner doubt on the efficacy of the
> limited professional self—on the usefulness of clear-eyed, patent-
> haired, inhumanly efficient defense secretaries, technicians, worshipers
> of military "intelligence"—than the disasters that followed every offi-
> cial optimistic pronouncement about Vietnam from the middle sixties
> onward.

Like many soldiers in Vietnam, many Americans at home felt betrayed
by their leaders, and like their soldiers, they suffered a sense of disorientation as a result. If their leaders had misled them, then perhaps not only
their leaders were corrupt. Maybe the mission—for soldiers, that of
fighting in Vietnam; for civilians, that of trying to perfect their professional proficiency in the domestic economy; for the nation, that of as-
suming the moral mantle of the world—was bankrupt. And if the mission was bankrupt, if the play had no script as it were, then what role
should they play?

For all the talk at the time of left and right, hawk and dove, such
disorientation went after its victims regardless of their political leanings.
Archconservative commentator James Fletcher could have been speaking
for many of his liberal "enemies" when he wrote, two weeks into the
Tet Offensive, that he feared "the destruction of the fundamental institutions of our political system and . . . the abandonment of the rational
control which has hitherto distinguished us as human." For conservatives
such as Fletcher, it was the antiwar protestors and their government
supporters, such as Senator William Fulbright, who had undermined
America's civic institutions and unleashed the forces of chaos. For liberals, the culprits were men such as William Westmoreland and Lyndon

Johnson. To both groups, however, Tet offered a glimpse of a world devoid of the social structures that gave their lives meaning. Having been raised to play their parts in the dramas of their national mythology, many feared they had stumbled onto an empty stage.

The Tet Offensive ended after two months, but it remained a watershed in the cultural representation of the war. In its wake, journalists ceased to describe the Vietnam War in terms of World War II or of "Wagon-Train GIs" and "Red-men." Vietnam was no longer a national mission, no longer "our" war; it came to be called simply "the" war. Where they once focused on American combat prowess, journalists now emphasized the sufferings of American troops. And the war itself, once the glowing model of what can happen when Americans put their rational, industrious minds to work, was now often referred to as "mad."

Nevertheless, the war went on and so did the riots at home. On April 4, 1968, days after the end of the Tet Offensive, Martin Luther King was assassinated. The reaction was predictable:

> Great streamers of acrid smoke, drifting from blazing shops in Washington's commercial center, twisted among the cherry blossoms near the Lincoln Memorial, where five years earlier Martin Luther King had proclaimed his vision of black and white harmony. Fires crackled three blocks from the White House, and from the air the capital looked like a bombed city.

Riots broke out in sixty-two cities across America. About 12,000 troops were called into the streets of each of the cities of Baltimore, Washington, and Chicago. In all, 25,000 people were arrested and 45 were killed. As it had during the ghetto riots of 1967, America itself looked like a war zone.

Americans' self-confidence continued to decline. In June, Robert Kennedy, one of the few white leaders trusted by large numbers of black citizens and an ardent opponent of the war, was assassinated. While it did not lead to riots, the second assassination in less than three months and the second killing of a Kennedy in five years spawned an excruciating period of self-examination. The murder, wrote the editors of *Time* soon afterward, "immediately prompted, at home and abroad, deep doubts about the stability of America. Many saw the unleashing of a dark, latent psychosis in the national character, a stain that had its start with the first settlement of a hostile continent." Americans' anxieties reached such a pitch that President Johnson went on national television to explain that "200 million Americans did not strike down Robert Kennedy. . . . It would be . . . wrong and . . . self-deceptive," he said, "to conclude from this act that our country itself is sick, that it's lost its balance, that it's lost its sense of direction, even its common decency."

Nevertheless, many reached just such a conclusion. In the summer of 1968, writes Lawrence Wright, Americans were suffering a collapse of national meaning, a collapse that sparked crises in individual identities:

> The country had gone wrong; it had slipped into a violent nightmare and couldn't wake up. I could feel the violence inside me, boiling over—i was frightened of myself. . . . Everything America stood for only a few years earlier now seemed to be all lies and illusion.

Benjamin DeMott explains that the assassinations of King and Kennedy spawned

> a flat rejection of past claims to value, principle or honor. For the seed of our traumas, whether assassinations or riots, seemed invariably to lie in racism, in a willful determination to treat millions of human beings as less than human. The contemplation of the deaths of heroes, in short, opened a door for us on our own self-deceit and on the self-deception practiced by our fathers. Neither they nor we had told it like it was. And they were apparently all unaware that because of their fantasies and obliviousness millions suffered.

For DeMott and others, America in 1968 was a world in which "value, principle [and] honor" were suspect. Like combat soldiers, he and Wright and many Americans had encountered a universe of dead heroes. Like combat veterans, they had become aware of a violence boiling inside them and of their "own self-deceit and the self-deception practiced by our fathers." And like soldiers, they found themselves alone. Neither wanted to be a member of a group whose "fantasies and obliviousness" had killed millions.

Together, the Tet Offensive and the assassinations of King and Kennedy opened a terrifying window on American mythology. In June 1969, after taking testimony throughout 1968, the National Commission on the Causes and Prevention of Violence, a blue-ribbon panel appointed by President Johnson in 1967, prefaced its final report thus:

> [S]o disturbing is today's civil commotion and its attendant widespread disillusionment that it invites a reaction against the comfortable old certitudes. Contemporary Americans, confronted as they are with overseas war and domestic turmoil, may be tempted to overcompensate for past patriotic excesses by equating the American experience instead with slavery and imperialism, Indian genocide, and Judge Lynch. Similarly, some contemporary European intellectuals, such as Jean-Paul Sartre, have come to regard "that super-European monstrosity, North America" as a bastard child or satanic mutation of a degraded Europe.

In 1968, Americans learned, as Arthur Schlesinger put it, that "life is not solid and predictable but infinitely chancy, that violence is not the deviation but the ever-present possibility." In 1968, chance was not only, as Philip Caputo wrote, the "one true god of modern war"; for civilians at home it had also become the god of daily life. Schlesinger must have felt that he was standing at the edge of an abyss when he wrote:

> [O]ur nation is in a state of incipient fragmentation. A series of tensions severely strain the social fabric: tensions between young and old, between poor and rich, between black and white, between educated and uneducated, between intellectuals and know-nothings. . . . No social emotion . . . is more vital in America today than a sense of personal helplessness, uselessness, and impotence. . . . Everyone more or less has the sense of existing in the shadow of vast uncontrollable structures, impervious to human desire or need.

So too, of course, did combat soldiers in Vietnam. Yet, it would be another year before Americans at home learned what many of their troops already knew: They could be helpless not only before "vast uncontrollable structures," but before their own violent impulses.

In the first months of 1969, American anxieties began to cool. General Westmoreland had been recalled from Vietnam and President

Johnson had stepped aside. The political party that many thought had gotten America into Vietnam had fallen from power. Now, a Republican, Richard Nixon, had taken over, bringing with him, he claimed, a secret plan to end the war. In October and November 1969, more than half a million Americans protested the war in Washington, D.C., but even as they did, those whom Nixon called the "silent majority" sat on the sidelines, waiting for the President's plan to take effect.

On the evening of November 24, many of those people were sitting in their living rooms, surrounded by friends and family, waiting to watch the *Apollo 12* astronauts splash down into the Pacific Ocean. This was supposed to be a moment of American triumph—no other nation could have sent these men to the moon—and millions of Americans had gathered around their televisions to share in the feeling of national power. Yet, when they tuned their sets to CBS, they saw not the smiling faces of astronauts, but the awkward, strained visage of Paul Meadlo. In a live interview, Meadlo was telling Mike Wallace how he had lined up a group of unarmed villagers in a hamlet called Pinkville and shot them, using four clips of ammunition in the process. Once they were dead, Meadlo and his lieutenant gathered others together and brought them to the edge of a ditch. "Lieutenant Calley," he said, "started pushing them off and shooting . . . off into the ravine. It was a ditch. And so we just pushed them off, and just started using automatics on them . . . men, women, children . . . and babies. . . ."

Wallace tried to bring the meaning of what Meadlo had done home to the audience:

WALLACE: You're married?

MEADLO: Right.

WALLACE: Children?

MEADLO: Two.

WALLACE: How old?

MEADLO: The boy is two and a half, and the little girl is a year and a half.

WALLACE: Well, obviously the question comes to mind . . . the father of two little kids like that . . . how can he shoot babies?

MEADLO: I don't know. It's just one of them things.

WALLACE: How many people would you imagine were killed that day?

MEADLO: I would say 370.

WALLACE: What did these civilians . . . these, particularly the women and children, the old men, what did they do? What did they say to you? They weren't begging or anything, "No . . . no," or . . . ?

MEADLO: Right . . . They were begging and saying, "No. No." And their mothers were hugging their children, but they kept on firing. Well, we kept on firing. They was waving their arms and begging . . .

WALLACE: Did you ever dream about all of this that went on in Pinkville?

MEADLO: Yes, I did . . . and I still dream about it.

WALLACE: What kinds of dreams?

MEADLO: I see the women and children in my sleep. Some days . . . some nights, I can't sleep. I just lay there thinking about it.

In the weeks ahead, Pinkville would come to be known by its name on American military maps, My Lai. Americans would learn that six months earlier, on March 16, 1968, the 105 men of Charlie Company, Americal Division, descended on the village in helicopters and proceeded to kill as many as 500 of the village's 700 inhabitants, virtually all of them old men, women, and children. Over the course of four hours, members of Charlie Company raped and sodomized the inhabitants of My Lai and mutilated their corpses. A handful of men refused to participate; one shot himself in the foot. At the end of the encounter, the men of Charlie Company reported to their superiors that they had killed 128 Viet Cong and found three weapons in the village. They were later congratulated for a successful action against the enemy by General William Westmoreland himself. In March 1969, an Army investigation would accuse nearly 30 officers, ranging in rank from lieutenant to general, of being involved in or covering up the massacre.

Yet, early on, it wasn't the cover-up but the massacre itself that stunned the public. The My Lai massacre wasn't the first war crime the press had covered. But it was unique in the vividness with which it was reported. Several weeks after Meadlo appeared on television, *Life* magazine published color photographs of the massacre. Taken by Army photographer Ronald Haeberle, the pictures show the soldiers landing near the village on what appeared to be an ordinary combat mission. But on the next page, the reader could see a group of women and children, cowering and clutching one another, terrified. Turning the page, the reader saw a pile of bloody, half-naked corpses, mostly of women and children. After that, the reader could see photographs of a wounded child, whom the caption explained was later killed. Then the reader could see soldiers burning houses and more bodies, again of women and children.

Like the Meadlo interview, the photographs in *Life* literally brought the massacre home to civilian Americans. In a letter to *Life,* Roger R. Eckert wrote: "Having been a Marine, a devoted American, a true believer in our great country, I took the massacre as one would the death of his child. The picture in your issue was like a knife in my heart." Almost immediately, the massacre broke open the safe in which many people kept their faith in America and their faith in themselves. To many, My Lai cast a shadow not only on the Vietnam War, but on the whole of American history. As a Native American from Pennsylvania wrote *Life:* "Yes, it *is* terrible, but history repeats itself and this is *not* the first time that American soldiers have cruelly murdered women and children. To name one instance, how about Wounded Knee, South Dakota on Dec. 29, 1890?" For many, the massacre gave evidence of a flaw deep within the country, but also deep within themselves. "One feels a need to place the blame for this latest horror," Mrs. Virginia Apsey wrote to *Life.* "All we need to do is look in our mirror."

My Lai challenged the self-image of millions of Americans since, as an Army report later explained, the men of Charlie Company were "A typical cross section of American youth assigned to most combat units." They were not monsters. When the face of Paul Meadlo stared out at them from their televisions, Americans saw a face they recognized, a face belonging to someone like them. No Nazi, no fanatical Kamikaze, he bore no resemblance to those whom so many Americans held responsible for the crimes of World War II. Looking at Meadlo, many Americans learned, as many of their soldiers in Vietnam already had, that "murder for no reason could be done by just about anybody." As Jonathan Schell wrote in *The New Yorker* at the time:

> We sense—all of us—that our best instincts are deserting us, and we are oppressed by a dim feeling that beneath our words and phrases, almost beneath our consciousnesses, we are quietly choking on the blood of innocents. . . . When others committed them, we looked on the atrocities through the eyes of the victims. Now we find ourselves, almost against our will, looking through the eyes of the perpetrators, and the landscape seems next to unrecognizable.

The threat My Lai posed to both national myth and individual civilians' psychological security can be measured by the variety of ways Americans found to deflect and deny its importance. Even as liberal politicians, such as Senator George McGovern (D–South Dakota), argued that My Lai had torn "the mask off the war" and put "a national policy on trial," conservative supporters of the war, such as George Wallace, the former governor of Alabama, refused to believe the massacre had happened at all. "I can't believe an American serviceman would purposely shoot any civilian," said Wallace. "Any atrocities in this war were caused by the Communists." What had happened in My Lai was so threatening that even a number of those who thought the war was wrong preferred to believe that the massacre hadn't occurred. A *Minneapolis Tribune* poll taken just before Christmas in 1969 revealed that 49 percent of the 600 people interviewed believed reports of the massacre were untrue; according to reporter Seymour Hersh, the man who broke the My Lai story nationwide, 43 percent of those same 600 people said that "they were horrified when they first heard the story and [then] decided that it wasn't true." "Our boys wouldn't do this," said one man who believed America should get out of Vietnam. "Something else is behind it."

Others suggested that in fact it wasn't "our boys" who were at fault here, but these specific boys. Writing in July 1970, the House Armed Services Committee explained: "What obviously happened at My Lai was wrong. In fact, it was so wrong and so foreign to the normal character and actions of our military forces as to immediately raise a question as to the legal sanity at the time of those men involved." In subsequent years, the assigning of "madness" to and the blaming of veterans for crimes committed in a larger sense by the nation as a whole was to become commonplace. In the wake of the massacre, this strategy served to deflect attention from a terrifying chain of metaphorical logic: If these soldiers had behaved like the German soldiers of World War II, then perhaps their commanders were Nazis and we at home were "good Germans." If they were simply "crazy," then perhaps they alone were responsible for the killings.

Other Americans found a way to blame neither the men of Charlie Company nor their leaders nor the war as a whole. "The most pertinent truth," wrote the editors of Time, "is less accusatory and more difficult for the U.S. to accept: it is that Americans as a people have too readily ignored and too little understood the presence of evil in the world." According to this line of thinking, what American soldiers had done to the citizens of My Lai was best blamed on the abstract and invisible forces of "evil." What's more, that evil did not reside in America or Americans, but instead, roamed "the world." Like the forces of war or disease, evil infected its victims regardless of their individual wishes or their social roles. Since they had been thus infected, men such as the soldiers of Charlie Company—or, for that matter, America's military and political leaders—could not be held entirely responsible for their horrific acts. Thanks to "the presence of evil in the world," Americans could commit war crimes in Vietnam without becoming war criminals.

Yet, even as they struggled to deny it, many American civilians saw themselves in the men of Charlie Company and the whole war in the My Lai massacre. Like combat soldiers, they encountered a world of unreason and gore not only around them, but within them. They began to sense what Joan Didion called an "amoral vacuum out there just beyond the eye's range" and to feel its pull. At the time, Robert Lifton, a psychiatrist who has devoted most of his career to the study of mass psychological trauma, described the condition of American civilians in the wake of My Lai as follows:

> Americans as a national group have become participants in, and survivors of, a sustained pattern of killing and dying which we inwardly sense to be not only brutal but ultimately absurd. . . . Our own justifications for our actions convince us incompletely, if at all, and we are left with the numbing and brutalization required to protect those justifications and fend off a sense of guilt. We are already experiencing the consequences of this general process, and our psychological scars are likely to be extensive and permanent.

To be sure, there remains a wide gap between the intensity of a combat soldier's "death immersion" and that of a civilian reading *Life* magazine at home. Even among combat soldiers there is a wide range of encounters with and responses to the traumatizing forces of combat. Yet it is also true that by the time of My Lai, many civilian Americans had begun to distrust their leaders, their country, and even themselves with a ferocity not unlike that displayed by traumatized combat veterans. If the North Vietnamese and the Viet Cong had undermined the twin myths of America's invincibility and its unique moral rectitude during the Tet Offensive, My Lai finished the job.

As the war wound down, Americans learned the lessons of Tet and My Lai over and over again. Like William Westmoreland on the eve of Tet, Nixon, in his 1968 campaign, had promised to end the war in a hurry; four years later, Americans were still fighting in Vietnam. When students at Kent State University protested the American invasion of Cambodia in 1970, National Guardsmen donned gas masks and shot four of them dead. In the early 1970s, Americans had to face not only the fact that their leaders were capable of waging an absurd and immoral war abroad, but the fact that their own sons could kill unarmed civilians at home. With the advent of Watergate and the resignation of President Nixon, and later, the revelations that the FBI and CIA had spied extensively on American citizens, Americans were reminded that their leaders regarded them with less than paternal affection. When, in 1975, as the

North Vietnamese Army marched toward Saigon, they saw American diplomats punching and kicking Vietnamese civilians who were frantically trying to climb on board the helicopters that would take the Americans to aircraft carriers offshore, they were reminded yet again that the American army, the same army that had marched to Berlin and occupied Tokyo, had been beaten by a people they had once called "gooks" and "slants."

In the final years of the war, Americans entered into a collective numbness not unlike that into which Robert Mason entered during combat. Like Mason, Americans had seen their faith in a benevolent moral and political universe radically undermined. By the end of the war, large numbers of both combat veterans and American civilians had sensed the existence of a world not ordered by national myth or a concern for one's personal safety, a world of random horror for whose creation they could themselves be held, at least in part, responsible. In the years to come, both veterans and civilians would struggle to make sense of this new, alien world.

CHAPTER THREE

BRINGING IT ALL BACK HOME:

THE VIETNAM WAR AS MENTAL ILLNESS

IN APRIL 1975, AS SOUTH VIETNAMESE TROOPS FELL BACK
before what would be the North Vietnamese Army's final onslaught,
Congressman Don Bonker of the state of Washington described the
American mood: "People are drained. They want to bury the memory
of Indochina. They regard it as a tragic chapter in American life, but
they want no further part in it." Journalists around the country brought
his point home with force. "Recriminations over 'who lost Vietnam,' "
wrote the editors of the *Philadelphia Inquirer,* would only "poison our
national atmosphere now and in the future." In an article entitled "How
Should Americans Feel?", the editors of *Time* explained that "There
cannot be an infinite cycle of protests, recrimination and guilt. The U.S.
has paid for Viet Nam—many times over. A phase of American history
has finished. It is time to begin anew."

Twenty years later it is hard to imagine that Americans could wage a
war for nearly a decade, a war that led to the deaths of more than three

million people, lose it, and then simply "begin anew." But as the war came to a close, Americans all across the country were trying to do just that. During the years preceding the official withdrawal of American forces from Vietnam, traumatized combat veterans had come home, folded up their uniforms, and tried to get on with their lives; now civilians, urged on by politicians and journalists, joined them in trying to lock the war away.

At the same time, though, neither traumatized veterans nor their civilian counterparts could quite put the war out of mind. For veterans, the fighting returned in terrifying nightmares, dreams that replayed recent battles, often precisely as they had happened, night after night. For civilians, the war returned in public fantasies, in films and television programs that were often every bit as violent as the private nightmares of their former soldiers.

In the last years of the war, newspaper and magazine reporters began to circulate tales of crazed returnees, veterans who were refighting the battles of Vietnam here in the United States. Television and film producers quickly ensured that these hyperviolent traumatized veterans—in reality, few in number—loomed large in the national imagination. In the early 1970s, moviegoers watched their veterans come home and form private armies *(The Stone Killer,* 1973), rape friendly American girls *(The Visitors,* 1972), and try to murder an entire stadium full of Super Bowl fans, including the President of the United States *(Black Sunday,* 1977). Those who watched television saw them deal drugs and commit sadistic murders *(Mannix,* 1974), kill for cash *(Columbo,* 1974), and blow themselves up with homemade bombs *(Hawaii Five-O,* 1974). As Robert Brewin, a disabled veteran, wrote in 1975, "if I acted according to what I have seen on television in the last six months or so, I would be harboring extreme psychopathic tendencies that prompt me to shoot up heroin with one hand while fashioning explosives with the other as my war-and-drug crazed mind flashes back to the rice paddy where I fragged my lieutenant [i.e., killed him with a fragmentation grenade]."

This public preoccupation with veterans' potential for psychotic violence was altogether new. During and after World War I, for instance, poets and novelists tended to depict shell-shocked soldiers as blasted, hollow men. Prone to weeping, these victims of combat recalled the grotesque violence of the front, but they rarely threatened to reenact it.

After World War II and Korea, many civilians worked hard to ignore what by then had come to be called "combat fatigue." In perhaps the best-known returning-vet film of the Second World War, *The Best Years of Our Lives* (1946), Fred Derry (Dana Andrews), a former bombardier, has a combat nightmare while sleeping at a buddy's house. During the nightmare, the buddy's daughter Peggy (Teresa Wright) swabs Derry's face with a cooling washcloth. "There's nothing to be afraid of," she whispers. "All you have to do is go to sleep." In the morning, after they have breakfast, he tells her, "You were very kind—you didn't even mention [that dream] this morning." Peggy smiles sweetly and later, after a courtship sparked by this moment of intimacy, they marry. By minimizing the symptoms of Fred's traumatic experiences, Peggy makes it possible for them both to go forward in their lives.

The question is: Why, after Vietnam, didn't Americans adopt a similar strategy? Why didn't they too sweep the sufferings of their soldiers out of sight?

Part of the answer, I think, lies in a fundamental similarity between traumatized combat veterans and the civilians who made and watched the films about them. By the end of the war, great numbers of both civilians and combat veterans were suffering a condition of split recollection. For members of both groups, the war had capsized some of their most fundamental beliefs about themselves and their world. But rather than drown in the new uncertainties, civilians and veterans clung to earlier, more innocent images of themselves. While they busied themselves with their daily lives, their psyches broke apart in such a way that two worlds—one present, the other past; one certain, the other chaotic—came to live side by side in their minds.

Naturally, this split was far more severe for traumatized combat veterans. Many had come back to the country they had been dreaming of during their tours only to find that they could not stop thinking about Vietnam. Brian Winhover, a three-tour veteran, came home and went to work maintaining airplane engines a hundred hours a week. He couldn't sleep, so in his off-hours he drank. But for all the effort he put into working and drinking, he found he couldn't escape his memories of the war. "Everything was Vietnam in my head," said Winhover. "Vietnam was just there constantly . . . even when you didn't want it. Sights, smells—you'd think you were back in Vietnam." Nor was Winhover unique. Combat often split soldiers' memories in such a way that now, as a former helicopter crew chief puts it, "What happened twenty years ago feels like yesterday and what happened yesterday feels like twenty years ago." Many traumatized veterans came to feel like they were living double lives. "Sometimes," said Brian Winhover, "it's as vivid as like I'm there [in Vietnam]. Everything is clear as a bell. Other times I can't remember a thing about Vietnam. It's like I'm totally in the present. It's either there or it's not there, and at times it's like: Was *I* really there?"

By the end of the war, many civilians might have echoed Winhover's words. In its last years, Vietnam had become a war that could be both there and not there in the public mind, a war about which a civilian could be forgiven for asking, "Are we really there?" In 1968, Americans elected Richard Nixon in part because he had promised to quickly end the war. But over the next four years they would watch their President engage in a bewildering and emotionally numbing series of simultaneous escalations and deescalations in the conflict. In 1969, soon after coming into office, Nixon and his advisers promulgated the policy of "Vietnamization," under which South Vietnamese troops were to do a greater part of the fighting as American troops were withdrawn. By the end of the year, he had pulled out 60,000 soldiers. In the same year, however, Nixon ordered American troops to bomb neutral Cambodia. In April of the following year, he ordered them to invade. Students across the country protested the attack, but many of their parents did not. To those who hoped the war was ending, Nixon had offered a withdrawal of troops; to those who still wanted to win, or at least to preserve the image of victory, Nixon had offered an invasion. In both cases, he had given the public just enough of what they wanted to allow them to ignore what they didn't want to see.

In February 1972, Nixon visited China; in May, he went to Moscow. All but the most conservative Americans (who feared a rapprochement with the Communists) applauded the visits as examples of visionary diplomacy. American soldiers continued to fight and die in Vietnam (more than 100,000 remained of a force that had peaked at 540,000 in 1968), but once again, Nixon had diverted the public's attention from the continued fighting. As he had in 1969 and 1970, he depicted himself as a peacemaker plausibly enough that Americans could continue to set aside questions of his—and their own—responsibility for the ongoing war. For those who wanted out, peace seemed near at hand; for those who wanted to stay, the fighting continued.

By 1972, large-scale antiwar protests had ceased. American feelings on the war continued to surge and ebb, but few took to the streets with their opinions. True, the government had infiltrated antiwar groups and disrupted their activities, while at Kent State, government troops had also shown that they were willing on occasion to kill those who spoke up. But the silence that settled over the antiwar movement in 1972 had less to do with government intimidation than simple exhaustion, numbness, and denial. By the last years of the war, many Americans had drifted into a state of simultaneously knowing and not knowing what was happening in Vietnam. Like Brian Winhover's memories of combat, the war had become too painful to think about and yet it continued, day after day, demanding to be thought about.

In his 1972 reelection campaign, Nixon effectively summed up the public's ambivalence toward the war in the phrase "peace with honor." Nixon wanted to end the war, he said, but not if it meant giving up South Vietnam, and with it, American "honor." The power of such logic made itself clear on the campaign trail. One day the President's campaign motorcade was driving through Ohio. In the small town of Mantua Corners, they saw a giant sign in front of a simple white house: MR. PRESIDENT MAY I PLEASE SHAKE YOUR HAND. WE LOST OUR SON IN VIET-NAM. Nixon stopped the motorcade and stepped out to talk to Mr. and Mrs. Frank Lorence, whose son Frank had died in Vietnam. The President shook hands with the couple and told them that he wished he "could bring him back. We're going to do everything we can to see that it doesn't happen to . . . other boys." To which Mrs. Lorence replied, "I don't want to feel like he went for nothing."

In the phrase "peace with honor," Nixon offered Americans a way to avoid the pain of thinking that their sons had in fact died "for nothing." While never quite defining just what American "honor" might be, Nixon did manage to suggest that the war had meant *something*. His opponent, on the other hand, offered Americans an unvarnished indictment of the war and their own roles in it. Senator George McGovern favored an immediate withdrawal of all American men and materials from Indochina, an exchange of prisoners of war, and an amnesty for draft dodgers. On the campaign trail, he claimed that "The Nixon

bombing policy in Indochina is the most barbaric action that any country has committed since Hitler's effort to exterminate the Jews in Germany in the 1930s." He suggested that "Our government would rather
burn down schoolhouses and schoolchildren in Asia than build schools
for Americans at home." Theodore White, perhaps the nation's most
experienced campaign journalist at the time, summed up McGovern's
condemnation of American conduct in Vietnam thus: "If Americans
themselves were not criminals," he claimed McGovern was suggesting,
"then at least they supported a government run by criminals."

In fact, as the Watergate revelations would soon show, the American
government *was* being run by criminals in 1972. And as the reports of
My Lai and subsequent atrocities had confirmed, some Americans had
behaved like criminals in Vietnam. But for many, both veterans and
civilians, the pain of those truths remained unapproachable in 1972. To
think that more than 50,000 Americans had given their lives in a criminal enterprise, or even in a merely pointless one, simply hurt too much
for a majority of Americans to consider. In November, 47,165,234
Americans—61 percent of those voting—pulled their levers for Richard
Nixon. George McGovern carried only the District of Columbia and
the state of Massachusetts.

And yet, even as Americans tried to put the war behind them at the
polls, they began to read strange stories about returning veterans in the
press. On May 26, 1971, *The New York Times* published a front-page
feature on Sergeant Dwight Johnson—the first of what was to become a
long string of stories in papers around the country on Vietnam veterans
who had run amok at home. In the housing projects where he grew up,
wrote reporter Jon Nordheimer, Johnson "had been the good boy on his
block . . . an altar boy and Explorer Scout, one of the few among the
thousands of poor black youngsters in Detroit who had struggled against
the grinding life of the ghetto and broken free." In Vietnam, his tank
patrol had been attacked and, after seeing his closest buddies burned to
death in their tank, Johnson had charged out after the North Vietnamese
soldiers, hunted them down, and shot between five and twenty with his
pistol and his submachine gun. "When it was all over," said a soldier
who was there, "it took three men and three shots of morphine to hold
Dwight down. He was raving. . . . They took him away to a hospital

in Pleiku in a straitjacket." For his actions, Johnson won a Congressional Medal of Honor.

The story went on to explain that after his return to Detroit, local dignitaries had offered Johnson jobs, cars, and public speaking engagements. As the only Medal of Honor winner in Michigan, Johnson became the toast of the state. He also began having psychological problems. Having reenlisted in the military and, at the Army's request, become a recruiter in Detroit's predominantly black high schools, Johnson went AWOL, ran up debts, and saw a psychiatrist at the Valley Forge Army Hospital in Pennsylvania. Then, on April 30, 1971, he walked into a Detroit grocery store and pulled a pistol on the manager. The manager drew his own gun. "I first hit him with two bullets," said the manager. "But he just stood there, with the gun in his hand, and said, 'I'm going to kill you. . . .' I kept pulling the trigger until my gun was empty."

At the Valley Forge hospital, Johnson had asked an Army psychiatrist, "What would happen if I lost control of myself in Detroit and behaved like I did in Vietnam?" The psychiatrist declined to answer. For the next several years, Johnson's question ricocheted through press reports of similar incidents. Vietnam veterans, wrote one reporter in 1973, were "the most alienated generation of trained killers in American history." In 1972, a Harvard sociologist who had studied sixty combat veterans in the Boston area told *Time* magazine that the violence of which they were capable "has no boundaries." In the same article, *Time*'s reporters described a former Green Beret who got into a barroom argument over a woman with a friend and shot him seven times. While his friend lay dead on the floor, the veteran, "thinking he had just killed an attacking Viet Cong, was stripping the body so that it could not be rigged with booby traps." During Richard Nixon's reelection campaign, his party platform had described the America of 1972 as a world of "reason and order and hope," a world in which war had faded from view and Americans had returned to their traditional peacetime concerns. The increasing number of stories of violent, traumatized veterans, however, suggested that behind that peaceful facade, Americans remained haunted by their recollections of the fighting in Vietnam.

Psychologists and sociologists soon developed a clinical language with which to describe men like Johnson, a language that codified not only the former soldiers' symptoms of traumatic stress, but the fears about themselves that American civilians had projected onto their veterans. In 1971, historian Murray Polner wrote:

> There may be emerging a "new" . . . veteran, different indeed from all the rest, a still small but growing minority who have what some are now calling PVS, Post-Vietnam Syndrome. Hardly a clear diagnostic category, PVS is rather a malaise that embraces intangibles undetected in past conflicts: moral corruption, alienation, guilt; having been compelled to be both "victim and executioner"; having been made to serve in a class war for no discernible reason, by a nation that cared little for them; being held morally responsible in an amoral whirlwind.

Polner's "intangibles" clearly embrace civilian as well as military behaviors and moods. By the early 1970s, millions of civilian Americans had, like their soldiers, become both victims and executioners. On the one hand, they had been lied to by their political and military leaders throughout the war. To the extent that they believed General William Westmoreland when he claimed on the eve of the Tet Offensive that the end of the war had "come into view" or earlier, President Johnson, when he claimed that he would never ask American boys to fight a war that wasn't theirs, the American public had suffered a national betrayal.

On the other hand, though, journalists and academics had been offering up fairly accurate assessments of the nature and probable duration of the fighting in Vietnam since the mid-1960s. To the extent that they ignored those reports and chose instead, particularly in the latter years of the war, to work for the local draft board, march in pro-Nixon and prowar demonstrations, or simply encourage their sons to "do what was right" and go to Vietnam, civilian Americans joined in the killing and dying of their soldier-sons. Lurking at the edge of Richard Nixon's rhetoric of "greatness" was the shadow of the American public's sense of its own "moral corruption, alienation, guilt." American leaders and American soldiers had not prosecuted the war entirely on their own, without public sanction. But rather than address the feelings stemming from that knowledge, many Americans assigned them to Vietnam veterans. By the end of the war, returning veterans carried with them not only the knowledge of combat, but the weight of the entire conflict. As Robert Lifton wrote in 1971:

> [T]he Vietnam veteran serves as a psychological crucible of the entire country's doubts and misgivings about the war. He has been the agent and victim of that confusion—of on the one hand our general desensitization to indiscriminate killing, and on the other our accumulating guilt and deep suspicion concerning our own actions. We sent him as an intruder in a revolution taking place in a small Asian society, and he returns as a tainted intruder in our own society.

Yet, in the early 1970s, it wasn't just any Vietnam veteran who intruded on American society. Rather, it was a mentally ill veteran whose dominant symptom was an uncontrollable urge to return to Vietnam. The urge might manifest itself subtly, in little tics and twitches, or floridly, in full-blown repetitions of combat behavior that inevitably entangled noncombatants. In the movies and on TV, and too often, in the real-life crime reports on men like Dwight Johnson, Vietnam veterans became cyclones of violence, sucking unsuspecting civilians away from their peaceful postwar lives and back into the kill-or-be-killed dynamics of Vietnam.

In the film *Welcome Home, Soldier Boys* (1972), for instance, four Green Berets who have just been mustered out of the Army set out for California in a used Cadillac. They pass through Oklahoma and Texas like a search-and-destroy team in the Mekong Delta. They pick up a hitchhiker, have sex with her, and throw her out of the fast-moving car, as if she had no more value than the one commonly assigned to prostitutes in Vietnam. A mechanic who fixes their car in Texas cheats them, much as Vietnamese hustlers once cheated GIs. When the foursome hits Hope, New Mexico, at dawn, they find a gas station owner who won't open his pumps. He takes a shot at them—the proverbial shot from the Vietnamese village that sparked its annihilation—and the former Green Berets go berserk. They unload a pile of weapons from their trunk and proceed to wipe the town off the map, doing to its inhabitants what real American GIs had done to the villagers of My Lai several years before. They stop only when a heavily armed contingent of the National Guard guns them down.

In Henry Jaglom's *Tracks* (1976), a film made less than a year after the fall of Saigon, Sergeant Jack Falen (Dennis Hopper) finds himself on a train, escorting the body of his best friend across the country. When he eventually arrives in the small town his dead friend came from, Falen is surprised to find only two undertakers waiting to meet him. His friend won the Congressional Medal of Honor and Falen had expected him to be welcomed and praised. But no one comes, either to the station or the cemetery. "He's the biggest hero here," says Falen at the grave, but "No one showed up. No one." As the undertakers lower the coffin into the ground, Falen goes berserk. Screaming "You motherfuckers! You motherfuckers!", he jumps on top of the coffin, tears off the American flag, and starts talking to his dead buddy. "You didn't just go into the Army," he says. "They sent you to Nam." Then he turns to the undertakers and the theater audience and howls: *"You want to go to Nam?!? You want to go to Nam?!? I'll take you there!"* On top of the coffin, now surreally draped with a South Vietnamese flag, Falen finds a helmet, a pair of M-16s, and clips of ammunition. And in the film's final scene, he bursts up out of the burial hole, fully armed for combat and ready to kill, shouting over and over again: *"You want to go to Nam? I'll take you there!"*

Like the Green Berets of *Welcome Home, Soldier Boys,* Falen stands ready to go to war on American civilians and—specifically—on the theater full of moviegoers watching his film. As he explodes up out of the grave, fully armed and enraged, he presents the audience with an emblem of their own violence toward the Vietnamese. At the same time, he offers them a chance to comprehend that violence, intellectually and emotionally. He has returned from the grave in order to invite the audience to return to the scene of battle, and with his craziness he offers the audience a chance to revisit and come to grips with their own.

In this respect, the stories of men like Falen and the Green Berets resembled the nightmares of traumatized veterans themselves. Since his return from Vietnam, for example, Brian Winhover has dreamed repeatedly of finding himself suddenly alone in the Vietnamese jungle. Unarmed, he hears the enemy approaching and hides in the bushes. Then he decides to run. "As fast as I run," he says, "it's almost slow motion. I never escape, but I never get caught either."

Winhover's actions in the dream, like those of the soldiers in *Welcome Home, Soldier Boys* and *Tracks,* recall real historical events. As a tank crewman, Brian Winhover spent his days driving the roads and trails of Vietnam, enduring repeated ambushes. At one point, a rocket hit his tank, killing his fellow crewmen and disabling the vehicle. While Winhover waited inside, surrounded by the corpses of the crew, enemy soldiers climbed up onto the tank's turret and attempted to break in. Before they could succeed, American helicopters strafed the area, killing them. Winhover opened the turret hatch and ran into the jungle, where he survived for three days. When he was eventually found by American troops, he could remember nothing after the moment he realized his tank was being overrun.

Winhover still cannot consciously remember what he did after he fled the tank. But in a dramatically compressed form, his dream tells the story for him. The facts of hiding in the jungle, of being hunted and alone, of being unarmed—all belong to the historical experience of the escape. So too does the emotion of terror and the ability, common in moments of great stress, to see everything in slow motion. Winhover has "imagined" none of it. Instead, like survivors of many different kinds of traumatic events, he has relived it. Even though, in the daytime, he has succeeded in "forgetting" the details of what had happened to him, those same details return to him at night.

In the early 1970s, films and newspaper stories featuring traumatized veterans performed a similar function in the culture at large. In editorials and political speeches, Americans stepped away from Vietnam. They neither assessed blame, nor even discussed the details of the fighting. Even those films involving former soldiers were set in the United States. Vietnam itself had faded from the screen, slipped over the horizon— vanished. And yet, at the same time, stories of what Americans had seen and done lived on, with more than a little historical accuracy, in the nightmarish tales of traumatized veterans who had brought the war back home.

Both *Tracks* and *Welcome Home, Soldier Boys* were relatively low-budget movies and neither attracted a mass audience. While extremely common, particularly on television, depictions of traumatized veterans in the early 1970s never garnered the audience share accorded to nostalgic depictions of prewar America, such as *American Graffiti* (1973) or *The Way We Were* (1973). Nor did they enjoy the popularity of films such as *M*A*S*H* (1970 and, from 1972 to 1983, a TV series) or *Slaughterhouse-*

Five (1972), films that transposed the absurdities of Vietnam to older, less emotionally charged battlegrounds.

In 1976, however, Martin Scorsese released perhaps the most famous "crazed vet" movie of all time, *Taxi Driver*. Like earlier films, *Taxi Driver* stars a man who clearly suffers many of the symptoms of post-traumatic stress disorder. A twenty-six-year-old ex-Marine, uneducated and addicted to junk food, Travis Bickle (Robert De Niro) drives a cab, he says, because he "can't sleep nights." Night after night, he patrols the streets of New York as if they were the trails of Vietnam. Hypervigilant, incapable of forming relationships, Bickle feels surrounded by a filth he despises: "All the animals come out at night," he says. "Whores, skunk pussies, buggers, queens, fairies, dopers, junkies. Sick, venal. Someday a real rain will come and wash all the scum off the streets."

By 1976, the image of a combat veteran returning to an America that looked like Vietnam and wanting to "wash all the scum off the streets" was nothing new. What *was* new was Bickle's resemblance to the people he wanted to hurt. When he claims that "All the animals come out at night," he implies that he too has become a beast. Like a soldier newly arrived in Vietnam, he feels disgust at local customs. Prostitutes, for instance, bring their johns into his taxi. Some nights, he says, he has to clean their cum and their blood off the backseat. Yet no sooner has he detailed the behavior of hookers and their clients than he strides into a porn theater and makes himself at home. In earlier films, such as *Welcome Home, Soldier Boys* or *Tracks,* veterans brought violence back with them from Vietnam in the form of stress disorders and inflicted it on unsuspecting and seemingly uninvolved civilians. They hoped, like Jack Falen, to teach Americans what they had done to their soldiers and to the Vietnamese. But in *Taxi Driver,* the veteran's symptoms of postcombat distress hardly leave him out of place. Rather, they help identify him as one of the urban animals.

In the best American tradition, Bickle aims at self-improvement. "I don't believe that one should devote his life to morbid self-attention," he tells the audience. "I believe that one should become a person like other people." Where earlier veterans remained incorrigible and often had to be killed in the end, Bickle hopes to reintegrate himself into American society. Scorsese grants him his wish. Like earlier sociopathic veterans, Bickle undertakes a mission against the forces of law and order in America, a mission that he suggests will be the "rain" the city so desperately needs. He shaves his head in a mohawk (a haircut Scorsese mistakenly believed to be common among Special Forces troops in Vietnam), straps a nasty pack of jungle weapons to his body, and sets out to assassinate the bombastic candidate for President, Charles Palantine.

Had he succeeded, Bickle might have become just another in a long fictional line of traumatized veterans who have compulsively replayed their combat experiences at the expense of innocent civilians and *Taxi Driver* might have faded from memory. At the last moment, though, Bickle lets Secret Service agents chase him away. Jack Falen or the Green Berets of *Welcome Home, Soldier Boys* would have stood and fought and probably died, but Bickle leaves the scene and seeks out Iris (Jodie Foster), a teenaged prostitute he has befriended. Arriving at the tenement where she works, he turns his guns on her pimp, her landlord, and one of her customers. After a frenzy of gunplay and gore that leaves only Iris unwounded, Bickle tries to shoot himself, but survives—the gun has run out of bullets. The police arrive, and in the final moments of the film, Scorsese lets his audience know that Bickle has been declared a hero. His camera reveals a letter from Iris's parents taped to his wall: "There is no way we can repay you for returning our Iris to us. We thought we had lost her and now our lives are full again. Needless to say, you are something of a hero around this household."

Where once it would have led to certain death, a traumatized Vietnam veteran's bizarre need to reenact combat has now led to heroism. He has restored Iris to her parents and, with her, the possibility of redemption to Americans as a whole. If earlier veterans embodied the unspoken guilt many Americans felt for what their countrymen had done in Vietnam, Bickle's choosing to go after the pimps rather than the politician suggested that that guilt could be rechanneled away from the war and toward the restoration of social order. If men like Jack Falen had in part exacted an imaginary revenge on behalf of the Vietnamese, then the Secret Service's ability to thwart Bickle's attempt on the candidate's life hinted that the time for retribution had passed, that as long as they were not antisocial "animals," such as pimps, civilians and their leaders would now be safe from reprisal. Leaders like Palantine and the people who voted for them had sent Americans into Vietnam, but in Bickle's New York, it was the local common crooks, rather than the national political villains, who would be punished.

When the film was released, critics debated the meaning of Bickle's actions with uncommon ferocity. Some argued that "there is no catharsis possible in the psychopathic nightmare of *Taxi Driver.*" Others argued that the film "forced the audience to . . . empathetically experience . . . the collective fantasy of liberating violence." Still others felt that *Taxi Driver* was nothing more than "the kind of adrenaline-pumping, unprincipled revenge melodrama which will do anything to arouse its audience." But whether they thought it was effective or not, the critics tended to agree that, as Julian Rice put it, Bickle resembled "the cowboy and the terrorist cubistically fused." Unlike Jack Falen or the Green Berets who wiped out Hope, New Mexico, Bickle was neither all crazy nor all bad. Instead, as Rice put it at the time, he assumed "simultaneously, the roles of the conventional hero and the ultimate modern villain." In other words, he had bridged what had, in earlier films, as well as many journalistic accounts of veterans' behavior, remained divided: the rift between the prewar world of the "conventional hero" and the villainous universe of Vietnam. Bickle was the mythical cowboy in which Americans saw themselves as they rode into Vietnam and, at the same time, he was the kind of crazed terrorizer of civilians Americans had seen their sons become at My Lai. Perhaps most surprising, he was terribly attractive to American moviegoers: *Taxi Driver* drew one of the largest audiences for any film released that year.

Taxi Driver marked a new stage in the recollection of the war. In the early and mid-1970s, films like *Welcome Home, Soldier Boys* and *Tracks* offered viewers fairly precise repetitions of combat that had actually taken place in Vietnam. But in the late 1970s, tales of veterans engaged in repetitive combat violence began to fade from the media. In films like *Taxi Driver,* or later *Heroes* (1977) or *Coming Home* (1978), the traumatized veteran began to lose his lunatic edge. If his character still retained some of its earlier naked, psychotic isolation, it also began to blend into traditional genre roles. In *Coming Home,* Bruce Dern's pinwheel-eyed veteran commits suicide, but not before playing the odd man out in a classic melodramatic love triangle. In *Heroes,* Henry Winkler's traumatized veteran endures terrible flashbacks, but not before winning the love of Sally Field in a conventional romance.

In their changes, these stories continued to resemble the dreams of traumatized veterans. To return to Brian Winhover: The central fact of his nightmare, a fact that many veterans' stories have in common, is Winhover's radical solitude. When the enemy overran his tank, Winhover found himself alone in a manner and to a degree that few who haven't seen combat could even imagine. Almost twenty years after returning home, though, Winhover began having another, very different dream. In this dream, he and his current wife are sitting in a bunker in Vietnam. A tank pulls up next to the bunker and a man steps out and tells them that it is time to leave, time to fly back to America. Winhover's wife doesn't want to leave and they look at each other. He then wakes up.

In this new dream, the historical accuracy of the chase dream has been violated. Vietnam has ceased to be Vietnam and even the past has ceased to be strictly the past. In the Vietnam in which his tank was overrun, a Vietnam he recalled in nightmares for years, Winhover was alone. Now he has begun to mingle past and present. In his dreams, he has eased the long isolation of combat with the companionship of his wife. At the same time, he has brought his memories of Vietnam out of psychological segregation, allowing them to mingle with his thoughts of the present. His buddies in Vietnam, many dead, actually speak to him and his wife, both now living. The two worlds—past and present, Vietnam and America—have become one, if only for a moment.

Likewise, in *Taxi Driver,* Vietnam and America have melded into a single dreamscape. Bickle's taxi could be a tank; his mission to save Iris could be the American mission to save South Vietnam. In the Technicolor-*noire* of Scorsese's camerawork, the urban jungle of New York becomes as alien as the triple-canopy forests of Vietnam. The pimps and johns Bickle kills blend into the population of this degraded city as well as the Viet Cong once blended into the population of Saigon. And like the American troops who leveled the city of Hué during the Tet Offensive, Bickle has had to destroy Iris's world in order to save it.

For Winhover, the dream of the bunker and his wife was both the result and the marker of tremendous psychological changes. For years his past had come after him, dragging him into flashbacks and nightmares. Now these torments came less often. In the late 1980s, around the time he first dreamed of his wife in Vietnam, Winhover began taking charge of his memories. He began organizing his recollections of combat into stories with clear narrative lines and telling those stories to members of his therapy group and to visiting doctors as well. Again and again he would voluntarily recall the war, and as he did, his involuntary recollections of combat faded.

In the wake of *Taxi Driver,* Americans entered a similar period of voluntary recall. In the early 1970s, Americans had by and large worked hard to avoid thinking about the fighting in Vietnam. Then, in the late 1970s, they turned back toward it in hordes. Between 1976 and 1980, Americans saw an outpouring of novels, memoirs, and films about the war, all of which recalled the details of combat that had been suppressed in public discourse and sublimated in the stories of returning veterans. Michael Herr's *Dispatches,* Ron Kovic's *Born on the Fourth of July,* Philip Caputo's *A Rumor of War,* James Webb's *Fields of Fire*—all came out between 1976 and 1978. Each told formerly forbidden stories of combat, whether from the point of view of a journalist (Herr), a grunt turned antiwarrior (Kovic), or a right-wing ex-Marine (Webb). In recent years, we've come to think of Vietnam veterans as a group whose voices have been largely ignored. But in the late 1970s, their voices could be heard booming from the center of the national stage. In 1979, veteran Tim O'Brien's Vietnam combat novel *Going After Cacciato* received the National Book Award for Fiction. That same year two films about returning veterans—*The Deer Hunter* and *Coming Home*—won Academy Awards. Twelve months later, Francis Ford Coppola's combat epic *Apocalypse Now* repeated their performance. By the end of the 1970s, the experience of combat could be openly and directly discussed in a way that only five years earlier it could not.

All across the country, Americans displayed a new sympathy for Vietnam veterans and particularly for those who still suffered, physically and psychologically. In April 1979, Congress recognized post-traumatic stress disorder as a valid medical condition and authorized Veterans Administration hospitals to treat it. Two months later, the House voted 342 to 0 to fund a string of veterans centers across the country, centers that would provide psychological counseling, along with alcohol and drug rehabilitation services—they had rejected a similar Senate bill four times in the previous eight years. Finally, in 1980, psychologists succeed in having the diagnosis of post-traumatic stress disorder included in the American Psychiatric Association's *Diagnostic and Statistical Manual of Mental Disorders,* the diagnostic sourcebook for the psychological professions.

Yet our seeming willingness to confront the legacy of the war masked a subtle and increasing obfuscation of the conflict's nature and causes. Like Brian Winhover after his dream of the bunker, Americans had begun to string their recollections of the war into coherent narratives. But rather than simply organize the facts of their experiences in the war, as Winhover's stories did, our public narratives began to recast the private experiences of civilians and soldiers in a more flattering mold. On May 28, 1979, for example, President Jimmy Carter announced the start of the first Vietnam Veterans Week. In a speech at the White House on May 30, Carter stood surrounded by veterans, many in wheelchairs, and explained that "the nation is ready to change its heart, its mind and its attitude about the men who had fought in the war." In the past, he told the veterans, Americans had not done enough "to respect, honor, recognize, and reward [your] special heroism." Today, he concluded, "We love you for what you were and what you stood for—and we love you for what you are and what you stand for."

Carter was notably vague about just what it was Vietnam veterans had been and what they stood for now. How had their heroism been "special"? Carter neglected to say, hinting only that risking one's life in Vietnam "require[d] an extra measure of patriotism and sacrifice." Whereas ten years before, George McGovern, a politician not too far to the left of Jimmy Carter, had called Vietnam an immoral war and implied that serving in such a war, however efficiently, was itself an immoral act, Carter focused on the rhetoric of affection and welcome.

In a parallel development, the framers of the diagnosis of post-traumatic stress disorder carefully pared away the social "intangibles" that had characterized earlier descriptions of post-Vietnam syndrome. Where Murray Polner and Robert Lifton had described the symptoms of post-traumatic stress as the inevitable results of having to play both victim and executioner in Vietnam, the psychologists who defined the disorder in the *Diagnostic and Statistical Manual* claimed that it was the result of "a psychologically traumatic event that is generally outside the range of usual human experience." Such an event, they wrote, "may be experienced alone (rape or assault) or in the company of groups of people (military combat)." In a telling bit of grammar and diction, the psychologists' definition suggested that what traumatized soldiers (and other trauma survivors) was simply being *in the presence* of certain events. The events, said the diagnosis, produced the disorder; traumatized people, it suggested, had passively "experienced" rape or combat and had been victimized by these events. But what of men who had brought about such events? Or of the fact that for working-class American men, including not only those of the Vietnam generation, but their fathers and grandfathers as well, the experience of combat was hardly "outside the range of usual human experience"? Whereas Murray Polner had seen traumatized soldiers as both victims and executioners, the authors of the *Diagnostic and Statistical Manual* presented them exclusively as victims.

Some critics continued to link the sufferings of veterans to questions of national psychology. In 1978, Jeffrey Jay echoed Robert Lifton's analysis of seven years before when he told the readers of *Harper's Magazine* that "The veteran's [psychological] conflicts are not his alone, but are bound to the trauma and guilt of the nation. And our failure to deal with our guilt renders the veteran the symptom-carrier for society and increases his moral and emotional burden." But where Robert Lifton had located the source of veterans' psychological conflicts in the soldiers' having been both the "agent and victim . . . of . . . our general desensitization to indiscriminate killing," Jeffrey Jay declares that it is "our failure to *deal with our guilt* [my italics]" which "isolates the veteran and will freeze him in an attitude of perpetual combat until the issues of the war are confronted in the national conscience."

According to Jay, the hallmark symptoms of post-traumatic stress disorder—the conditions of perpetual combat, of being isolated and suspicious—derive not from a veteran's having killed and seen others killed in a war, let alone such a militarily and morally confusing war, but from his having been neglected when he returned:

> Although the nation hastens on to new issues, the veteran—years after discharge—repeatedly reviews the events of his Vietnam duty. He seeks to justify his war experiences in a society that now denies them

any meaning. The veteran cannot reconcile the beliefs that propelled him through combat with his current social isolation; he cannot accept the status of social pariah. *It may well be that isolation, the burden of conflicted feelings, and not being heard makes people crazy* [my italics].

In fact, as numerous psychological studies have shown, it is the exposure to and participation in killing, dying, and acts of abusive violence, such as torture and mutilation, that "makes people crazy" with post-traumatic stress disorder. Social isolation and stigmatization certainly complicate and increase a traumatized veteran's sufferings, but they do not cause them.

In the early 1970s, Americans' guilt over what they had done (and were still doing) in Vietnam and their guilt over how they had ignored their veterans had been intertwined. By the end of the decade, the fighting in Vietnam had faded and the specter of neglected veterans at home had risen up to take its place. On August 18, 1980, presidential candidate Ronald Reagan told a convention of the Veterans of Foreign Wars:

> For too long, we have lived with the "Vietnam Syndrome". . . . It is time that we recognized that ours was, in truth, a noble cause. A small country, newly free from colonial rule, sought our help in establishing self-rule and the means of self-defense against a totalitarian neighbor bent on conquest. . . . We dishonor the memory of 50,000 young Americans who died in that cause when we give way to feelings of guilt as if we were doing something shameful, and we have been shabby in our treatment of those who returned. They fought as well and as bravely as any Americans have ever fought in any war. They deserve our gratitude, our respect, and our continuing concern.

In Reagan's America, "our continuing concern" for Vietnam veterans would come to replace our guilt and our suspicion that ours was not "a noble cause." The former understanding of the veteran as both victim and executioner, along with the notion that those roles made veterans sick with post-traumatic stress disorder, had slipped from public view. Only one word of the old phrase remained: the word "victim." In 1979, a Harris poll revealed that 73 percent of Americans felt that "The trouble was that our troops were asked to fight in a war which our ⌐ders in Washington would not let them win." The image of Vietnam as an "amoral whirlwind" or as a place where Americans participated in "indiscriminate killing" had largely disappeared.

A few stray voices on the left sought to remind Americans of what they were losing. Six months after Reagan addressed the Veterans of Foreign Wars, writer Peter Marin published a long and thoughtful essay in *Harper's Magazine* that tackled the moral legacy of the war head on. "None of us," he wrote,

> has faced the specter of his *own* culpability—not Nixon's, not Kissinger's—but the way in which each one of us, actively or passively, contributed to the killing, the taxes we paid, officials we elected, lessons we taught in the classroom, obedience we taught, the endless round of incipient [sic] and explicit influences that made countless young men willing to kill for the worst of causes in the worst of ways. We have skirted the sort of passionate and open self-investigation that members of a democratic society must conduct to protect others from themselves, a rethinking of values and allegiances that have had brutal effects.

But even as they renamed the sources of the guilt that civilians had for so long loaded onto the shoulders of veterans, Marin and others turned back to traumatized veterans and asked them to heal the nation once again. "It is [veterans'] voices—real voices, grounded in the real," wrote Marin, "that may have the power to call us back from our illusions to the discomforting concreteness of our acts." The fact that "some of them are forced . . . to struggle inwardly, and apparently endlessly" with their memories of the fighting and its moral conflicts makes veterans uniquely qualified to save the civilian population: "for who else," asked Marin, "has it in their power to keep us straight, and who else has the knowledge required to do it?"

Throughout the 1980s and early 1990s, the traumatized veterans of the popular media have in fact devoted themselves to keeping us—and each other—straight, although not perhaps in the way that Marin intended. Stories of men like Dwight Johnson have faded from the papers, just as characters like Jack Falen have disappeared from the movies. If on occasion a veteran goes haywire, whether in real life or fiction, his reen-actments of combat have been identified as the symptoms of a *medical* rather than *cultural* disorder. The chord linking his behavior at home to his nation's behavior in Vietnam has been cut. Where once he commit-ted himself to killing everything in sight, the traumatized veteran charac-ter has now turned to restoring the social order and to healing himself, his buddies, and his audience.

In the films and TV programs of the early 1980s, for example, post-traumatic stress disorder became a mark of experience for otherwise traditional superheroes. Thomas Magnum (Tom Selleck), the broad-chested star of the enormously popular detective series *Magnum, P.I.* (CBS, 1980–1988), used to be a Navy frogman in Vietnam. He now employs his combat skills (and a few of his old combat buddies) to catch criminals in Hawaii. Periodically he suffers flashbacks, but these rarely bother him for more than a moment. Instead, like references to the planet Krypton in a *Superman* comic strip, they remind Magnum—and his audience—of the origins of his unusual strength.

Even Sylvester Stallone's John Rambo, probably the best-known veteran character of the 1980s, turns his traumatic memories to account. In *First Blood* (1982), for instance, the first of the Rambo films, Rambo takes on a small-town sheriff's department in the jungle-like woods of the American Northwest. While he was hitchhiking through the town, the sheriff had harassed and arrested him. Fearing that the sheriff might torture him as the Vietnamese once had, Rambo flees the town jail. Chased by the sheriff and his posse, Rambo slips into an extended flash-back and begins to kill off the deputies one by one. But even as he does, Rambo remains a sympathetic character. He is less a psychopath than a combat-hardened, gun-toting Robin Hood, a victim of police brutality who has the skills to fight back. When Rambo does fight back, full of post-traumatic fury, he fights for the very right to live his life as he sees fit that the sheriff and his men were supposed to protect. Even as he disobeys the law, he upholds its spirit.

In the early 1970s, traumatized veteran characters like Jack Falen let loose a nasty, helter-skelter violence on Americans, a violence akin to that of real combat. In the 1980s, characters like Magnum or Rambo kill only when they have to and then with smooth control. Like their prede-cessors, they appear to be refighting the war, but in fact, they bring little of the reality of combat to the screen. Instead, they help bind the stories of Vietnam veterans to the big-screen myths of John Wayne, and even to older tales, such as those of Superman or Robin Hood. Their violence serves, rather than threatens, the maintenance of social order.

So too does their mental illness. In 1989, for instance, just thirteen years after he prowled the jungles of New York in *Taxi Driver,* Robert De Niro sets out to save an old Army buddy in the melodrama *Jackknife.* With a shaggy beard and a personality as soft and worn as an old slipper, De Niro's Megs is everything his Travis Bickle was not: emotionally collected, self-aware, warm. He still suffers from his memories of the war, but rather than act them out, he talks them through at a local veterans' rap group. His pal Dave (Ed Harris) remains consumed by his memories of the war and his guilt over his behavior there. But even he is hardly dangerous. His sister Martha (Kathy Baker), with whom he lives, puts it neatly when she tells him, "You're like a mold in this house. You eat what's put in front of you and grunt when spoken to. Shit. I'd be better off with a Saint Bernard. At least I wouldn't have to worry about him killing himself every time I went out at night." In a movie made a decade before, Martha might well have had to worry that Dave would kill *her.*

In *Taxi Driver,* Travis Bickle's commando demeanor and his familiarity with weapons suggested he had killed a great deal in Vietnam and implied that it was the killing he had done in combat, rather than, say, the loss of friends or his fear of death, that haunted him in later years. In *Jackknife,* the filmmakers never suggest that Dave or Megs killed anyone in Vietnam at all. Instead, they show that what haunts them is having *watched* someone die. In a series of flashbacks, the audience sees Dave and Megs pinned down during a firefight as a helicopter comes to get them out. Their friend Bobby loads Dave onto the chopper and then goes back for Megs. Dave, not wanting Bobby to get killed, tells him that Megs is dead. Bobby goes anyway, gets shot, and dies.

During the fighting, the Vietnamese remain invisible behind the trees. Afterward, a single old man in black pajamas appears, but otherwise the audience sees little evidence of a specifically Vietnamese enemy and almost none of American aggression. The Americans concern themselves with rescuing their friends and getting out of the line of fire. The moments that bother Dave and Megs today involve only Americans and their behavior toward one another. Where the veterans of earlier films came back to America and reenacted a conflict in which American troops wreaked havoc on innocent foreign civilians, Dave and Megs suffer a suicidal guilt from having fought a battle among themselves.

Megs tries to alleviate his guilt by rescuing Dave from the isolation of post-traumatic stress disorder. As he does, he not only imitates Bobby's attempt to rescue *him* in combat, but also hints at a right-wing reinterpretation of the war. On the one hand, Bobby's effort to save Megs can be read simply as an image of personal heroism, an emblem of moral behavior in the midst of an immoral or, at the very least, meaningless war. On the other hand, though, it can also be seen as an echo of the interpretation Ronald Reagan proposed in 1980: Just as Bobby was trying to keep Megs from being crushed by an overwhelming enemy, so perhaps Americans were indeed trying to protect "a small country, newly free from colonial rule" from "a totalitarian neighbor bent on conquest." Likewise, as he works to heal Dave by pressing him to acknowledge what actually happened in Vietnam, Megs offers his audience a chance to take refuge from their memories of national aggression in the soothing notion that, twenty-five years before, maybe they too were just trying to help.

At the end of the film, Megs finds his way back into society by putting the past away. One night he was considering suicide, but then, he tells Martha, "I prayed and I felt better. What was done [in Vietnam] was done. I couldn't change it. For some reason, we lost old Bobby and it was up to me to make that reason a good one, 'cause old Bobby, he deserved it."

What *was* the reason they "lost old Bobby"? What *was* the reason Americans lost so many Bobbys? De Niro's Megs never quite lets on, nor do other cinematic vets. One after another, the traumatized former soldiers of films like *Birdy* (1984), *Cease Fire* (1984), *Distant Thunder* (1988), and *In Country* (1989) reach out to one another and to civilians, comforting those whom their predecessors had formerly attacked and smothering the complicated origins and the grisly nature of the war in the emotional honey of recovery. The sheer absence of Vietnamese in these films, along with the repeated, detailed attention the moviemakers pay to healing the rifts between individual veterans, suggest to viewers that Vietnam was in fact an exclusively American war, a war between brothers, as it were, and that its wounds linger only for us.

In 1990, the producers of *Jacob's Ladder* used a traumatized veteran to make that point explicitly. Like the mirror image of a stock early-1970s veteran, the film's central character, Jacob Singer (Tim Robbins), suffers a series of flash*forwards*. As he lies dying from wounds in Vietnam, he projects himself into the future and imagines that he has returned home to the United States. Demons, clearly meant to parallel the hallucinated characters of traumatized veterans' flash*backs,* chase him through the streets. The demons keep after him, until another veteran takes Singer aside and explains that he was killed not by the enemy, but by his own comrades—men whom the government had fed an experimental drug designed to bring out "the dark side" of their natures. Having acquired this new knowledge of the meaning of his suffering, Jacob reconciles himself to his fate and allows himself to die on the battlefield.

Like *Jackknife, Jacob's Ladder* suggests that once Americans recognize that they were only fighting themselves in Vietnam (as now, confronting the symptoms of their traumas, veterans fight among themselves in order to heal), they will be able to put the war to rest. For the makers of *Jackknife* and *Jacob's Ladder,* the war was an individual rather than an international problem. In their versions of the war, Americans killed each other, not millions of Vietnamese. And now, like the symptoms of post-traumatic stress disorder, the war has become something to be accepted, lived with, and recovered from—not something to be reexamined or critiqued.

In part, perhaps, these new and flattering interpretations of what Americans did in Vietnam are the result of a natural process of making sense of a cataclysmic event. Not long ago, Brian Winhover tried to explain to me what it had meant for him to be diagnosed with post-traumatic stress disorder. "If I didn't have PTSD," he said, "I'd be one sick bastard." In Vietnam, Winhover had witnessed and participated in several atrocities. When he came home, he lashed out at friends and family members and, at times, strangers on the street. As he put it, "For the first ten years [after I got back from Vietnam], I didn't have PTSD and I was one cold bastard. I didn't have no feelings. I could cut somebody's throat and smile about it." For Winhover, the diagnosis of post-traumatic stress disorder offered a way to make sense of what otherwise might have appeared to be senseless behavior. By describing his numbness and his violence as reactions to combat in Vietnam, they allowed Winhover to see himself not as a monstrous killer, but as a survivor of a series of horrors: "I'm normal for what I went through," he said, repeating himself to make sure I understood. "I'm normal for what I went through."

Over the years, depictions of traumatized veterans in the popular media have played a role in our society not unlike the role the diagnosis of post-traumatic stress disorder has played in the mind of Brian Winhover. In the early 1970s, they offered us a way to frame and comprehend our own violent behavior. In the late 1970s, and on through the 1980s and 1990s, they offered us a way to forgive ourselves for our violence. And to that extent, they have served as a healing force in our society.

At the same time, though, as we have changed our perceptions of the causes of PTSD, we have also altered our memories of the nature of the fighting in Vietnam. In 1990, Senator Alan Cranston, the chairman of the Senate Committee on Veterans' Affairs and a longtime advocate of services for Vietnam veterans, described what he believed to be the origins of post-traumatic stress disorder:

> The reasons for the dramatic psychological impact of fighting the Vietnam War on those who fought it remain a matter of controversy, as, indeed, does the war itself. Certainly the unrest at home played a part. Whereas veterans from other wars returned to heroes' welcomes and were allowed, if not encouraged, to discuss their war experiences, Vietnam veterans received no such welcome and little encouragement or understanding. Another factor may have been the lack of time to decompress after the war experience. Within a twenty-four-hour period, a soldier could be transported from the jungle to the streets of San Francisco. Another factor may have been the relatively short-term, one-year experience in-country, which inhibited both the willingness of the soldier to form cohesive bonds within their units and the natural development of those bonds.
>
> What can no longer be in controversy is our need to respond to these problems.

Twenty years ago Americans saw their traumatized soldiers as men made ill largely by their nation's aggressive violence overseas. The post-Vietnam syndrome of the 1970s was "a malaise that embraces . . . moral corruption, alienation, guilt." The post-traumatic stress disorder of the 1990s, however, has come to be blamed on "the unrest at home," on the fact that returning veterans received "little encouragement or understanding." Likewise, those who suffer from PTSD are no longer the anguished survivors of an unnecessary war, but the victims of an overly efficient transportation system, a too-short "experience in-country," a chilly welcome at home. In public discussions of post-traumatic stress today, the combat that Robert Lifton described as "indiscriminate killing," the war that even the Republican Party platform of 1972 called "so bloody, so costly, so bitterly divisive," has faded from view.

So too has the memory of American responsibility for that combat. In the early 1960s, Americans hoped to save the South Vietnamese from the plague of communism. But in the postwar years, the Vietnamese have slipped from sight. Rewritten as a conflict among Americans alone, the war now offers us new victims—traumatized American veterans. At the same time, it flatters us into reprising the roles in which we first began to fight. In the new drama of post-traumatic stress disorder, as in the old drama of infectious communism, Americans can take the stage as healers and saviors of blameless victims. This time, though, the victims are Americans too.

CHAPTER FOUR

REBUILDING
THE HERO:

FANTASY, AGENCY, AND
THE PORNOGRAPHY OF WAR

NEARLY A HUNDRED YEARS BEFORE AMERICAN TROOPS went to war in Southeast Asia, one of George Armstrong Custer's aides, Major Marcus Reno, found himself and his men trapped by Indians during the Battle of Little Big Horn. Hunkered down in a cluster of cottonwood trees, Reno called one of his own Indian scouts, a man named Bloody Knife, over to his side. While they were talking, a bullet hit Bloody Knife in the face, spraying his blood, flesh, and brains onto Reno, who collapsed. According to a witness, "his mouth and beard [were] white with foam, which dripped down, and his eyes were wild and rolling." He could give no commands or even speak in coherent sentences. No one knows how long he remained this way, but the reports of some witnesses suggest he may have been unable to command his troops for an entire day.

Although the major did recover, his experience reveals much about what traumatizes participants in wars, including American soldiers in

Vietnam. Reno was neither young nor new to combat. He had fought in the Civil War and had been cited for gallantry. As far as we know, he had no predisposition to breaking under the stress of battle. But the phrase "the stress of battle" doesn't quite capture the experience of watching a close and trusted colleague's body burst apart. When Bloody Knife was shot, Reno came face-to-face with his own mortality and, at the same time, he saw that bodies that appear solid, bodies that have offered advice and comradeship, can come apart in an instant. As his reaction testified, such knowledge can so challenge a person's perceptions of the world around him that he literally ceases to perceive that world at all.

In Vietnam, hundreds of thousands of men had the opportunity to witness and, often, cause such deaths. Men saw mines blow the legs off their friends, bullets tear open their chests, shrapnel fracture their skulls. Perhaps they helped hook a Vietnamese prisoner up to a field telephone and watched as his skin smoked when they cranked up the electricity. Or maybe they came upon the dismembered corpses of villagers scattered in the wake of an air raid. If they were in combat, soldiers soon learned how fragile the human body, both their enemy's and their own, could be.

So too did American civilians at home. During the Vietnam War, newspapers, magazines, and even TV reports presented civilians with an astonishing array of images of bodily disintegration. Day after day, particularly in the wake of the 1968 Tet Offensive, Americans could see images of limbless American GIs, napalmed Vietnamese children, and piles of bloody corpses, both civilian and military. Clearly, seeing death in a magazine is infinitely less psychologically damaging than witnessing it firsthand or bringing it about. Yet I believe that part of what has made the Vietnam War linger so long and painfully in our popular memory is the fact that even when safely framed in the two-dimensional confines of a magazine page or a TV screen, images of violent deaths connected to the war, both American and Vietnamese, traumatized their viewers.

In part, civilian audiences suffered from a simple confrontation with mortality. When readers and viewers saw pictures of dying or wounded young men who looked like their brothers, their sons, or their grandsons, they could imagine themselves at their own moments of death. But the pictures of atrocity and gore that came to define the Vietnam War also forced viewers to confront the mortality of an idealized national self-image. In earlier, more popular wars, press photographs of American and enemy dead tended to reinforce civilians' sense of their nation as honorable and its military mission as right. The press almost never depicted American corpses that were not whole and clothed. And when, as in World War II, they showed the charred or hacked-apart corpses of the enemy, they rarely offended their readers. Instead, they reminded them that just as enemy soldiers could be killed, so enemy nations could be beaten.

In Vietnam, however, pictures of both Vietnamese and American deaths suggested that the American mission in Southeast Asia was at least impractical and perhaps immoral. On February 2, 1968, for instance, *The New York Times* published Eddie Adams's photograph of a suspected Viet Cong guerrilla, his hands tied behind his back, being shot in the head by the chief of the South Vietnamese National Police, General Nguyen Ngoc Loan. After news footage of the killing had been broadcast on national television and after still pictures had been reprinted across the country, columnist Shana Alexander asked of the picture, "Is this the sort of 'freedom and justice' that over half a million Americans are in Vietnam to fight for? Is this what some 18,000 already have died to defend?" In perhaps the most famous instance of this phenomenon, Ronald Haeberle's photographs of the My Lai massacre sparked a massive questioning of American morality. Mrs. Carling Dinkler, a Miami socialite, was not the only one who felt, as she put it in a letter to the editors of *Life,* an "utter mortal fright at an episode so contrary to the American ideal, where we have thought of ourselves as protecting women, children and the oppressed."

As the war dragged on, even traditional formats for honoring the dead took on subversive overtones. In June 1969, for example, *Life* magazine printed the photographs of 217 of the 242 Americans who had been killed in action between May 28 and June 3. Above an image of a young man's face, a close-up out of which all evidence of masculinity and youthful strength had been cropped, the magazine headlined: "The Faces of the American Dead in Vietnam: One Week's Toll." Inside, it printed a yearbook-style collection of head shots showing smiling young men, some in uniform, some not. Such layouts had been a convention of war reporting since the Spanish Civil War, but in the past, they had appeared under headlines like "Our Nation's Roll of Honor" (in World

War I) or "From Their Hour of Joy . . . These Went to Duty . . . and Death" (in Korea). Now the editors of *Life* had chosen this format to present deaths entirely divorced from any notion of duty or honor, deaths that were simply a "toll." For some time, the government had been using the body count as a measure of success in Vietnam. With their pictures of the men behind the numbers, the editors of *Life* not only humanized the statistics of that particular week, but suggested that the government's practice of measuring the war's progress numerically was inhuman.

Three weeks later *Life* printed some of the 1,300 letters they received in response to the story. "The 'faces' show us that these young men are *all* our cousins, brothers, husbands and sons," wrote Geraldine L. Barrett from Saratoga, California. As J. Hartman, a veteran, pointed out in his letter, however, these young men were not muscular bearers of national morality that their movie heroes had been:

> I grew up on a diet of Hollywood war films. The heroism, the ro-
> mance, the adventure, and even the death excited my interest. For
> these were men. When I entered the service I was astonished that no
> Fredric Marches, Clark Gables, Humphrey Bogarts were to be found
> in my barracks. Only young kids like myself (17), half-frightened, con-
> fused, immature kids stumbling through the senselessness of combat.

The deaths of such innocents suggested to many that it was time to pull out of the war. "Ever since the beginning of the 'conflict in Vietnam,' I have been an adamant hawk," wrote Tony Cook from San Bernardino, California. "However, your article is causing an agonizing 180-degree change of attitude. This perpetual bloodletting of the American youth must end."

Where in earlier wars Americans had seen their soldiers die for "duty" and "honor," in Vietnam they saw them perish on behalf of nothing more noble than a "perpetual bloodletting." As a result, Americans grieved not only their dead sons and brothers, but for their own loss of a sense of collective meaning. In the wake of World War II, on through Korea, and even into the first years of Vietnam, men like John Wayne, Gary Cooper, and the future President of the United States, Ronald Reagan, embodied the entire nation's aspirations, its youth, and its moral rectitude. When they fought the cinematic battles of the Old West or World War II, their handsome male bodies offered proof that Americans inhabited a secure moral universe.

But in Vietnam, as photograph after photograph showed, the bodies of young American men were being torn apart. Just as the muscles of John Wayne had once confirmed the morality of the American mission, so now the vulnerability of their soldiers' bodies reminded Americans that their mission in Vietnam might not be the right one after all. In combat, each violent death they witnessed corroded soldiers' confidence in the solidity of their own bodies and of the world they inhabited. Likewise, at home, each image of a wounded American teenager, a bloody Vietnamese baby, or a pile of Vietnamese corpses wore away at American civilians' confidence not only in the safety of their physical world, but in the moral integrity of the American body politic. Like Major Reno before them, combat soldiers and American civilians came face-to-face in Vietnam with a terrifying fragility.

Both on the battlefield and off, Americans responded to that fragility by becoming havoc-makers themselves. When combat soldiers arrived in Vietnam, they were frequently shocked by the violence of their comrades. "When I went over there, I was *appalled* by the American soldier," says Brian Winhover. "I was appalled by the torture, the dehumanization. And then I turned into one of them. I hated every fucking thing over there and whatever I hated I destroyed." In large part, what changed men like Winhover was an ever-increasing exposure to bodily injury. As death came closer to them by claiming their friends, soldiers became terrified and enraged. In a nonmilitary setting, they might have run for their lives, but of course, as soldiers who could be severely punished for desertion, let alone soldiers in a jungle thousands of miles from home, they had nowhere to go. Many pushed away their fears by doing to others what they were most afraid the enemy might do to them. Some became particularly proficient killers; others went beyond that, to cutting ears off corpses or to torturing prisoners. "The war works on you until you become part of it," wrote combat veteran Larry Heinemann in his novel *Close Quarters,* "and then you start working on it instead of it working on you, and you get deep-down mean. Not just kidding mean; not movie-style John Wayne mean, you get mean for real." Said another veteran, whose unit found the corpses of tortured GIs and began mutilating enemy bodies in return, "Everybody was cold. We didn't know it. I have a picture of me with a head in each hand and a necklace of fifteen ears. I was proud. That didn't bother me."

In combat, soldiers came to associate both their emotional coldness and their awesome destructive power with their maleness. You could "call me a piece of ice," recalls Brian Winhover. "You couldn't impregnate me with anything. I was hard." Each time a soldier survived an enemy attack, he became harder. A former Airborne trooper remembers hiding in a banana grove while the Viet Cong machine guns sprayed the area so completely that they cut down most of the trees. "They didn't touch me," says the trooper, "so I got to be invincible." During a firefight, a soldier's adrenaline would pump so fiercely that he would often come to believe—and behave as if—he had superhuman powers. "Fucking Carl Lewis couldn't run half as fast as I could," says the former trooper. "We were stronger," says Brian Winhover. "Bullets would bounce off me. That's how it felt."

For these super-hard men, killing sometimes became a symbolic form of sexual intercourse. In boot camp, drill sergeants had routinely ordered future riflemen to grip their crotches with one hand and their rifles with the other and to chant "This is my rifle and this [penis] is my gun. One is for killing, one is for fun." In Vietnam, soldiers took that training to heart. In *Dispatches,* Michael Herr describes watching helicopter gunships attacking a fortified enemy position with an American captain:

> It was incredible, those little ships were the most beautiful things flying
> in Vietnam (you had to stop once in a while and admire the machin-
> ery), they just hung there outside a nest. "That's sex," the captain said.
> "That's pure sex."

Some soldiers could actually feel the pleasure of killing in their genitals. After a while, says one veteran, "I started to enjoy it. I enjoyed the shooting and killing. I was literally turned on when I saw a gook get shot."

In 1984, journalist William Broyles, who served as a Marine lieutenant in Vietnam, wrote an essay for *Esquire* magazine in which he claimed that "The love of war stems from the union, deep in the core of our

being, between sex and destruction, beauty and horror, love and death."
As if to prove the point, he recalled the body of a dead Viet Cong
guerrilla his men brought back to the base. "I later found the dead man
propped against some C-ration boxes. He had on sunglasses, and a *Playboy* magazine lay open in his lap; a cigarette dangled jauntily from his
mouth, and on his head was perched a large and perfectly formed piece
of shit."

By laying a *Playboy* on their victim's lap, Broyles's men had proven
beyond a doubt that their former enemy could no longer "fuck" with
them, literally or figuratively. Nor could he "shit" on them. With their
macabre bit of stagecraft, Broyles's men brought to life a psychological
fiction underlying much of the fighting in Vietnam: that winners were
males whose bodies were whole and powerful and that losers, their bodies punctured, dismembered, penetrated in a thousand ways, were no
longer males at all. In combat, many soldiers so sexualized their terror
and rage that they fought the enemy in large part to defend their own
masculinity. Their guns *became* their penises, and what potent members
they were: "As anyone who has fired a bazooka or an M-60 machine
gun knows," wrote Broyles,

> there is something to that power in your finger, the soft, seductive
> touch of the trigger. It's like the magic sword, a grunt's Excalibur: all
> you do is move that finger so imperceptibly, just a wish flashing across
> your mind like a shadow, not even a full brain synapse, and *poof!* in a
> blast of sound and energy and light a truck or a house or even people
> disappear, everything flying and settling back into dust.

The trouble was, as many soldiers soon found out, neither their
penises nor their guns were potent enough to render them invulnerable.
No matter how hard they became, no matter how big their guns were,
no matter how badly they wanted to "fuck up" the enemy, the North
Vietnamese and the Viet Cong kept coming. Mines kept exploding,
friends kept going home in body bags. A platoon would sweep through a
village, theoretically clearing it of Viet Cong, only to get caught in an
ambush on their way out. A unit would carve up the corpses of several
Viet Cong only to find their own dead, several days later, mutilated too.
No sooner would soldiers assert their masculinity than the Viet Cong

would symbolically emasculate them. For all their powerful technology, their training, their youth, and their muscles, Americans continued to suffer devastating losses.

In that sense, the combat soldier's predicament resembled a national one. The United States entered the war much as many soldiers entered their first battle, with full confidence in its might and the rightness of its mission. They had only to display their superior technology, thought many American leaders, and the North Vietnamese would pack it in. As the years passed, Americans saw to their dismay that for all their country's technological prowess, their Vietnamese enemies continued to fight. Terrified by the possibility of their own defeat, American leaders responded by trying to terrorize the enemy; they created free-fire zones, relocated whole villages, defoliated thousands of acres of farmland and jungle, dropped thousands of tons of bombs.

Certainly these displays of violence had short-term tactical purposes—to destroy this base, to wipe out that enemy unit—but they also had the larger purpose of demonstrating the American will to win. In 1964, for instance, the Joint Chiefs of Staff prepared a plan to mine North Vietnamese ports and bomb bridges, railroads, and, according to *The Pentagon Papers,* "such targets as would have the maximum psychological effect on the North's willingness to stop insurgency." Much as soldiers who mutilate the corpses of their enemies hope to destroy the survivors' will to fight, the Joint Chiefs hoped to crush "the *will* of the DRV [Democratic Republic of Vietnam] leaders [italics in the original]." Victory, wrote Johnson's Assistant Secretary of Defense John Mc-Naughton, "means that we succeed in demonstrating to the Viet Cong that they cannot win."

In the early years of the war, military planners hoped to stage those demonstrations by degrees. As an individual soldier might gradually intensify his efforts to intimidate the enemy, moving from cutting ears off corpses, to mutilating corpses, to torturing living prisoners, so the United States planned to "use selected and carefully graduated military force against North Vietnam." After each turn of the military thumbscrew, the North Vietnamese would be given the chance to give up; if they failed to take it, more pain would be applied. But as the war progressed and opposition to it at home heated up, the mask of reason and precision began to crack. Politicians felt compelled to show their enemies that America was still hard enough, still tough enough, to get the job done. Again and again, like combat soldiers run amok, American leaders ordered up grotesque spectacles of violence—napalm bombings, white phosphorous attacks, the midnight assassinations of the Phoenix program—so as to put fear into the hearts of their enemies.

Presidents Johnson and Nixon often envisioned such spectacles in sexual and excremental terms. In February 1965, for example, Lyndon Johnson told the syndicated columnists Evans and Novack that China would not intervene on behalf of the North Vietnamese because

> the slow escalation of the air war in the North and the increasing pressure on Ho Chi Minh was seduction, not rape. If China should suddenly react to slow escalation, by threatening to retaliate (a slap in the face, to continue the metaphor), the United States would have plenty of time to ease off the bombing. On the other hand, if the United States were to unleash an all-out, total assault on the North— rape rather than seduction—there could be no turning back, and Chinese reaction might be instant and total.

Later that spring, Johnson told Senator George McGovern that he was watching North Vietnamese reactions to American bombing campaigns "very closely. I'm going up her leg an inch at a time. . . . I'll get to the snatch before they know what's happening, you see."

In December 1972, almost eight years later, Richard Nixon ordered Admiral Thomas Moorer, chairman of the Joint Chiefs of Staff, to prepare a series of massive air raids on industrial targets in Hanoi and Haiphong. Nixon's National Security Adviser Henry Kissinger had recently returned from stalled peace negotiations and had told Nixon that bombings might be needed to bring the North Vietnamese back to the table. "They're just a bunch of shits," said Kissinger of the Communists. "Tawdry, filthy shits." Said Nixon to Moorer, "I don't want any more of this crap about the fact that we couldn't hit this target or that one. This is your chance to use military power to win this war, and if you don't, I'll hold you responsible." Like the men of William Broyles's platoon, Nixon and Kissinger saw themselves inhabiting a world in which a man either "shit" on his enemies or "got shit on" himself.

Strength meant potency, the ability, as Lyndon Johnson saw it, to get to the enemy's "snatch" before they knew what was happening.

On the home front, thousands of young Americans reacted to their leaders' and their soldiers' misogynistic displays in Vietnam by adopting styles conventionally associated with femininity. Men grew their hair as long as their girlfriends'; women threaded their hair with flowers. Sex stereotypes blurred as antiwar men sought to project the image of vulnerability that had traditionally belonged to women. Some protestors believed that the only way to stop America's leaders was to imitate them. "How do you take a society away from madmen?" asked Norman Mailer in 1968. "By getting weapons and charging the castle where the madmen have barricaded themselves and are terrifying the countryside." But the great majority of antiwar protestors rejected calls for violent action and, with them, the imagery of threat and penetration.

Supporters of the government, on the other hand, sought to project confidence in traditional sex roles and in their leaders' masculine firmness of purpose. Prowar men kept their hair short, their faces free of beards. Women marched in support of the war wearing long gloves and carefully teased hair. Where the antiwar crowd was "soft," they were "hard." When they charged into the ranks of antiwar demonstrators at the Democratic National Convention of 1968, the Chicago police wore helmets and short-sleeved shirts that emphasized their thickly muscled arms. When construction workers marched through the streets of Manhattan to support President Nixon's conduct of the war, they wore hard hats that symbolized not only their trade, but the intensity of their commitment to their political position.

In the final years of the war, it looked to many Americans on both the left and the right as though the country might come apart at the seams. "Hardness" versus "softness," short hair versus long, the "will to win" versus the urge to "accommodate" the enemy—these became the terms by which Americans understood the potential fragmentation of their nation. As the last helicopters lifted off from the American Embassy in Saigon, leaving thousands of panicked, clambering Vietnamese allies below, the American nation remained intact, yet the memory of its potential dissolution lingered. With its protests broken up by tear gas and gunfire, its Weathermen and its riot cops, the Vietnam War had demonstrated that the body politic could be dismembered. Americans had suffered a radical disruption of their fundamental sense of the order of the world, a disruption similar in kind, if not in degree, to the one Major Marcus Reno had endured a hundred years earlier. As the bullet that killed Bloody Knife had taught Reno that the bonds of friendship could be severed in an instant, so the war had taught Americans that the ties that held them together as a nation, ties many Americans had long taken for granted as permanent and strong, could be cut.

How then, in the postwar world, were Americans to move forward? What was to keep them, as individual veterans or as a nation, from falling apart like Marcus Reno? How could they acknowledge their vulnerability in Vietnam and still retain some connection to their prewar heroes and ideals, to the parts of their mythology that made them feel capable, whole, and strong?

I believe the experiences of survivors of other traumas, particularly sexual traumas, offer a number of intriguing clues. Like combat veterans, survivors of sexual traumas have often suffered attacks on their corporal integrity. Like both veterans and civilians, they have seen their pretraumatic expectations that the world will be consistent and benevolent radically undermined. Many have felt robbed of their own agency, particularly their sexual agency, as well as of their confidence in the social and moral order. In order to move forward with their lives, these survivors of sexual abuse, like post-Vietnam Americans, have had to find some way to restore their faith in their own ability to act, particularly in sexualized ways, and to renew their confidence in the solidity and goodness of the society to which they belong.

According to Dr. Judith Herman, a professor at the Harvard Medical School and a therapist who has worked extensively with victims of incest and domestic violence, "The conflict between the will to deny horrible events and the will to proclaim them aloud is the central dialectic of psychological trauma." In her well-known book on the process of healing from psychological wounds, *Trauma and Recovery,* Herman writes that, in order to recover, survivors must cease to deny their traumas and must instead make them part of a fully felt narrative. They must tell "the story of the trauma," she writes, "in depth and in detail. This work of reconstruction actually transforms the traumatic memory, so that it can be integrated into the survivor's life story." Survivors must also mourn the losses the trauma has caused. Quoting Freud and his colleague Josef

Breuer, Herman points out that "recollection without affect [e.g., emotion] almost invariably produces no result." As they integrate the trauma and the feelings it aroused into their lives, survivors gain control over their memories. "Helplessness constitutes the essential insult of trauma," writes Herman; as they tell a story of events, survivors reverse their former helplessness and put themselves in a position of power.

Yet, as Herman and a number of others have pointed out, survivors rarely tell these healing stories early on in their recoveries. Instead, they endure cycles of denial and intrusive recollection. Unable to put what they experienced into a complete verbal narrative, they often reenact their traumas. Rape survivors return to the alleys where they were attacked; combat medics go to work in hospital emergency rooms; survivors of incest dare older men to attack them. At the same time, many dream of revenge. "The revenge fantasy," writes Herman, "is one form of the wish for catharsis. The victim imagines that she can get rid of the terror, shame, and pain of the trauma by retaliating against the perpetrator. . . . In her humiliated fury, the victim imagines that revenge is the only way to restore her sense of power." But neither revenge nor reenactment offers an effective catharsis. Compulsive and strange, such fantasies leave survivors not empowered but, rather, groping to integrate their traumas into their lives.

Between revenge and reenactment, psychologists have described a third dynamic, one which, together with the first two, has characterized much of the psychology of the American recovery from Vietnam: perversion. In his landmark study of the psychodynamics of sexual perversion and pornography, *Perversion: The Erotic Form of Hatred,* psychoanalyst Robert Stoller points out that perverse behaviors such as transvestism, voyeurism, or pedophilia are in fact retellings of historical traumas. Like their verbal counterparts, they both recall the past and mark an attempt to master it. Each detail of the perverse fantasy, writes Stoller, has its place "in reassuring the perverse person that now he is safe. This time, the attack on him, which is reenacted in fantasy, will turn into an offensive against his old vanquisher; this time, exact revenge will be wrested out. The former assailant will have to suffer precisely those sensations that afflicted the child-victim."

By way of illustration, Stoller tells the story of a middle-aged transvestite he treated. Until this patient was three years old, he had been raised as a male by both his mother and father. At that point, his mother became sick and was taken to the hospital; she died two years later. After putting the boy in the care of an aunt, his father left the family. That aunt and her daughter, quietly enraged at the boy's emerging masculinity, regularly dressed him in girls' clothes. On his fourth birthday, his terminally ill mother came home for a visit. "On that occasion," writes Stoller, "the aunt and cousin introduced his mother to 'a new neighbor girl,' in fact the dying woman's son, and took photographs to memorialize the joke." Today the man does not recall this incident. What he does remember is the "voluptuous feeling" of a pair of stockings a woman forced him to wear several years later and the fact that when he arrived at puberty, cross-dressing became his primary source of sexual pleasure. Even now, writes Stoller, "he is fully potent only when cross-dressed."

In his cross-dressing, explains Stoller, this patient has simultaneously memorialized his humiliation and turned the tables on his aunt and her daughter. Every time he puts on women's clothes, he does to himself what his relatives did to him on his fourth birthday. But this time, rather than feel himself under attack, he finds himself in charge and sexually powerful. Where his aunt and her daughter hoped to frustrate him, to constrain his masculinity, by dressing him in girls' clothes, he has frustrated *them* by reasserting it. Each time he has an orgasm while dressed as a woman, he proves that they have failed to destroy his maleness. He has even turned the specific instruments of his humiliation—women's skirts and underwear, their stockings and shoes—into the tools of his triumph.

It is precisely these dynamics of perverse retribution that have driven the postwar fantasy lives of many traumatized combat veterans and their civilian counterparts. Unlike Stoller's patient, Americans in Southeast Asia were not exclusively innocent victims. They had brought the fighting in Vietnam on themselves and had sustained it long after the possibility (and even the definition) of victory had slipped away. Even so, the war was a direct attack on the nation's young male soldiers and on its symbolically masculine national identity, an attack to which both veterans and civilians have responded, like many survivors of sexual traumas, by breeding fantasies of revenge. Whether acted out in violent rages or brought to life in books and on movie screens, these fantasies have memorialized American suffering in Vietnam. But like the perverse fantasies of survivors of sexual traumas, they have also turned that suffering on its head. In pulp fiction and action movies, they have allowed us to tear apart enemy bodies as the enemy once tore apart ours. They have taken the instruments of our humiliation—booby traps, handmade weapons, an intimate knowledge of the battlefield—and made them the instruments of our heroes' triumphs. As dressing up in women's clothes did for Stoller's patient, these fantasies have given Americans a chance to prove their potency in the face of their old humiliations.

In his book *Warrior Dreams: Paramilitary Culture in Post-Vietnam America,* the most thorough exploration of these fantasies to date, sociologist James William Gibson points out that at the end of the Vietnam War, men all across America began to imagine themselves as paramilitary warriors. In 1975, the year Saigon fell, writes Gibson, a former Special Forces captain and Vietnam combat veteran named Robert K. Brown founded *Soldier of Fortune: The Journal for Professional Adventurers.* In 1974, Brown had gotten hold of a forty-page packet describing how to join the Omani Army as a mercenary. He decided to market this information and put an ad in a leading gun magazine, *Shotgun News.* The replies he got surprised him. "Some of the responses came from recently discharged soldiers, which made sense," he later wrote, "but a lot came from lawyers, doctors, police, the too young and the too old. Now these people obviously were not going to go off to Oman, but it was clear to me they wanted to read about going off to Oman as a soldier of fortune."

When it was founded, *Soldier of Fortune* had 4,500 subscribers; by the mid-1980s, it was selling 250,000 copies a month and had an estimated readership of about one million men, most of them between the ages of eighteen and thirty-four. What these men received for their money was the chance to imagine themselves as warriors. As Gibson points out, "Nearly every article appearing in *SOF* was written *as if* the reader was a soldier or a mercenary who might go off to war *tomorrow.*" Articles in which writers field-tested various weapons "gave the impression . . . that the reader's life might well depend upon his quick mastery of an alien firearm." Stories in which men traveled to El Salvador, Nicaragua, and Afghanistan "read like intelligence reports addressed to soldiers on a mission, men who needed to know the deployment of enemy forces, their patrolling patterns, their armaments and morale."

This, of course, was exactly the information soldiers had needed to know in Vietnam. By reading *Soldier of Fortune,* men could fantasize not only that they were soldiers, but that they were soldiers who possessed the intelligence information that Americans in Southeast Asia had so often lacked. In their imaginations, they could take themselves to a guerrilla war, master its alien battlefields, and come out victorious. In short, they could become men who would win just the kind of war our army had lost in Vietnam.

Over the same period that *Soldier of Fortune* was building its readership, the pulp fiction industry began to draw hundreds of thousands of readers to graphic tales of military and guerrilla violence. Packed with scenes of hand-to-hand combat and automatic rifle fire, these stories attracted such a readership that by the mid-1980s, publishers were running off between 60,000 and 250,000 copies of each new volume in more than half a dozen separate series. Like the articles in *Soldier of Fortune,* these books offered armchair warriors a chance to picture themselves in battle, often in Southeast Asia. But in these stories, more than a tactical victory was at stake. With titles like *Cherry-Boy Body Bag, Rivers of Flesh,* and *Boonie-Rat Body Burning,* these books brought their readers straight back to the questions of corporal integrity raised by the fighting in Vietnam. They depicted threats to male bodies very explicitly and, as they did, they presented their readers with a chance to relive and thus repair the helplessness of individual soldiers in combat and the breakdown of a masculinized national self-image in the war as a whole.

In postwar pulp fiction, as on the real battlefields of Southeast Asia, injury and death are highly sexualized events. The war threatens to emasculate not only individual soldiers, but the entire American army. In Jonathan Cain's *Cherry-Boy Body Bag,* for example, the fourth volume in a long-running series of adventures starring American military policemen in Saigon, one American infantryman remarks that the Vietnamese jungle "is a lady: gobble, gobble, gobble." In Cain's imagination, the landscape of Vietnam and even the war itself threaten to gobble up Americans' maleness. Throughout postwar pulp fiction, to fail in combat is to have one's body entered, penetrated, fucked. Failure is almost always linked to female genitalia: In *Cherry-Boy Body Bag,* for instance, characters mark each others' mistakes by calling each other "douche-bag," "dildo-breath," and "cunt." To succeed in combat, however, is to do the entering, the penetrating, the fucking—in short, to put one's male organ powerfully to work. In Jack Hamilton Teed's *The Killing Zone,* for example, the first in the highly successful *Gunships* series, a villainous American soldier kills a man named Meeker:

> Stocker moaned with pleasure. It felt like he was on fire. He sent half the mag slamming into Meeker, punching him over backwards. Meeker hit the tree and slithered down it, crumpling to the earth, leaving a sticky slime of blood down the bark. Stocker hobbled over to the twisted body and emptied the gun into it at point-blank range, opening it up, unzipping it, tearing it apart. Blood splashed and sprayed as the rounds tore into the bucking, jerking thing on the ground.
>
> Stocker dropped the gun and fell to his knees, clutching at his groin, his body shuddering and quaking in paroxysms of shrill, squealing laughter.

Scenes such as these proliferate in pulp fiction about the war. With the slow-motion eye they cast over body movements ("bucking, jerking") and the exchange of body fluids ("splashed and sprayed"), these scenes of violence, like pornographic descriptions of sex, place their viewers in the presence of terror yet allow them to remain safe. Simply because they are reading the scene, rather than living it, readers can experience some of the fear and excitement associated with violent death while knowing that their bodies are intact and that they are risking nothing. The threat—sex in pornography, combat here—remains trapped on the page.

But the resemblance between postwar pulp fiction and sexual pornography does not stop at individual scenes. As Robert Stoller has pointed out, the images and stories of sexual pornography can encapsulate not only a reader's fantasies, but his memories as well. For the perverse person, he suggests, each pornographic text recalls and redresses a historical sexual trauma, using a predictable series of plot devices to do so. The same can be said of postwar pulp fiction about Vietnam. Like pornographic stories of sex, these graphic stories of war return their readers to a scene of historical suffering and ameliorate that suffering through a predictable and consistent set of tale-telling strategies.

Foremost among these strategies is something Stoller calls the "guilt-removing device." One day, says Stoller, his transvestite patient brought him a pornographic book entitled *Panty Raid . . . and other stories of TRANSVESTISM & FEMALE IMPERSONATION.* The book tells the story of Bruce King, a fraternity pledge sent to capture the under-clothes of a nearby sorority. A normal male at the start of the story (as was Stoller's patient at the start of his life), King finds himself captured and overwhelmed by "victorious vixens who thrilled at the helpless struggles of their male captive." They strip off his khakis and button-down Oxford shirt and replace them with "a gossamer silk" gown of "Vampire Red" (much as his aunt and cousin once re-dressed the pa-tient). At first Bruce resists, but soon "he was breathless with eager anticipation. He dared not admit his true feelings to anyone; even to himself!" When he leaves, he and the women promise to meet again, in drag, as friends.

Stoller points out that this bit of pornography clearly retells the story of his patient's personal humiliation. And yet, rather than feel victimized when he reads this story (as he did when he lived it), the patient becomes sexually excited. One key to his excitement, writes Stoller, is the fact that Bruce King was overwhelmed by the sorority girls. He tried to fight back, but couldn't. As a result, he could not be blamed for falling in love with women's clothes—and neither could the reader, Stoller's patient. The guilt-removing device of the overwhelming attack has made it pos-sible for Stoller's patient to take control of, rather than simply replay, his humiliation as a child. Having been relieved of responsibility for his pleasure, Bruce King can come to enjoy the prerogatives of the very people who have humiliated him. By the end of the story, he can dress himself up, toy with his masculinity, and, in effect, treat himself as the "victorious vixens" once treated him. So too can Stoller's patient, who, when he reads the story, can identify not only with his victimized self (Bruce King at the start of the story), but with the people who humili-ated him as well (in the person of Bruce King and his female "friends" at the end). Where in reality he was simply a victim, the patient is now, in fantasy, a victor.

The same dynamic is at work for readers of stories like *The Killing Zone.* Postwar pulp novels of combat employ a consistent set of plots. The warriors who become heroes in these books begin life as ordinary men. Only after they suffer a devastating loss—such as finding the bodies of their friends and families, or seeing their platoons wiped out—do they go in search of revenge. If they seek help, the authorities prove incompetent or corrupt. Again and again, the heroes of postwar pulp fiction find themselves betrayed by higher-ups.

Like the overwhelming attack on Bruce King, these betrayals serve as a guilt-removing device: By forcing the hero to leave behind his allegiance to one side of the conflict at hand, they allow him to borrow freely from the weapons, tactics, and moral strengths of the other side. In *The Killing Zone,* for instance, the murderer Stocker turns out to work for a General Dempsey, who in turn is selling secrets to the North Vietnamese. The hero of the book, Special Forces Colonel Hardin (pun no doubt intended), has assembled a team of former misfits and is working to disrupt Dempsey's operation. Left by the American military to fend for themselves, Hardin and his men become solo operators—part regular army, part guerrilla, even part Viet Cong. They wear American uniforms, but they set ambushes with a stealth and efficiency that in the real Vietnam War marked the tactics of America's enemies. What's more, they set their ambushes to trap both North Vietnamese and corrupt *American* soldiers. Hardin and his men not only fight the *way* the Viet Cong fought, but they also confront some of the same enemies.

When they take on the Americans, they grant their American readers permission to take pleasure in what once tormented them. In *The Killing Zone,* Hardin and his men guide their readers across the no-man's-land of patriotism and show them the original scene of the American humiliation in Vietnam through enemy eyes, as well as their own. With this new view, the readers of pulp adventures no longer need to confront the question of who was responsible for the real fighting in Southeast Asia. Instead, like Stoller's patients, they can make "friends" with those who once humiliated them. As he read, writes Stoller, his patient could incorporate both the victim Bruce King and the "victorious vixens" into himself. When he dressed up in women's clothing, he literally put on both roles. Consequently, he never had to blame his aunt or his cousin for humiliating him—or himself for not being strong enough to prevent his humiliation. As Stoller's patient could avoid challenging his oppressors, so readers of *The Killing Zone* can stow away whatever anger they might feel toward their government or the Vietnamese for causing so many Americans to be killed—or toward themselves for supporting the war. Like Stoller's patient, they have revisited their past miseries, come to believe that they were not responsible for them, and left them triumphantly behind.

Such rewritings of the past would matter less if they were not so popular. Unlike the pornography of transvestism, the stories told in books like *The Killing Zone* have appealed to a wide audience. The twenty years since the war have seen these stories filter out into the culture at large. Their plots have become the plots of hundreds of action films and tens of television shows, some set in Vietnam *(Missing in Action, Uncommon Valor),* some set here at home (the *Lethal Weapon* series, *Magnum, P.I.*). Their cartoonish heroes have become objects of national adulation. Sylvester Stallone, Arnold Schwarzenegger, Chuck Norris— one after another, these action-pic mannequins have flexed their extraordinary, hypermasculine muscles, fired their weapons, and watched as bullets tore into the flesh of their enemies. Even if they never fall to the ground clutching their penises as their pulp fiction counterparts do, the heroes of film and television act out much the same fantasies of masculinity and revenge. Like Colonel Hardin, they repeatedly demonstrate that, even as their weapons penetrate the bodies of their enemies, male Americans can keep their own bodies intact and efficient.

Few such heroes have accomplished their missions as efficiently as Sylvester Stallone's John Rambo. In each of the three Rambo films— *First Blood* (1982), *Rambo: First Blood Part II* (1985), and *Rambo III* (1988)—the former Green Beret returns to fantasy versions of the battlefields of Vietnam on behalf of his audience. In *First Blood,* Rambo roams the rain forests of the American Northwest, fighting a guerrilla war against a heavily armed and highly mechanized army of policemen. In *Rambo: First Blood Part II,* he returns to Vietnam itself, where he takes on not only our former enemies, but also another heavily armed and highly mechanized occupying army (this time Russian). The same holds true in *Rambo III.* In the mountains of Afghanistan, he has joined up with a band of indigenous Third World revolutionaries, not unlike the Viet Cong, to attack yet another occupying army, one that happens to be Russian, but one that in its tactics and equipment closely resembles the American army in Vietnam.

From the outset, the Rambo films offer up Rambo's body as an emblem for the nation. When, in *First Blood,* the filmmakers show Rambo being tortured by the Vietnamese, they remind viewers that just

as his torturers have bound Rambo's wrists and are forcing him to endure great pain, so the Vietnamese once tied down the American army,
made it helpless, mutilated its members. Rambo's body stands in for
America itself and the scars he earned in Vietnam become the wounds
borne by the nation. As Bruce King did for Stoller's patient, Rambo
offers his viewers a stylized vision of themselves.

The Rambo films also incorporate a series of guilt-removing devices. In *First Blood,* a small-town sheriff harasses him until he has no
choice but to take to the woods and rewage the Vietnam War. In *Rambo:
First Blood Part II,* he heads into the jungle to rescue American prisoners
of war in Vietnam, but when he finds some alive, the American in
charge of his mission betrays him and allows him to be captured by the
Vietnamese. In *Rambo III,* he goes to Afghanistan to rescue his mentor
and surrogate father, Green Beret Colonel Trautman. But before he
leaves, his State Department handler tells him, "If you're captured or if
this leaks . . . we'll deny any knowledge of your existence." Says
Rambo, "I'm used to it."

These repeated betrayals force Rambo to renounce his allegiance to
the American military and allow him to incorporate the powers of
America's historical enemies, the North Vietnamese and the Viet Cong.
Film critics have often read the Rambo movies as Reagan-era *agit prop,*
blunt attacks on Communists everywhere. While they certainly are that,
the Rambo films also offer their viewers a way to claim as their own the
qualities they admired in the Communists who beat them in Vietnam. In
each film, the enemies Rambo takes on behave much like the American
military in Vietnam. In *First Blood,* the uniformed police stumble
through the rain forest like clumsy grunts in the jungles of Southeast
Asia. In *Rambo: First Blood Part II,* Rambo's enemies are Vietnamese and
Russian, but their tactics are American. The Russians wield precisely the
weapons that defined the American battle plan in Vietnam—helicopters
and automatic rifles. Together with their Vietnamese allies they cling to a
fortified base (here, a prison camp) and defend it against the sapper
Rambo. Even in *Rambo III* the Russians hunker down in their mountain
redoubt, waiting to be attacked by the native population, every bit as out
of place in feudal Afghanistan as the Americans were on their firebases in
the mountains of Vietnam.

Rambo himself has a number of characteristics and skills for which the Viet Cong were once famous. Rambo is "an expert in guerrilla warfare," says Colonel Trautman in *First Blood,* "a man who's been trained to ignore pain, to live off the land, to eat things that would make a billy goat puke." During the Vietnam War, American soldiers and civilians frequently remarked on the Viet Cong's ability to melt into the jungle and to survive on small quantities of strange foods. American troops, in contrast, depended on canned rations and resupply by air. One of the greatest frustrations for Americans during the Vietnam War was the enemy's ability to inflict injury with low-technology weapons such as punji pits, while they themselves were failing to defeat the enemy with the most high-tech weaponry available. In the Rambo movies, the film-makers have reversed this situation: Armed primarily with an oversized knife and, in the second two films, with explosive-tipped arrows, Rambo defeats opponents equipped with the same helicopters, tanks, and automatic rifles that Americans fought with in Vietnam. Like the Viet Cong, he knows the land. In *Rambo: First Blood Part II,* he knows it so well that he disappears into a wall of mud and emerges, as the Viet Cong once emerged from spider holes and tunnels, only to ambush his enemy.

Just in case his audience has missed Rambo's link to the Viet Cong, Stallone makes it explicit in *Rambo III.* Early in the film, he finds himself captured by the evil Russian Colonel Zaysen, who tells him, "It is just a matter of time before we [Russians] achieve victory [over the Afghanis]." Rambo replies:

> There won't be a victory. Every day your war machines lose ground to a bunch of poorly armed, poorly equipped freedom fighters. The fact is that you underestimated your competition. If you'd studied your history, you'd know that these people have never given up to anyone. They'd rather die than be slaves to an invading army. You can't defeat people like that. We tried. We already had our Vietnam. Now you're going to have yours.

With this history lesson for Zaysen, Rambo has also delivered a set of viewing instructions to his audience. These battles in Afghanistan, he suggests, will be replays of Vietnam. But this time, the Americans, in the person of Rambo, will fight on the side of the Vietnamese. And so they do: Dressed in black fatigues not unlike the black pajamas of the Viet Cong, Rambo ranges among the Afghanis, adopts their strange tribal customs (including playing tug-of-war on horseback with the corpse of a goat), and in the end, leads them through the fortifications of the occupying army and on to victory.

As he does, he behaves much like Colonel Hardin of *The Killing Zone*. Like Hardin, Rambo has fled corrupt higher-ups, thus granting his audience views of the historical battlefield of Vietnam from several different angles. Rambo can be an American killer, a Vietnamese-style guerrilla, a refugee from society's rules, and the defender of a higher law. He can be the scarred survivor of Vietnamese torture in *First Blood* and the torturer of a Russian with a body as hard as his own in *Rambo: First Blood Part II*. As they identify with him, moviegoers too can travel back to the battlefields of Vietnam in their imaginations. But rather than simply be Americans, they can see the war from the enemy's point of view as well.

This new view offers our culture a perverse power over the past. When he dressed up in women's clothes, Stoller's patient both restaged his humiliation and adopted the appearance of his oppressors. In fact, it was the adoption of their *appearance* that restored to him the sense of personal power and, at the moment of orgasm, masculine integrity that his aunt and cousin had stolen. Likewise, when Rambo adopts the dress and behaviors of America's former enemies, he not only returns Americans to the historic site of their humiliation, but he appropriates the power of the victors there on behalf of the vanquished. The Vietnamese who defeated our army can no longer intimidate us because, in the person of John Rambo, *we* have become *them*.

With his seemingly indestructible, hypermasculine physique, Rambo restores to Americans the vision of individual and national corporal integrity that the Vietnam War destroyed. Like Colonel Hardin in *The Killing Zone* or like the mercenary journalists of *Soldier of Fortune*, he presents his countrymen with a fantasy world in which their masculine bodies are whole and efficient. In the process, he invites them to think back to a time before the corporal destruction wrought by the Vietnam

War, to a mythical America of backwoods marksmen and westward expansion. As James William Gibson and others have pointed out, Rambo is half-Indian, half-German, a Medal of Honor winner, and a clear descendant of frontiersmen like Kit Carson and Daniel Boone. He is a historical collage, as much an embodiment of the American past as John Wayne or Gary Cooper. Thus, when he returns to Vietnam and wins, he argues with his body for the incorporation of the war into the body of American myth. We are still the people who won World War II and who conquered the West, he claims. We are still masculine, still whole. "The home of the brave will never fall," sings Sylvester Stallone's brother, Frank, as the credits roll at the end of *Rambo: First Blood Part II.* "The strength of our nation belongs to us all."

Although the Rambo films, and particularly *Rambo: First Blood Part II,* were among the most popular movies of the 1980s, they were hardly an isolated phenomenon. Action films starring violent, overmuscled men have raked in millions of dollars over the last fifteen years. Only some of those films have been set in Vietnam *(Missing in Action, Rambo: First Blood Part II)* or dealt with Vietnam veteran characters *(Lethal Weapon,* Arnold Schwarzenegger's *Predator).* Many others, such as Bruce Willis's *Die Hard* or Peter Weller's *RoboCop,* have been set in the United States or in a sci-fi fantasy world and have not seemed to have anything to do with Vietnam. And yet even those films that might appear to be the farthest removed from Southeast Asia have employed the plot devices and characterizations that define the Rambo films. Whether their names are Magnum or Terminator or Rambo, the hammer-headed heroes of these films place their bodies between America's present and its past. In their rippling torsos they incorporate both the American defeat in Vietnam and the Viet Cong victory. They meld the two sides into a single rock-hard character—a character whose body is a living, breathing emblem of the nation itself.

These characters and their stories are both banal and terribly appealing to American audiences. Perhaps one way to understand their appeal is to understand the magnetic pull stories of combat exert on traumatized veterans. Watching graphically violent Vietnam combat films or reading memoirs and novels about the fighting, said one veteran, "is like an addiction. It gets the adrenaline running. It totally fucks me up." Many

veterans have found themselves searching books and movies for depictions of specific combat behaviors and have sat in judgment on their
cinematic peers. "We're watching somebody dissecting a frog," explained Edward Ravitch, a former infantryman, "and we have dissected
frogs and we can say, 'Yes, that's how you dissect frogs.' " But behind
that quest for details there lurks a desire to return to the past in a position
of power. In combat, soldiers often watched their friends die, helpless to
save them and under attack themselves. In a movie theater, they can
revisit those moments from the safety of a well-padded chair. Ravitch
recalled that when he attended one film he saw soldiers' bodies get
blown apart: "Watching people blow up without being committed [to
the battle himself] . . . felt good. . . . I could picture so-and-so
when he got blown up by an M-80 [shell]. It relieves my anxiety."

Perhaps as we watch Rambo blow North Vietnamese officers to
smithereens in *Rambo: First Blood Part II,* we feel a similar relief. Not
only can we take an imaginary revenge on our former enemies, but we
can remember that the Vietnam War is over and that we are sitting safely
in a theater many years later. Our nation, even if it is as scarred as
Rambo's body, has remained whole and powerful and, as we sit in the
dark, surrounded by fellow citizens, perhaps we do partake of its power.

Yet, in my interviews with traumatized veterans, I've found that
survivors of combat in Vietnam often turn to war movies not only to feel
safe, but to mourn. The images on the screen offer them a way into
rooms of emotion they keep otherwise locked up. "For that split second," said Ravitch, "that one segment in a film that rips our hearts out,
that's it. It's only that brief segment that brings truth to us. It allows us
the anger and fear and crying." And this is where movies like the
Rambo films or books like *The Killing Zone* fail us. To the extent that
their settings resemble the battlefields of Southeast Asia and their heroes
the men—of both sides—who fought there, our postwar fairy tales of
male bodies in action do put us in the presence of the details of our
traumas. But where other kinds of stories, particularly memoirs, have
aimed to help their audiences feel the "anger and fear and crying" those
traumas sparked in their survivors, these stories, like sexual pornography,
have steered their audiences away from the emotions of mourning and
toward the adrenaline rush of temporary mastery. As they run with
Rambo through the jungles of a Hollywood Vietnam, Americans might

truly feel invincible, might actually feel as if "the strength of our nation belongs to us all." But when they leave the theater, the vulnerability they knew in Vietnam—a vulnerability before the attacks of the North Vietnamese, before the lies of their own government, and even before their own violent impulses—still waits to be acknowledged and felt.

CHAPTER FIVE

EMOTIONAL RESCUE:

MAKING MEANING OF LOSS

EVERY FEW MONTHS ALBERT MAHONEY RETREATS TO the small room at the back of his apartment, the one farthest from the front door. He sits in a large armchair and watches TV or stares out the back window at a parking lot. Sometimes he eats Army surplus C rations, the same ones he ate in the field in Vietnam. He calls his apartment his "bunker" and he stays there for days or weeks at a time. "I'm as in fear of my well-being now as I was in Nam," he explains. On the street, he says, "Every person is a potential threat. Every car—if I don't watch them—they'll run me over." But in his "bunker," he feels safe.

For Albert Mahoney, as well as thousands of other traumatized combat veterans, the experience of war has all but vanquished the ability to trust. For them, the America of today, like the Vietnam of twenty-five years ago, presents a hostile territory inhabited by enemies disguised as allies, a landscape prone to erupt into uncontrollable violence. These men also know that they can become destroyers themselves: Having fought in a war in which the moral restraints on violence, particularly toward civilians, often fell away, they fear that if they become angry enough, those restraints could vanish again and they could harm even their own friends and families. This knowledge leaves them profoundly depressed and deeply ashamed. Many days, says Mahoney, "I'm just waiting to die. I don't feel alive. I don't feel like I'm a participant. I'm just this piece of shit that's still holding on to breath."

Since the final years of the war, a similar, if far less debilitating, species of fear and shame has entangled civilian Americans. During the late 1960s and early 1970s, news of the My Lai massacre, the murders at Kent State, and other atrocities drew civilians into the moral vacuum of combat in Vietnam. Like Albert Mahoney, many glimpsed a world in which moral laws could be set aside, one in which they and their country could suffer and commit ferocious acts of violence. In the years immediately after the war and on through the 1980s, a "Vietnam syndrome" took hold: Americans became almost as reluctant to send their army overseas as Albert Mahoney has been to leave his apartment. Faced with the takeover of the American Embassy in Tehran by Iranian militants in 1979, President Carter waited five months before attempting a military rescue of embassy personnel. When the Reagan Administration began to hint that it might take American troops to defeat communism in Nicaragua and El Salvador, the public balked. And since 1975, each time an American President has succeeded in sending American troops into combat he has had to claim that *this* time, the soldiers' mission was honorable and their victory assured.

Even as Americans became more reluctant to use their military power, they came to fear and demonize the outside world much as Albert Mahoney does the streets of his neighborhood. In the last twenty years, Americans have seen their Marines massacred in Lebanon and their helicopter pilots dragged through the alleys of Mogadishu. They have lined up at the gas pumps during an Arab oil embargo, witnessed a rash of jetliner hijackings on the evening news, and in Southern and Western states particularly, watched with dismay as thousands of illegal immigrants slipped into their cities and towns. Since the fall of Saigon, many Americans have begun to worry that the world beyond our borders is one in which, to paraphrase Mahoney, every country is a potential threat.

That fear, of course, has helped spark our fantasies of revenge, our fascination with the muscle-bound epics of Sylvester Stallone and Arnold Schwarzenegger. Yet it has also given rise to another, equally powerful preoccupation: missions of rescue. Even as they have dreamed of becoming a reborn warrior nation, Americans have sought to restore their moral and military self-confidence by staging fantasies of heroic redemption. In complex, private dramas of emergency and deliverance, veterans like Albert Mahoney, men sometimes so traumatized as to be unable to function in almost any other context, have taken effective, concerted action to save one another, their families, and their friends. At the national level, both veterans and civilians have imagined that American prisoners of war are still alive in Southeast Asia and that we can bring them home. More ominously, Presidents Reagan and Bush have used the rhetoric of rescue to justify a series of military interventions abroad.

Throughout the 1980s and the early 1990s, rescue missions, whether real or imagined, have allowed Americans to recall and redeem our mission in Southeast Asia. They have also offered us a way to integrate the Vietnam War into the larger framework of American myth.

Since the seventeenth century, Americans have seen themselves as a nation of rescuers. As they sailed across the Atlantic from England, the country's first European settlers imagined that they were God's chosen people, the Israelites, cast out from Egypt. In the wilderness of the Americas, they thought they would create a country that would be, as the Puritan minister John Winthrop put it, "a City upon a Hill," a shining example of piety and prosperity that might light the way for other nations.

When the Pilgrims arrived in the New World, however, they found themselves surrounded by vast and gloomy forests, thick swamps, and hostile Indians. Seventeenth-century America was no Eden. Confronted with such a seemingly godless world, they began to tell each other stories in which settlers, usually women or ministers, fell into the hands of Indians, resisted the heathens' punishments and temptations by means of their faith in God, and were eventually restored to their communities. Known as "captivity narratives," these stories recounted the real kidnappings of actual settlers. But they also told the story of the burgeoning

American nation in miniature: Carried away from their homes (in England), the colonists had found themselves surrounded by devils (the Indians, the wilderness) and had been rescued by God on account of their faith. When He saved the leading characters of captivity narratives from their enemies, God saved the colonists as a whole from their fears that the eyes of the world might not be upon them, that they might have journeyed to the edge of the known world for no good reason at all. These stories reminded the colonists of their redemptory mission: As God had saved the Israelites in the Bible and individual Christians in captivity narratives, so now the colonists of New England would set about saving the world.

When they arrived on the shores of North America, the settlers hoped to build a community of saints whose pious examples of righteous living might inspire others elsewhere to follow in their path. When they arrived in Vietnam three centuries later, Americans hoped to save the South Vietnamese from the heathen menace of the Communist North by force of arms. South Vietnam, said Lyndon Johnson in 1965, was a "small and brave nation" that found itself caught in "a war of unparalleled brutality," like a Puritan woman in a captivity narrative. Its "simple farmers," said Johnson, "are the targets of assassination and kidnapping," while its "helpless villages are ravaged by sneak attacks. Large-scale raids are conducted on towns, and terror strikes in the heart of cities." He could have just as easily been describing New England during the Indian wars of the 1670s, and it was clear to Johnson that it was now up to America to save another "small and brave nation."

No single artifact from the war embodies this paternalistic attitude better than John Wayne's 1968 propaganda film *The Green Berets,* in which Wayne plays a Green Beret colonel sent to run a Special Forces base (called "Dodge City") in the mountains of Vietnam. In the words of the film's opening song, the Green Berets appear to be "Fighting soldiers from the sky, fearless men who jump and die." Their job is to rescue the South Vietnamese, who in turn appear diminutive, determined, and helpless. As a group, the South Vietnamese are personified by Hamchunk, an orphan boy adopted first by Peterson, one of Wayne's men, and, in the end, by Wayne himself. When Hamchunk's dog is killed by Viet Cong shelling, the following dialogue ensues:

PETERSON: He was all you had in the world, wasn't he?

HAMCHUNK: Except you.

PETERSON (*picking Hamchunk up*): Yeah.

After Peterson has died and as the sun is setting over the South China Sea (a geographic impossibility, since the Vietnamese coast faces east and southeast), Hamchunk asks the giant, overmuscled Wayne, "What's going to happen to me now?" "You let me worry about that," says Wayne. "You're what this is all about." As God once saved the colonists of New England, so now, Wayne implies, the ancestors of those colonists will save another helpless people.

The soldiers sent to do this rescuing, however, soon learned that Vietnam was no more the colonial landscape of settlers and Indians than early New England had been the wilderness of biblical Canaan. Contrary to Lyndon Johnson's vigorous assertions that South Vietnam was an independent country under attack from the North, combat troops quickly discovered that they faced a largely indigenous uprising. Its "simple farmers" often turned out to be Viet Cong riflemen who launched sneak attacks on American outposts. In such a war, soldiers soon let go of the historical and mythical meanings of their mission and settled for their own survival. "The hardest thing to come to grips with is that making it through Vietnam—surviving—is probably the only worthwhile part of the experience," said one veteran. "It wasn't going over there and saving the world from communism or defending the country. The matter of survival was the only thing you could get any gratification from."

In a war in which the survival of oneself and one's comrades offered the ultimate value of combat, acts of rescue took on a unique significance. All wars present soldiers with opportunities to rescue one another and Vietnam was no exception: Soldiers pulled each other out of lines of fire, called in medevac helicopters to take out the wounded, called in artillery rounds to save trapped platoons, and sacrificed themselves to save their buddies. Particularly in the middle and later years of the war, when the moral framework of the larger American rescue mission in Vietnam had begun to collapse, individual acts of rescue reassured soldiers that there might still be a moral significance to at least part of their work.

In the late 1960s, Americans at home needed a moral vision of themselves almost as much as their soldiers in the field did. In the wake of the Tet Offensive, they saw that Lyndon Johnson's attempt to rescue the Vietnamese had run aground. Soon thereafter they confronted the assassinations of Martin Luther King and Robert Kennedy, the brutalization of antiwar protestors at the Democratic National Convention, and the news of My Lai.

Like their soldiers, civilians turned to images of rescue for comfort. But where soldiers drew on acts of military competence and even heroism for their imagery, civilians at home drew on a government propaganda campaign. In March 1969, less than three months after his inauguration, Richard Nixon launched a massive publicity drive called Go Public to rally Americans behind the idea that the North Vietnamese were mistreating American prisoners of war and should immediately release them. "The Communist side," wrote the editors of *The New York Times,* toting the Nixon line, was "inhuman" and "the prisoner-of-war question [was] a humanitarian, not a political issue." Despite the facts that the United States was *at war* with North Vietnam and that the United States had never given up all of *its* prisoners of war before hostilities had ceased, Nixon continued to berate the North Vietnamese for "the barbaric use of our prisoners as negotiating pawns" and to call for "the immediate and unconditional release of all prisoners of war throughout Indochina."

The campaign garnered immediate and widespread support and, over the next year and a half, getting the POWs out of enemy hands became a national obsession. In 1970 alone, the post office issued 135 million POW-MIA stamps, Richard Nixon changed the official name of Veterans Day to Prisoner of War Day, Senator Robert Dole staged an elaborate POW rally in Washington's Constitution Hall, and POW advocates set up tableaux in state capitol buildings across the country modeled after the one set up in the U.S. Capitol Building by future presidential candidate H. Ross Perot, then head of the Richard M. Nixon Foundation. Perot's exhibit depicted two miserable POWs: "One sits in the corner of a bare cell," wrote *The New York Times,* "staring bleakly at an empty bowl and chopsticks on which a huge cockroach is perched.

On the floor are other cockroaches and a large rat. The other figure lies in a bamboo cage, ankles shackled."

What could Americans do to help these men? In the spring of 1970, an organization called Voices in Vital America (known until 1969 as the Victory in Vietnam Association) provided the answer. Led by Gloria Coppin, the wife of an industrialist whose company supplied airplane parts to military contractors, and bankrolled by such leading hawks as Barry Goldwater, Alexander Haig, and California Governor Ronald Reagan, VIVA created and marketed metal bracelets engraved with the names of prisoners of war and men who were missing in action. Buyers of the bracelets promised not to remove them until their prisoner or missing man had returned from Vietnam or had been shown to be dead. Wearing their bracelets day and night, concerned citizens only had to look at their wrists to remember one of our soldiers in Vietnam. By midsummer 1972, VIVA was selling 11,000 of these bracelets a day; by the time of the 1973 peace accords, somewhere between four million and ten million Americans were wearing them, including such celebrities as Richard Nixon, Charlton Heston, Bill Cosby, Cher and Sonny Bono, and Bob Hope.

The Nixon Administration's campaign to highlight the plight of the POWs had a powerful effect on the public's perception of the war. By 1972, wrote Jonathan Schell, the POWs and MIAs had become "the objects of a virtual cult, and many people were persuaded that the United States was fighting in Vietnam in order to get its prisoners back. . . . Following the President's lead, people began to speak as though the North Vietnamese had kidnapped four hundred Americans and the United States had gone to war to retrieve them." In the early 1970s, explains historian H. Bruce Franklin, "America's vision of the war was being transformed. The *actual* photographs and TV footage of massacred villagers, napalmed children, Vietnamese prisoners being tortured and murdered, wounded GIs screaming in agony, and body bags being loaded by the dozen for shipment back home were being replaced by *simulated* images of American POWs in the savage hands of Asian Communists [italics mine]."

In much the same way that the notion of rescue offered soldiers in the field an acceptable moral framework for acting in combat ("I'm killing to save my buddies"), the POWs and MIAs of the early 1970s offered Americans at home a way to imagine that the war in Vietnam remained, as many had thought it was in the beginning, a form of altruism. If, after Tet, Americans could no longer imagine themselves rescuing the "small and brave nation" of South Vietnam, they could at least imagine themselves saving their own helpless soldiers.

The national obsession with the POWs crested in February 1973, when the POWs returned in the wake of the Paris peace accords. Christened Operation Homecoming, the return was handled with higher degrees of precision and visibility than most combat campaigns. "The U.S. military's planning for the operation had been meticulous, and even loving, in an official way," wrote *Time* magazine. Huge jets delivered handsome, lanky airmen into the arms of their wives and children. Crowds swarmed the runways with banners reading WE LOVE YOU while news photographers snapped away. "Operation Homecoming," wrote *Time* magazine, set off "A Celebration of Men Redeemed" and "a ritual of resurrection":

> For the U.S., the war in Viet Nam had gone ambiguously: the nation's longest battle had ended in nothing like glory but in a kind of complex suspension. The nation could at least find its consolation, even its celebration, in the return of the prisoners. Here, at last, was something that the war had always denied—the sense of men redeemed, the satisfaction of something retrieved from the tragedy.

When they used the language of redemption and salvation, the editors of *Time* echoed the authors of colonial captivity narratives. Once again the rescue of helpless, faithful individuals offered American citizens a way to console themselves for "the tragedy" of their sufferings in an alien wilderness. In the same way that the moral dramas of captivity narratives had reassured the lonely colonists of seventeenth-century New England of God's love for them, so Operation Homecoming reassured war-weary Americans that they were a strong and moral people whose mission in Vietnam had not been undertaken in vain. With the return of the POWs, Americans could temporarily displace the shame they felt for their military and moral failures in Southeast Asia with the fantasy that they were, as they always had been, citizens of a redeemer nation.

After the fall of Saigon, few Americans felt more in need of redemption than traumatized combat veterans. They were the ones who had done the killing and dying that the rest of the nation was so anxious to put behind them. "I came back with a lot of guilt," says Brian Winhover. "I asked myself three million times, 'Why did I ever come back?' I never knew. . . ." Why had they survived when their friends had not? What had they become in Vietnam? Would they be as violent in America as they had been in Southeast Asia?

The relative calm of American streets made little sense to men who had been alert to ambushes almost every moment of every day for a year. Their finely honed ability to react with maximum violence to the first sign of an attack, an ability that saved lives in battle, did little to help veterans of heavy combat accomplish the tasks of daily civilian life. Targeting a mortar, standing still in the jungle all night ten feet from an enemy trail, hitting fleeing enemy soldiers with a machine gun fired from a helicopter moving 150 miles per hour—none of these skills had meaning in civilian life. For many veterans, returning home was like entering a combat nightmare. Lost in an alien landscape, unarmed and cut off from their units, many felt surrounded by hostile forces. They knew they had to move forward, but in what direction? And even as they tried to look ahead, they kept thinking about the dead they had left behind. Why hadn't *they* survived as well?

Confronted with such isolation and emotional confusion, many traumatized veterans have turned to versions of the patterns of behavior that gave meaning to the chaos of Vietnam: missions, especially ones of rescue. These missions can take an hour or a lifetime to complete. From pulling a stranger from a burning building to falling in love with and marrying a barely functioning alcoholic, these missions can turn veterans into rescuers or create situations in which they have to be rescued by someone else. As Dr. James Munroe, a Veterans Administration psychologist who has treated traumatized Vietnam veterans for more than twenty years, explains, "There's endless variation and it doesn't matter in a way. Their skills suddenly become obvious. There's suddenly a chance for rest." Veterans who wonder whether their lives have meaning can stop questioning themselves. For the moment, says Munroe, the rescue mission "defines one task as 'This is it' " and demands the veteran's entire concentration. "Within that mission there is relevance," explains

Munroe. "If [traumatized veterans] can find a mission, it allows them to function."

For some traumatized veterans, the only way to come to respect another person is to see how they perform on a mission. "You want to be my friend?" asks James Munroe. "Well, let's go have an emergency and see if you're good enough to save my life. If you are, you can be my friend." What's at stake on the mission is not merely skill, but commitment. "Rescue usually means putting yourself in grave danger," says Munroe. "That's the measure. Will you sacrifice yourself for me? If so, we have love. Trauma reduces trust to the point where rescue can be the only thing that counts. No relationship is possible without emergency."

Such a mission, for instance, cemented Albert Mahoney's friendship with Brian Winhover. One evening, a number of years after he returned from Vietnam, Mahoney went to a low-rent bar. He had become increasingly anxious in the last week and he had had a few drinks for the first time in four years. He stepped into the bar wearing several thousand dollars' worth of jewelry, he said, and got into an argument with several other patrons. When Mahoney left the bar, they followed him and one robbed him of a necklace. He didn't call the police. Instead, he called his wife, who came and picked him up. When Mahoney got back to his apartment, he loaded a shotgun he kept in his bedroom and started shouting, "I'm gonna kill him! I'm gonna kill him!" Like the infantryman he used to be, he was getting ready to head back out into enemy territory and blow the bad guys away.

His wife could have called the police, but having seen this kind of behavior before, she called Winhover. "Things were getting out of control," says Winhover matter-of-factly. "I just went over and did my thing." By the time Winhover arrived, Mahoney's brothers, who lived nearby, had called the police. As they stood outside the apartment's front door, Winhover walked into Mahoney's bedroom, took the loaded shotgun out of his hands, cracked it open, and put the shells in his pocket. He then presented Mahoney to the police, who took him into temporary protective custody and placed him in jail. To this day, Mahoney and Winhover remain the best of friends. "I know I can trust him," says Mahoney, "and I know he feels the way I feel. . . . The whole basis is mutual respect. I have to have total respect."

Yet rescue missions offer more than the chance to establish social bonds. Rescue, says a former Marine, "takes you away from your own grief." Where formerly a man might have sunk into despair as he thought of dead and wounded comrades or of the parts of himself he had lost in Vietnam, he could now rise up and act with confidence. As he rescued a beloved friend or family member in the present, he could also act out the fantasy of returning to Vietnam and somehow bringing the dead men he loved there back to life. Instead of simply lamenting the loss of his comrades, he could, in fantasy at least, rescue them from their fates. And by rescuing others, he could see himself not as a "piece of shit that's still holding on to breath," but as a good man. One former infantryman has long felt ashamed of a time when his unit in Vietnam accidentally ambushed and killed a group of unarmed villagers. He now takes care of two granddaughters who were abandoned by their mother. As he does, he thinks of himself not as a haphazard killer, but as a friend to the helpless. "The savior of the underdog . . . that's what my life's been," says the former soldier. "Somebody fucks with somebody and he gets into their faces . . . I can be sitting here with fevers and puking— I'm dying—and then I get a mission and I'm living."

Rescue missions, says James Munroe, give traumatized veterans a taste of true healing, but only a taste. On a mission, men "have the ability to rest, have control over their lives, do what they want, have the ability to plan, have meaning"—all characteristics of a person who has recovered from psychological trauma. They create these conditions, however, by reenacting the dynamics of the events that traumatized them in the first place. "As long as you keep running the mission," says Munroe, "you continue the victim/abuser, rescuer/rescued dynamic. You reverse the roles, but you perpetuate the basic interaction." When Brian Winhover rescued Albert Mahoney, for instance, they became two buddies in the same platoon, surrounded by hostile thieves and policemen as they had once each been surrounded by hostile Vietnamese. Even as they sought to break free of the roles they had played in combat, they reprised them.

In this respect, veterans' rescue missions resemble their dreams of revenge. For survivors of trauma, writes Judith Herman, "the revenge fantasy is often a mirror image of the traumatic memory, in which the roles of perpetrator and victim are reversed. It often has the same grotesque, frozen, and wordless quality as the traumatic memory itself." And like revenge fantasies, rescue missions defend against the pain of grieving. For a moment, they rid traumatized veterans of their crippling shame and despair and restore them to the purposeful, moral, socially connected condition they enjoyed before the war. But as soon as the missions end, the memories of the purposeless, amoral, isolated combatants that these men became in Vietnam inevitably return, demanding to be mourned.

Like their traumatized veterans, many civilians entered the post-Vietnam era desperately unsure of their places in American society. Long-cherished national myths had broken down in Vietnam, as had Americans' faith in their leaders and institutions. As a result, many felt cut off from a sense of purpose and personal efficacy. In 1976, soon after the fall of Saigon and the Watergate crisis, a Harris poll reported that an all-time high of 62 percent of Americans felt "alienated from the centers of power." That same year 64 percent reported that "what I think doesn't count much anymore." Even as Americans faced rampant inflation and growing job insecurity, their society continued to undergo social changes begun during the war. Schools that less than two decades before would not have admitted a black student were now fully integrated. Women who might have stayed home with their children just ten years earlier now held full-time jobs—jobs that sometimes paid more than their husbands'. The pace of change was dizzying: By 1980, nearly half of all Americans felt that they were "left out of the things going on around me."

As the sense of individual helplessness and alienation spread through the American public, events overseas reinforced the notion that the nation as a whole had lost its strength. On November 4, 1979, a group of Iranian students broke through the gates of the American Embassy in Tehran and took more than 60 Americans hostage. The television images were riveting: bearded, gloating Third World students marching white middle-class Americans, with their eyes blindfolded and their hands tied behind their backs, through an angry mob. As helpless as ministers or women kidnapped by Indians in seventeenth-century New England, the diplomats became the protagonists of a new captivity narrative, one in which, as ABC newscasts put it daily, "America [was] Held Hostage." Every evening television network news programs began and ended by listing the number of days the hostages had been held, and in effect, the diplomats became the Vietnam POWs all over again. Families all across the country tied yellow ribbons around trees in their front yards. Volunteers met in shopping malls to send Christmas cards to the hostages. Like the POWs at the end of the Vietnam War, the hostages became the object of cultlike affections.

In April 1980, five months after the hostages were taken, President Carter sent a commando team to rescue them. On the night of April 24, three helicopters transporting the team suffered mechanical failures. At a staging area in the Iranian desert, a fourth crashed into a C-130 transport plane, killing eight servicemen and severely burning five more. Over the next few days, the news media would bombard Americans with pictures of the wreckage and of charred American corpses. Each image reinforced the sense that America was not what it used to be. "A once dominant military machine," wrote *Time* magazine, "first humbled in its agonizing standoff in Viet Nam, now looked incapable of keeping its aircraft aloft even when no enemy knew they were there." With the failure of the rescue attempt, the logic of the Iranian hostage captivity narrative flipped: A story that should have shown Americans as uniquely favored by God now suggested that they might have been abandoned by God or, at the very least, that they were incapable of playing their traditional role as a redeemer nation. As journalist and historian Haynes Johnson explains, "this latest debacle became another symbol of a muscle-bound country whose might amounted to naught, proof that America had become the Gulliver of the age, a giant stuck in the sand."

Along with an economic recession and an Arab oil embargo, the disaster in the desert also helped cost Jimmy Carter the 1980 election. During the Iranian hostage crisis, Americans had seen their national mythology begin to crack in much the same places it had come apart during the Vietnam War. They had felt helpless, both individually and on behalf of their nation. With his cardigan sweaters and his soft Georgia accent, Jimmy Carter had come to embody those feelings, as well as the national inability to get rid of them. He was America's Hamlet, said several columnists, weak and indecisive. When presented with the traditional script for national redemption—the captivity narrative—he had failed to play his part. Under Carter, wrote *Time* essayist Roger Rosenblatt, Americans had started "to fear that the future [was] over."

In order to restore that future, Americans turned to an actor who rode into Washington like a rescuing hero from our mythic frontier. "Out of the Past," headlined the editors of *Time* in January 1981, as they named him "Man of the Year," Ronald Reagan brought "Fresh Choices for the Future." Along with the article, the editors presented readers with a full-page oil portrait of Reagan, mounted on a dun stallion, white hat on his head, his eyes fixed on the horizon. "At 6 ft. 1 in., 185 lbs., his body is tight, as tight as it can be on a large frame," wrote Roger Rosenblatt of the sixty-nine-year-old President-to-be. But the health of his body, suggested Rosenblatt, was simply a sign of the power of his mission:

> What we can see in Reagan is a vision of America, of America's future, at once so simple and deep as to incur every emotion from elation to terror. It is a little like the vision of the Hudson River school of painting—the brooding serenity of turquoise skies, patriarchal clouds and trees, very still, doll-like people (white and red), infinite promise, potential self-deception, and above all, perfect containment—the individual and the land, man and God locked in a snakeless Eden . . . an ideal America in which everyone ruled his own vast estate, his own civilization. . . .

With his overheated prose, Rosenblatt has conjured up the world of the Puritan captivity narrative. The Pilgrims of the seventeenth century had hoped that their new home would indeed be "a snakeless Eden," though they feared a "potential self-deception." As God once led Puritans out of captivity, Rosenblatt's encomium implied, Ronald Reagan would now help the nation break free of its paralyzing guilt and shame. He would once again make America the "City upon a Hill" our forefathers had intended it to be.

Yet, even as Reagan played his part in a national drama of resurrection, he and his followers brought with them into office a vision of a world outside America's borders every bit as dangerous to Americans as the world outside Albert Mahoney's apartment. "You and I live in a real world, where disasters are overtaking our nation," Reagan told delegates to the Republican National Convention in 1980. America, he said, was an "island of freedom," created by "Divine Providence." Around its shores, he explained in a later speech, swirled a hostile ocean of "totalitarian forces . . . who seek subversion and conflict around the globe to further their barbarous assault on the human spirit." It was America's job, said Reagan, to "commit our resources and risk the lives of those in our armed forces to rescue others from bloodshed and turmoil and to prevent humankind from drowning in a sea of tyranny. . . ."

Even if they did not see the world in such stark terms, a majority of Americans tended to agree that they and their country faced serious threats from abroad. That did not mean, however, that they were ready to let Reagan send American troops overseas to meet those threats. In the first years of his Administration, for instance, Reagan pointed to El Salvador and Nicaragua as arenas in which America would have to confront the specter of Soviet communism. A Marxist-led guerrilla movement was besieging the right-wing government of El Salvador, while Marxist rebels had already overthrown the government of Nicaraguan dictator Anastasio Somoza. According to Reagan, both actions could have a "domino effect" on the region that would ultimately threaten the United States. Public opinion polls from the time show that most Americans agreed. In 1982, two out of three people polled felt a "pro-Communist" takeover of El Salvador would threaten "the security of the United States," while in 1983, 51 percent said the Nicaraguan government already did. But even though they felt threatened, most Americans also believed that America should not intervene in Central American affairs. Throughout the Reagan years, the great majority of the American public opposed support for right-wing rebels in Nicaragua and for the right-wing government in El Salvador.

Many, if not most, did so because they feared that Central America would erupt into a long, drawn-out war of attrition like Vietnam. With their talk of the threat of communism and the domino effect, Reagan Administration officials did little to allay their fears. Like Albert Mahoney today, many Americans in the early 1980s felt under siege, but also like Mahoney, they had seen enough fighting in Southeast Asia to want to avoid excursions into foreign territory for some time.

In October 1983, Reagan ordered an invasion that he hoped would ease that reluctance. That month Maurice Bishop, the left-wing Prime Minister of the tiny Caribbean nation of Grenada, was murdered by revolutionaries from within his own government. The Reagan Administration had never much cared for the Bishop regime, which since coming to power in 1979 had sought economic support from Cuba and bought weapons from the Soviet Union. According to Reagan, Grenada "was a Soviet–Cuban colony being readied as a major military base to export terror and undermine democracy." The overthrow of Bishop and the ensuing chaos provided just the excuse the Administration needed to stamp out Grenadian communism before, as Reagan cast it, Grenada could "spread the virus among its neighbors."

Yet, rather than call the Grenada intervention an "invasion," Reagan insisted that it was a "rescue mission." Under the Bishop regime, said Jeane Kirkpatrick, Reagan's Ambassador to the United Nations, "Grenada's . . . people were helpless in the grip of terror." Now that the situation had worsened, it was America's job to pull them out. But Reagan also claimed to be rescuing American citizens. At the time of Bishop's overthrow, between 800 and 1,000 Americans were studying at St. George's University School of Medicine on the island of Grenada. Under Bishop, the school's students had long enjoyed the island's hospitality and after the coup d'état, the revolutionaries had taken special pains to assure the university of its students' safety. Nevertheless, Reagan voiced his fear that they might be taken hostage. He launched the invasion first and foremost, he said, to preserve their "personal safety."

Early in the morning of October 25, 1983, 1,900 U.S. Marines and Army paratroopers, along with 300 soldiers from various Caribbean allies, stormed ashore. Within four days, they had overwhelmed the Grenadian army and militia and the island's 784 Cuban construction workers. Eighty-seven people were dead, including 18 Americans, more than 500 were wounded, and after several days of waiting for the Marines to reach their campus, fewer than 600 American medical students had been evacuated.

At its start, Americans on the left and in the center had condemned the invasion of Grenada as pointless and immoral. But their objections were soon drowned out: "We have heard the terms 'warmonger' and 'gunboat diplomacy' used," said Congressman Dan Burton, a Republican from Indiana. "Well, last night we saw the results of that action. Students were getting off the plane. They were kissing the ground. They were saying, 'God Bless America.' They were thanking the President for sending in the Marines and the Rangers." By staging a brief, dramatic, and relatively low-casualty rescue operation, Reagan began to erase the memories of the hostages in Iran and of America in Vietnam. "Grenada by itself cannot be taken to signify a resurgence of American power," wrote neoconservative Norman Podhoretz, but it certainly helped alleviate "the shell-shocked condition that has muddled our minds and paralyzed our national will since Vietnam."

The irony here is that the Reagan Administration eased that "shell-shocked condition" by reenacting in miniature the war that caused it. On the one hand, like Lyndon Johnson, Reagan had sent troops into a tropical Third World country to rescue a people of a nonwhite race from a communism that he claimed had been foisted on them unwillingly. On the other hand, like Richard Nixon, Reagan had suggested that he was sending in the troops in large part to rescue threatened Americans. That Grenada was a comparatively minuscule country that lacked an army anything like the North Vietnamese and Viet Cong forces or that the medical students were never in danger of becoming POWs made little difference: Reagan seemed to have returned to the scene of America's defeat in Vietnam and brought back victory.

In that sense, the invasion of Grenada was as much a mission of memory as a military operation. By the early 1980s, like traumatized veterans of the Vietnam War who longed to return to the battlefield and to bring their dead comrades back to life, many American civilians longed to erase their memories of the war and to restore their national self-confidence. As veterans tried to fulfill their longings by staging rescues of one another, so Reagan offered Americans a chance to return to and repair the wounds of the past when he staged the rescues of Grenadian civilians and American medical students. When they kissed the pavement of various runways, the returning students became the hostages coming home from Iran and the POWs, back from Hanoi. In essence, they became the images of an America no longer held hostage, either by foreign powers or by recollections of its own impotence, and all across the country, Americans cheered what they thought was their newfound independence from the past.

The boost to our national self-image did not last long, though. Like the confidence and sense of purpose that rescue missions grant individual veterans, the sense of power and righteousness the invasion of Grenada

gave so many Americans quickly faded. For a more consistent affirma-
tion of their moral standing, Americans would have to turn away from
the material, political realm and toward the fantasies of television and
film. From the late 1970s through the mid-1980s, tales of rescue
streamed across TV and movie screens. Audiences cheered as Luke
Skywalker and his comrades wiped out the Death Star and saved their
new nation in George Lucas's *Star Wars* (1977) and as Indiana Jones saved
the woman he loved from the Nazis in Steven Spielberg's *Raiders of the
Lost Ark* (1981). Each week from December 1980 through September
1988, Americans tracked Tom Selleck's *Magnum, P.I.* and his team of
Vietnam vets through the tropical wilds of Hawaii as they chased down
criminals and rescued clients in distress. And in the wake of *Magnum*'s
success, TV viewers could follow similar Vietnam veteran/action heroes
on *The A Team* (1983–1987), *Riptide* (1984–1986), *Simon & Simon*
(1981–1988), and *Miami Vice* (1984–1989).

Apart from their profusion, what distinguished these rescue fantasies was the way in which they linked the war in Southeast Asia to
traditional American myths. Whether set in Hawaii, Miami, or outer
space, the rescue fables of the 1980s offered their viewers a mirror
image—with the original often distorted, but always visible—of their
nation's failures in Vietnam. In Vietnam, for instance, Lyndon Johnson had claimed (and many Americans had believed) that they were
taking on a criminal North Vietnamese regime in order to save a
helpless South Vietnamese people. In *Magnum, P.I.*, Thomas Magnum
takes on a series of criminals in order to pull his helpless, often fe
male, clients from their clutches. Part traditional captivity narratives,
part rewrites of the history of the Vietnam War, programs like *Magnum, P.I.* allowed Americans to imagine that the fighting in Southeast
Asia had not only failed to rupture American myths, but had in fact
conformed to them.

Perhaps no program better exemplifies this process than *The A Team*.
Slapstick, tongue-in-cheek, and banal beyond belief, *The A Team* featured a Vietnam Special Forces group that had committed crimes in
Vietnam (not the atrocities that real A Teams sometimes committed, but
a burglary of the "Bank of Hanoi"!) and had come back to the States on
the lam. "They survive as soldiers of fortune," the show's opening
voice-over announced each week. "If you have a problem and no one

else can help, if you can find them, maybe you can hire the A Team." In their pilot episode, a two-hour made-for-TV movie broadcast immediately after the Super Bowl in 1983 (and, according to its producers, watched by more than 50 million people), a reporter hires the A Team to rescue a colleague who has been captured by Communist rebels in Mexico. When they arrive south of the border, they discover that the rebels have been terrorizing local villagers. The A Team enlists the villagers to take on the rebels much as U.S. troops once enlisted South Vietnamese farmers against the Viet Cong. But whereas the South Vietnamese forces often cut and ran, the Mexican villagers stand firm, allowing the A Team to rescue not only the missing journalist, but the citizens of the entire region.

Like Ronald Reagan's invasion of Grenada, the first episode of *The A Team* saw crack American troops return to the Tropics and rescue an otherwise helpless Third World people. And once again American soldiers saved not only the natives, but captive Americans as well. This time, though, the soldiers were out of uniform. Where the invasion of Grenada demonstrated that the government and its troops could in fact win a tropical Third World war, however brief, the plot of *The A Team*'s premiere episode suggested that if they were going to complete their rescue mission, American fighters would have to step outside the law.

By shedding their uniforms, the men of the A Team acknowledged particular American mistakes in Vietnam, even as they hung them with the trappings of American frontier mythology. In the wake of the pilot episode, government incompetence and venality became a running joke. Week after week, the A Team eluded the goofball commander of the Fort Bragg military prison who had been sent to apprehend them. With their clever evasions, they pointed up not only the commander's personal bungling, but the horrific ignorance and clumsiness with which American military leaders conducted the Vietnam War. At the same time, the Vietnam veterans of the A Team became twentieth-century Davy Crocketts and Daniel Boones, violent captains of a frontier beyond government jurisdiction. Rescuers of damsels in distress, they obeyed a higher law than their erstwhile government masters—a law as righteous as that which governed the actions of the heroes of seventeenth-century captivity narratives.

In that sense, the A Team offered American civilians a way to lay the blame for the conduct and outcome of the Vietnam War at the feet of their politicians and generals and to forgive both ordinary soldiers and themselves for their roles in the conflict. In Vietnam and afterward, the men of the A Team had played by the rules of American mythology— and perhaps, they implied, other ordinary Americans had as well. Could either the fictional A Team or, by extension, its audience be held responsible if their government had not?

The men of the A Team were not the only figures to offer Americans this brand of absolution. In the early 1980s, the leaders of a revitalized POW-MIA movement too offered Americans a chance to imagine themselves caught between a callous government and a venal enemy and to see themselves as actors in a national morality play. Since the end of the war, little concrete evidence had appeared to support the idea that the governments of Southeast Asia were still holding American prisoners of war. On the contrary, in the wake of Operation Homecoming, several government studies concluded that no Americans remained in captivity. But even after these reports had been published, members of one of the most prominent POW-MIA lobbying groups, the National League of Families of American Prisoners and Missing in Southeast Asia (many of whom, after the war, were not in fact family members of missing men), as well as numerous freelance activists, insisted that the Vietnamese had held back American prisoners. Henry Kissinger and Richard Nixon, they claimed, had promised the Vietnamese $3.25 billion in war reparations; the Vietnamese had withheld the POWs as insurance that the money would be paid. When it wasn't, they kept the men.

Throughout the Ford and Carter administrations, the POW-MIA issue received a modest amount of attention. But in the early 1980s, as Americans renewed their interest in the war in general and their affection for the men who fought it in particular, the POW-MIA movement returned to something like the prominence it had enjoyed under Richard Nixon. The press reported that at war's end anywhere between 100 and 1,250 Americans had been left behind in Southeast Asia. Responding to public interest in the issue, Ronald Reagan tripled the size of the POW-MIA section of the Defense Intelligence Agency. Many veterans took up the cause of the missing men as well, buying and selling POW-MIA T-shirts and banners, building grassroots networks, and lobbying their congressmen.

One of those veterans was Sarge Hulbein, a man whose experience sheds some light on the broader appeal of the POW-MIA movement. In addition to being a full-time fireman, Hulbein runs a computer bulletin board for people interested in the POW-MIA issue out of his house. He carries a business card, printed in red, white, and blue, with a picture of an eagle whose talons tug at a chain. I WALK IN FREEDOM FOR THOSE WHO CAN'T! says the card. WHEN ONE AMERICAN IS NOT WORTH THE EFFORT TO BE FOUND, WE AS AMERICANS HAVE LOST!

With his words I WALK IN FREEDOM FOR THOSE WHO CAN'T!, Hulbein has acknowledged his own sense of guilt at having survived the war. Like many Americans after the war, Hulbein felt himself adrift for years, yet by working on the POW-MIA issue, he has gained a mission and a meaning for his life. "That's my new war," says Hulbein, "to not allow people to forget. Why did this happen? What was this really all about? If I allow them to forget, I know they're going to do it again." But what Hulbein wants Americans to remember is unclear. Does he want them to remember his friends who died? The Vietnamese whose deaths Americans caused? The fact that America lost the war? "I want them to know every friggin' thing the government did that was wrong. . . . As long as I breathe, even if nobody walks out of that jungle, I can't let them forget what happened. They did so many things over there that were wrong and I can't let them forget." And yet, says Hulbein, he himself played a role in Vietnam, a role he could neither forget nor accept. "I felt used by my own government," he explains. "This [war] wasn't about people. This wasn't about human rights. This wasn't any-thing that was noble. Sometimes I get mad. I should have known more. I shouldn't have just closed my eyes and did what I was told."

At times Hulbein admits that he suspects no POWs remain in South-east Asia. But by working on the POW-MIA issue anyway, he has found a way to remain vigilant. Each evening, as he returns from the fire station and checks in with his bulletin board, he scans the digital landscape for telltale signs of U.S. government perfidy as once he might have searched the tree lines of Vietnam for hidden enemies. He is a soldier again, albeit on a new and morally much-improved mission. And within his work on the POW-MIA issue, as within all such missions, there remains a seed pearl of historical truth. In Vietnam, many Americans *did* commit acts of violence for no high moral purpose. Sarge Hulbein and millions of other

Americans *did* close their eyes to the war. To the extent that the POW-MIA movement acknowledges those truths, it offers many Americans the chance to mourn not only their dead and missing men, but the fact that they themselves helped wage—even if only by refusing to protest—an immoral war.

For the most part, though, the movement has encased the history of the war in a narrative in which the American government harms *only* its own soldiers and one in which the Vietnamese remain a demonized enemy. Like Ronald Reagan, the POW-MIA activists of the last fifteen years have imagined Americans surrounded by hostile forces. They have dreamed of military missions with which they might rescue these prisoners "from bloodshed and turmoil" and prevent them "from drowning in a sea of tyranny." And throughout the 1980s and the early 1990s, these dreams became enormously popular not only with activists, but with the public at large. Novelists told stories of American POWs who had become "vestiges of men," their "arms and hands . . . discolored to a purplish black and swollen to twice their normal size." Like the prisoners of seventeenth-century captivity narratives, these men often called out to God: "Help him, sweet Jesus. . . . Help him in his hour of need." But it wasn't God who came to the fictional rescue—it was Americans. Usually freelancers, often veterans, Americans rode to the rescue of their POWs in such highly popular mainstream novels as J. C. Pollock's *Mission M.I.A.* (which inspired several POW rescue films) and Tom Clancy's *Without Remorse* (a *New York Times* bestseller in 1993), as well as numerous pulp titles, including Jack Buchanan's well-known *M.I.A. Hunter* series, which premiered in 1985.

Pressed to keep up with the flow of prose, Hollywood has churned out more than a dozen films featuring American POWs. The most popular of those movies—*Rambo: First Blood Part II* (1985), *Missing in Action* (1984), and *Uncommon Valor* (1983)—featured veterans who returned to Southeast Asia, alone or in teams, and freed the prisoners their government had abandoned a decade before. Like the real invasion of Grenada, these fantasy missions allowed their audiences to imagine winning a war they had lost. Vietnam, these films implied, had been a noble effort, a rescue mission gone wrong, yet this time it would go right.

As their private rescue missions did for individual traumatized veterans, these films allowed their viewers to feel a part of a tight-knit com-

munity. In *Uncommon Valor,* for instance, Colonel Jason Rhodes (Gene
Hackman) puts together a team of veterans in order to rescue American
POWs held secretly in Laos, all the while hoping that his son, who was
captured during the war, will be among the men he saves. As he addresses his rescue team, Rhodes symbolically restores the American social
cohesion that the Vietnam War once destroyed. "There's a bond between you men," he tells his team, "as strong as the bond between my
son and me." Given an emergency, he implies, Americans can work
together as his mercenaries have, as members of a national "family."

Even as they allowed Americans to refight the Vietnam War in their
imaginations, win it, and restore the prewar social order at home, these
films gave their viewers a chance to acknowledge their country's immoral behavior in Vietnam and to restore their sense of themselves as
moral men. Says Colonel Rhodes to his team:

> You seem to have a strong sense of loyalty [to each other] because
> you're thought of as criminals because of Vietnam. You know why?
> Because you lost. And in this country that's like going bankrupt. . . .
> They want to forget about you. You cost too much and you didn't turn
> a profit. That's why they won't go over there and pick up our buddies
> and bring 'em back home, because there's no gain in it. . . . Now
> they say they've been negotiating for ten years. Well, the other side's
> not buying. . . . So we're going back there. And this time, this time,
> nobody can dispute the rightness of what we're doing.

By assessing his Vietnam veterans in economic terms, Rhodes taps into
moviegoers' fiscal, as well as political, anxieties. But when he refers to
"criminals" and "bankruptcy," Rhodes also recalls the American public's broad-based suspicion during the final years of the war that our
soldiers' work in Vietnam was in fact criminal, was in fact morally bankrupt. But rather than mourn that moral breakdown, Rhodes makes it an
occasion for renewed loyalty.

By the end of the 1980s, characters like Colonel Rhodes and John
Rambo, together with the POW-MIA movement, had had an enormous
influence on the American public. In August 1991, despite nearly
twenty years of evidence to the contrary, a *Wall Street Journal*/NBC poll

showed that 69 percent of Americans believed that American POWs were still being held in Southeast Asia.

Such wide acceptance of the POW captivity myth gave George Bush a deep reservoir of feeling on which to draw for support of the American invasion of Iraq. In the years before Iraq invaded Kuwait, Americans had shown a strong reluctance to commit their troops to the Middle East, even on behalf of such staunch American allies as Saudi Arabia. When the Iraqi army moved into Kuwait on August 2, 1990, and the United States began sending troops to Saudi Arabia in Operation Desert Shield, many Americans remained reluctant to send their troops into combat. There had been "nothing like [Iraq's attack on Kuwait] since World War II," said Bush, but a substantial portion of the public disagreed. They felt that the primary reason their troops had been sent to the Persian Gulf was "to protect our oil supplies." In January 1991, when the Bush Administration transformed Operation Desert Shield into Operation Desert Storm and attacked Iraq, thousands of protestors took to the streets. On January 19, police estimated that 25,000 marched against the war in Washington, D.C. One week later a similar march drew three times that many protestors.

Yet neither those marches nor the highly publicized refusals of a number of soldiers to fight in the Gulf hindered the Bush Administration's ability to fight the war. Instead, by drawing on the rhetoric of rescue, the Bush Administration managed to neutralize such protests. "While the world waited," said Bush, "Saddam Hussein systematically raped, pillaged, and plundered a tiny nation [that posed] no threat to his own." With Kuwait held hostage, it was up to Americans to step in and free the "small and helpless nation." But the American forces would not only be rescuing the citizens of Kuwait. In the fall of 1990, during the American troop buildup, Saddam Hussein had taken a number of Americans, Japanese, and Western Europeans hostage. In the wake of their release, Secretary of State James Baker stated that "We must act so that innocent men and women and diplomats are protected, not held hostage, in the post–Cold War world." As Ronald Reagan had collapsed Grenadian citizens and American medical students into a single community during the invasion of Grenada, Secretary Baker now conflated Kuwaitis and American men, women, and diplomats. By rescuing the Kuwaitis, Baker implied, Americans would be rescuing themselves.

By the start of Operation Desert Storm, a great many Americans had
already begun to act out a version of the hostage drama to which Baker
referred. Not long after Bush began sending troops to Saudi Arabia,
Americans at home began tying yellow ribbons around trees in their
front yards. Soon McDonald's restaurants were serving coffee in cups
painted with yellow ribbons and American flags, the citizens of San
Diego were wrapping a skyscraper in yellow bunting, and the Franklin
Mint was selling commemorative yellow ribbon plates. The same public
symbol that once represented American *hostages* now became an emblem
of American *troops*. As they had during the Iranian hostage crisis and
earlier, during Nixon's Go Public campaign for the Vietnam POWs,
masses of Americans devoted huge amounts of emotional energy to
waiting for their men to come home. But at the same time, they subtly
redefined their soldiers' mission: Having symbolically marked them as
hostages, Americans could imagine their troops in the Middle East not as
military aggressors, but simply as men and women trying to survive.

The trouble was, our soldiers in the Gulf War were neither hostages
nor POWs. No hostile Third World nation held them captive. No mobs
of bearded students marched them through the streets. No matter how
President Bush demonized Saddam Hussein, many Americans continued
to believe that their troops had been sent in large part to ensure the flow
of Mideast oil to the United States. And yet the logic of the post-
Vietnam captivity narrative, as summed up in the act of tying yellow
ribbons around trees, allowed Americans to reconcile themselves to
Bush's policies. "I have told the American people before that this will
not be another Vietnam," said Bush as he announced the start of Operation Desert Storm. "Our troops will have the best possible support in the
entire world, and they will not be asked to fight with one hand tied
behind their back." According to Bush and other conservatives, Americans had lost the war in Vietnam because someone, either the American
government or the antiwar protestors, had kept American troops from
going all out. While factually inaccurate, this view had been kept alive as
part of the POW–MIA rescue myth. According to POW–MIA rescue
fantasists, the government's unwillingness to rescue its POWs was nothing more than a repetition of the American government's unwillingness
to support its troops in the field during the Vietnam War. Americans had

lost the war in Vietnam, said former POW John Rambo in *First Blood,* because "somebody wouldn't let us win."

During the Gulf War, relatively few Americans wanted to be that "somebody." By tying yellow ribbons around trees and praying for the safe return of their soldiers, Americans could assert that no matter how they felt about the war itself, they "supported" the troops. At the same time, if they objected to the war, they could find a nonverbal and relatively nonthreatening language in which to express their objections. By draping their yards with yellow ribbons, they could think of their soldiers as victims of the Bush Administration, as prisoners of its war, and they could imagine that at some level they were taking action against that Administration. In their prayers for the safe return of their soldiers, Americans could imaginatively snatch their sons and daughters not only from the clutches of Saddam Hussein, but from the hands of George Bush as well.

According to the Defense Intelligence Agency, American troops in the Gulf killed between 50,000 and 100,000 Iraqis and wounded three times that many. A total of 148 Americans lost their lives and 467 were wounded in action. But despite these casualties, Americans at the end of the war reveled in the efficiency of their army. Strong and swift, our army had not only restored the Kuwaiti emirs to power, but had also brought back to life the pre-Vietnam image of America as a redeemer nation. Said George Bush to a joint session of Congress:

> I am sure that many of you saw on the television the unforgettable scene of four terrified Iraqi soldiers surrendering. They emerged from their bunker—broken, tears streaming from their eyes, fearing the worst. And then there was an American soldier. Remember what he said? He said: "It's okay. You're all right now. You're all right now." That scene says a lot about America, a lot about who we are. . . . We are a good people, a generous people. Let us always be caring and good and generous in all we do.

According to George Bush, American troops in the Gulf were not so much attacking Iraqi troops as pulling them out of harm's way. Images of Iraqi corpses charred by American bombs faded away behind Bush's assertion that "We are a good people, a generous people." So too did the images of the corpses at My Lai. In the immediate postwar euphoria, many Americans believed their President when he told them, "we have finally kicked the Vietnam syndrome."

But the effect didn't last. Less than a year and a half later, Bush's approval rating had dropped from a wartime high of 89 percent to a mere 29 percent. No matter how often Bush recalled the war along the campaign trail, voters refused to rally. Like traumatized veterans in the wake of private rescue missions, they had reverted to their former lack of trust in leaders. "Sometimes we seek missions out," says Brian Winhover. "We need them. It's a relief. It's almost like being on morphine." But when the missions end, says another veteran, "the letdown is the killer. The adrenaline wears off and then you start to hurt." For all the President's claims to the contrary, the Persian Gulf War had erased the memory of Vietnam only temporarily, as had the invasion of Grenada and the endless stream of POW rescue films. As the euphoria of victory wore off, Americans once again encountered the fear of helplessness that had beset them since the fall of Saigon. Like Albert Mahoney, they once again found themselves surrounded by hostile forces—the economic powerhouses of Japan and Germany threatening to steal America's world-market share, the crumbling nations of Haiti and Cuba spewing emigrants northward, the countries of the Far East luring away manufacturing jobs from American workers. They were not the same forces that had threatened Americans in the 1960s and 1970s, but they were just as powerful, perhaps more so. And the rescue missions of the 1980s and 1990s had done nothing to make them go away.

CHAPTER SIX

IN FROM
THE JUNGLE:

RESTORING COMMUNITY IN
THE WAKE OF MORAL TRESPASS

IN DECEMBER 1970, IN THE FIRST OF WHAT WOULD SOON become hundreds of therapeutic "rap groups," twelve Vietnam veterans sat down with psychiatrists Robert Lifton and Chaim Shatan at the New York City offices of Vietnam Veterans Against the War (VVAW). Since their return from Southeast Asia, the veterans had suffered from their memories of combat and from the pressures of friends and families to keep those memories to themselves. Some had met with private psychoanalysts, others with Veterans Administration psychologists, but neither of these more traditional forms of therapy had provided the comfort or insight they sought. For some, the distanced professionalism of conventional psychiatrists echoed that of their former officers in the field. When they went for treatment, these veterans had found themselves at the bottom of a medical hierarchy as seemingly soulless as the military hierarchy in Vietnam. For others, therapy itself was the problem: Some veterans felt that with its focus on individual suffering, conventional psychiatry abetted a national tendency to deny the collective nature of the war that had injured them.

The meetings at the VVAW, though, would be different. As Robert Lifton later wrote, "professionals [at the meetings] had no special podium from which to avoid self-examination. We too could be challenged, questioned about anything." Having worked extensively with traumatized survivors of World War II, both he and Shatan could offer the veterans the benefit of their clinical expertise, but they would not treat the veterans per se. In fact, they and the veterans had chosen to call their meetings "rap groups" precisely in order to avoid implying that the veterans were in any way patients presenting themselves to be healed. Instead, veterans and therapists were to be a community of equals, learning from one another.

In this respect and in others, the rap groups offered an antidote to memories of the military and of combat. They became places in which veterans could reclaim the empathy they had given up in combat, let go of fantasies of rescue and revenge, and begin to mourn their losses. "The process [of working in the meetings]," wrote Arthur Egendorf, one of the first twelve veterans and later a psychotherapist himself, "feels to us like reverse basic training, undoing what the military did to and with us and trying to analyze, understand, and unravel the earlier experiences that made us ripe for the military's treatment." Where the army had taught them to accept their place in the chain of command, the rap groups allowed these veterans to question their place in society. Where the army had expected them to follow orders, their peers in the rap groups encouraged them to listen to and follow their own emotions and beliefs. Where their friends and families hoped they would keep silent about what they had seen and done in Vietnam, the members of the rap groups hoped they would speak up. "We see ourselves as members of a society that strains to dismiss the war from conscious thought and to avoid the implications of that collective experience," wrote Egendorf. "The group . . . confirms as nothing else does that we carry a legacy of the war in our memories, that we exist as veterans despite the denials within and around us."

Over the next two decades, the meetings at the VVAW offices became models for therapeutic communities across America. By the early 1980s, rap groups and related group therapies could be found from the most ramshackle storefront vet centers to the most high-tech Veterans Administration hospitals. As they spread, these groups came to offer thousands of veterans a safe haven in which to acknowledge and explore their feelings about the war—and particularly about combat.

In the same years that veterans were finding their way into rap groups, civilian Americans were seeking out more public forums in which to make sense of their memories. Like traumatized veterans, many civilians felt betrayed by their government and by their own support for it. During the war, many feared they had labored at the bottom of huge, emotionless corporate and political hierarchies. Many also felt a measure of responsibility for their army's violence in Southeast Asia. In the wake of the war, they, like veterans, required forums in which to articulate and confront these feelings, arenas in which they could recover a national sense of community.

Beginning at the end of the 1970s and continuing through the 1980s and 1990s, writers and filmmakers created those forums in their art. In darkened movie theaters and well-lit library reading rooms, they told *stories* of the war, *therapeutic narratives* whose conventionalized dynamics of character and plot, crisis and resolution offered Americans a highly formalized and emotionally secure environment in which to recall the chaotic, rage-provoking years of conflict. Unlike cartoonish tales of hard-bodied revenge or two-dimensional fantasies of rescue, these thera-peutic narratives focused not on a renewed American potency, but on images of fellowship. In films such as *Platoon* (1986) and *Casualties of War* (1989), or in novels such as John Del Vecchio's *The 13th Valley* (1982), and even to a lesser extent in memoirs such as Philip Caputo's *A Rumor of War* (1977), authors brought to life combat units into which readers and viewers could enter much as they might a room full of veterans. Like literary therapists, writers and filmmakers borrowed the genre conven-tions of family melodramas, coming-of-age stories, and even gung-ho World War II action flicks and used them to frame and normalize their audiences' recollections of combat.

To understand the appeal of such narratives, it is important to re-member how many Americans, and perhaps especially those who spoke out against the war, felt implicated in the killing and dying their soldiers were doing in Southeast Asia. Some twenty years after the war's end, many tend to see those who protested the war and those who fought it as

members of opposing camps. Since 1980, when Ronald Reagan declared the war a "noble cause," many Americans, particularly those on
the right, have heralded Vietnam veterans as the heroes of a misunder-
stood conflict and dismissed antiwar protestors as ignorant, longhaired
children or as creatures of the political fringe. In fact, even in the earliest
years of the conflict, events in Vietnam had drawn soldiers and antiwar
civilians toward a remarkably similar sense of the war's atrocious violence.

On January 31, 1967, when a group of clergy and laymen gathered
in Washington, D.C., to protest the war, their message reflected widespread feelings of shame and complicity. "Ours is an assembly of shock,
contrition, and dismay," exclaimed the rabbi Abraham Heschel as he led
the group in prayer. "Who would have believed that we life-loving
Americans are capable of bringing death and destruction to so many
innocent people? We are startled to discover how unmerciful, how
beastly we ourselves can be." In a later essay, Heschel explained that the
fact that he was a civilian offered him no escape from a sense of complicity in the fighting. Simply participating in the American economy implied a measure of responsibility. "I am personally involved in the
torment of the people injured in battle on the front and in the hamlets,
in the shipping of explosives, in the triggering of guns," he wrote.
"Though deaf to the distant cry of the orphaned and the maimed, I
know that my own integrity is being slashed in that slaughter." Even
before the Tet Offensive of 1968 and the revelations of the My Lai
massacre in 1969, Heschel felt as if he and his country were drowning in
a sea of violence:

> The groan deepens, the combat burns, the wailing cry does not abate.
> . . . For on horror's head horrors accumulate. We are in danger of
> being swept away—against our will, despite circumspection—by a ve-
> hement current and compulsive course. . . . Force unleashed moves
> on its own momentum, breaks all constraint, reaching intensities which
> man can no longer control.

Despite his distance from the battlefield, Heschel could well have
been describing the lessons American troops were learning in combat.

By 1967, the whirlwind of horror Heschel described had already up-
rooted thousands of combat soldiers, torn them away from the emotional
foundations of their youth, and sent them spinning through a topsy-
turvy moral universe. In the same year in which Heschel wrote his essay,
Brian Winhover arrived in Vietnam. He was eighteen years old, a Cath-
olic, and a virgin. Within a year he would become, by his own description, a highly proficient killer. "We weren't ready for it," says Winhover
of himself and the men in his unit. "The world . . . just exploded. The
world that was wrong—you were taught for eighteen years—became
right. And you *enjoyed* it." The violence of the combat zone snuck up on
men, almost against their will and, often, despite their circumspection. "I
raped a girl one time," said a former infantryman, "and I prayed: 'God
forgive me for doing that,' because I knew that I was losing my mind. It
made me think that I was just another animal, just like everybody else.
Killing . . . that was all they thought about . . . tearing up . . . destroying everything."

In recent years, largely thanks to the rescue fantasies of right-wing
filmmakers and POW-MIA activists, it has become common for Americans to imagine that they abandoned and ignored their soldiers in Vietnam. In reality, both prowar and antiwar Americans made powerful
emotional investments in their soldiers in the field. In a Harris poll taken
in January 1966, for instance, 73 percent of Americans reported feeling
"deeply concerned" about the war and 61 percent felt "personally involved"—this despite the fact that only a minority actually knew someone serving in Vietnam. As the war progressed, that emotional invest-
ment paid a devastating psychological dividend. When American soldiers
committed outright atrocities or when they simply did their jobs in a war
that many felt should never have been waged, they came to offer an
indictment of the American character.

In July 1971, journalist Fred Branfman printed a conversation between an American pilot and an information officer that captured the
passionless ease with which many civilians now feared their soldiers
could kill:

PILOT: Our five-hundred-pound nape canisters are newer, they have a
    better dispersal pattern than the older one-thousand-pounders.

INFORMATION OFFICER: Hey, you're not supposed to talk about the napalm.

PILOT: No shit. Why not?

INFORMATION OFFICER: Well, you know those college kids. Pretty soon they're going to get poor Dow Chemical out of business.

PILOT: It seems pretty ridiculous for people to get so emotional about how you kill people. What's so bad about nape anyway?

A year later the editors of *Life* answered his question with a photograph of a naked Vietnamese child, her clothes burned off by napalm, running down a road, screaming. For Americans against the war, the numbness of men like the pilot and their blissful ignorance of the damage their weapons were doing summed up the emotional detachment of all those who supported the war, including civilians.

Yet this attitude also conjured up a vision of a dangerous, all-pervasive affection for technology that entangled even those who opposed the war. For the men who were managing the conflict, the mechanisms of production on the home front and of killing overseas shared a marvelous efficiency. "Today," wrote General William Westmoreland, "machines and technology are permitting economy of manpower on the battlefield, as indeed they are in the factory. . . . I am confident the American people expect this country to take full advantage of its technology—to welcome and applaud the developments that will replace wherever possible the man with the machine." For Americans against the war, however, the analogy had terrifying implications. If our soldiers in Vietnam were simply worker bees in a great hive of destruction, then perhaps so too were all those who labored at home in America's factories and in its civilian industries. Perhaps millions of Americans, each as "deaf to the distant cry of the orphaned and the maimed" as Fred Branfman's pilot, could be held accountable for the killing in Vietnam.

If they could, some wondered, were they any different from those they had most abhorred—the Germans of World War II? Had America become, like Nazi Germany, a paragon of evil? No less a figure than Telford Taylor, America's chief counsel at the Nazi war crimes trials at

Nuremberg in 1946, felt compelled to ask whether the Americans in Vietnam, like the Germans in Europe, had stepped outside the bounds of morality and international law. In a closely reasoned volume entitled *Nuremberg and Vietnam: An American Tragedy,* published in 1970, Taylor examined America's bombings of civilian targets, its treatment of prisoners of war, and its use of free-fire zones in the light of Nazi tactics in World War II. With great regret he concluded that America's behavior in Southeast Asia had often resembled that of its former enemies. "We have smashed the country [of Vietnam] to bits," he wrote, "and will not even take the trouble to clean up the blood and rubble. . . . Somehow we failed ourselves to learn the lessons we undertook to teach at Nuremberg, and that failure is today's American tragedy."

By the end of the Vietnam War, great numbers of Americans shared Taylor's views. Where once they had held German and Japanese generals responsible for atrocities, they now accused smooth, professional Americans, such as General William Westmoreland. Nor did they point their fingers at only military men: Antiwar Americans (who, by the end of the war, constituted the great majority of the public) condemned a wide variety of leaders for drawing them into a pointless and immoral conflict. From Harvard intellectuals, such as Henry Kissinger, to Presidents Johnson and Nixon, the cream of America's political, intellectual, and military crop seemed tainted by the war.

Many ordinary citizens too felt debased by the conflict in ways they had not by earlier wars. During World War II, Americans had seen themselves and their soldiers making sacrifices for a worthwhile cause. Women and children on "the home front" squirreled away tin cans for recycling, restitched worn-out nylons, bought savings bonds—and each small sacrifice they made linked them to the sacrifices of life and limb their sons and brothers were making overseas. During Vietnam, on the other hand, Americans at home found themselves linked to their soldiers abroad not through acts of meaningful sacrifice, but through the shared suspicion that the killing and dying in Vietnam meant nothing.

In the immediate wake of the war, Americans found few opportunities to allay those suspicions or to restore the moral codes that the war had broken down. Unlike the Germans and Japanese after World War II, they faced no war crimes trials, no broad accounting of their actions. Nor did they undertake any large-scale public self-examination. Instead, as Saigon fell, they heeded the advice of President Ford and turned their backs on what he called "a war that is finished—as far as America is concerned."

By doing so, however, they ensured their continued preoccupation with the conflict. Throughout the last two decades, most Americans have remained convinced that in Vietnam their country stepped outside the boundaries of international law and its own traditional moral code. In 1975, two months after the fall of Saigon, a Roper opinion poll revealed that some 66 percent of Americans thought of the war as "the wrong thing." Two years later, a Gallup poll suggested that seven out of every ten Americans believed that Vietnam had been "More than a mistake, fundamentally wrong and immoral." From that time to the present, surveys have consistently noted that more than half of all Americans (and often as many as 70 percent) have felt the same way.

In that sense, their dilemma has resembled the postwar predicaments of those soldiers who went berserk on the battlefield. Driven temporarily insane by the deaths of friends, by their own near-annihilation, or perhaps by betrayal by a leader, these men, like some soldiers in all wars, charged off into enemy lines, utterly fearless and seemingly indestructible, to kill and mutilate their foes. While in this frenzied state, writes the psychiatrist Jonathan Shay, a soldier "feels like a god." Imagining himself invulnerable, he behaves accordingly.

The price of his imagined invulnerability, however, is a radical moral isolation. "All of our virtues," explains Shay, "come from *not* being gods: Generosity is meaningless to a god, who never suffers shortage or want; courage is meaningless to a god, who is immortal and can never suffer permanent injury; and so on. Our virtues and our dignity arise from our mortality. . . ." What's more, to the extent that a soldier feels like a god, he no longer needs to answer to mortal rules. He breaks free of the moral and legal constraints that govern civilian behavior and that bind civilian societies together. Reflecting on this sense of moral collapse, one veteran told Shay, "I became a fucking animal. I started putting fucking heads on poles. Leaving fucking notes for the motherfuckers. . . ." In Vietnam, whole units stepped outside the bounds of their prewar moral codes, while in many areas officers encouraged acts of abusive violence. After firefights, when soldiers sat weeping over the deaths of their friends, officers often stepped up and told them, "Don't get sad! Get even!" In such a climate, explains psychologist James Munroe, "There is no authority anymore. There is no one left to sanction you. Suddenly you're out there on your own. You're outside morality. You're the judge and executioner. You can do whatever you want to do."

For the formerly berserk soldier, as for survivors of other, noncombat traumas, one of the most effective avenues for social reentry has been the therapy group. As Robert Lifton wrote in 1973, Vietnam presented soldiers with "a counterfeit universe, in which all-pervasive, spiritually-reinforced inner corruption [became] the price of survival." The kind of therapy groups that have evolved out of the rap groups of the early 1970s, on the other hand, offer communities in which emotional and spiritual honesty are the price of membership. Although they come in many shapes and sizes (some with leaders, some without, some lasting for weeks, others for years) and although some focus on specific traumatic events, while others pay more attention to the post-traumatic lives of their members, virtually all such groups offer veterans a renewed sense of camaraderie. The soldier who once found himself alone, cut off from his feelings, disengaged from the moral and social networks into which he was born, now finds himself surrounded by others who understand and empathize with his experience. "Since Vietnam I'd never had a friend, someone I could call at four o'clock in the morning and say I feel like putting a .45 in my mouth," said one veteran. But when he joined a therapy group, he found companions. "These guys perfectly understood when I started talking," he said. "I felt this overwhelming relief."

Such relief mirrors the kind of emotional release men like Albert Mahoney and Brian Winhover have sought through rescue missions. Yet, unlike rescue missions, therapy groups do not ask veterans to replay their combat roles. On the contrary: Regardless of their particular focus and structure, therapy groups offer survivors of combat a set of values and behaviors diametrically opposed to those they encountered in the field. In Vietnam, survival required that soldiers identify themselves and the people around them as either allies or enemies, aggressors or victims. "Whenever you tried to be human in Vietnam," recalls one veteran, "you got screwed." Therapy groups, however, demand that veterans recognize one another as both aggressors and victims simultaneously and that they acknowledge these parts of themselves with compassion.

This process begins with trust, an acceptance of safety, and leads toward a renewed faith in moral order. In combat, men saw and were at times urged to commit acts of unrestrained violence, whereas in therapy groups, they are encouraged to follow rules that contain and govern expressions of violent emotion. As a result, a veteran in a therapy group soon discovers that he and others can describe experiences that enrage them, particularly combat experiences, without doing actual physical damage. "The whole thing is control," says Brian Winhover, a former member of a long-term therapy group. "You start talking about combat, you're going to go out of control. Who knows what's going to happen?" Over time, though, a veteran learns that the group around him can accept the violence of his impulses and can listen to his stories of destruction in combat without themselves being destroyed. He discovers that even though he remembers being a killer, the act of remembering will not kill others.

Nor will it kill the veteran himself. Having tested the ability of the group to contain and absorb the emotions associated with combat, a veteran can begin to recognize those emotions consciously. At first, he may feel so ashamed of his actions in Vietnam or so afraid of his feelings about them that he cannot acknowledge them. Instead, he perceives them first mirrored in the men around him, men he cares for in ways that, trapped by his own shame and fear, he cannot yet care for himself. Gradually, as he looks at the men in his group, he begins to see himself. He finds that he can feel their shame and fear and, as he does, he discovers that he can begin to bear his own emotions. Once he can feel those emotions and at the same time, know that he is not going to go berserk, the veteran can retake his place in civilian society. Neither god nor beast, he sees himself as human once again.

With his humanity, the veteran finds a renewed ability and desire to make moral choices. He comes to believe, as Arthur Egendorf explains, that "the cure for a life diminished by the fearful refusal to care is to call courageously on that capacity and to express caring in ways that make it real." He takes on tasks that reinforce his newfound moral confidence, tasks ranging from keeping the streets of his neighborhood clean to helping resettle Vietnamese refugees. Unlike rescue missions or revenge fantasies, these new activities arise out of empathy and they ask the former soldier not to reprise the combat roles of aggressor and victim, but to carve out a new emotional and moral niche. Having rediscovered the sense of safety and community that he lost in combat, having acknowledged his violence and mourned both the damage he did in Vietnam and his own lost innocence, the veteran can again perceive the existence of beneficence in himself and others. "I still revert back," says Brian Winhover. "There's still times when the combat soldier comes out. I still feel that power. But most of the time, I am a good father and a good guy in the neighborhood."

For American civilians, the sense of belonging and moral efficacy that men like Winhover have discovered in therapy groups can be found in works of film, fiction, and memoir. Like therapeutic gatherings of former soldiers, postwar narratives have drawn their audiences through the stages of trust, mirroring, confrontation, and emotional relief. Much as the rules and structures of therapy groups have given traumatized veterans a feeling of safety, the established patterns of narrative genres have reassured civilian moviegoers and readers that dangerous ideas and feelings can be contained. In the same way that a veteran might identify with other veterans in his therapy group and thus come to deal with otherwise unbearable emotions in himself, a viewer of a postwar film can identify with the characters on the screen and thus explore his own feelings about the conflict. Like a veteran in a therapy group, he can touch on the rage and shame his recollections evoke and learn that he no longer needs to act on those emotions, that what was once a psychologically threatening reality has now become a realistic, but far less dangerous, *memory*. With the emotional weight of the war thus lifted from their shoulders, civilians, like veterans, can turn toward the future with renewed hope.

Authors and filmmakers, many of them veterans, first began to lay down the rules of Vietnam narratives in the final years of the war. By 1984, critics could discern the existence of what C. D. B. Bryan, writing in *Harper's Magazine,* called the "Generic Vietnam War Narrative." Such a story, wrote Bryan, "charts the gradual deterioration of order, the disintegration of idealism, the breakdown of character, the alienation from those at home, and, finally, the loss of all sensibility save the will to survive." It does so, however, within an increasingly standardized narrative framework. Bryan explained that in the 1970s, a great many writers built their stories around a soldier's tour of duty. Their tales would begin by following a "vital, confident, self-consciously patriotic" young man into the Marines, then on through boot camp to Vietnam. There, the hero would "replace a kid who didn't last long enough for anyone to learn his name." Gradually he would blend into his new, multiracial, multiclass combat unit. He would go through combat for the first time (and find it more real than any John Wayne movie), see a comrade die in battle, witness or even participate in an atrocity, find a bar girl for "boom-boom," and finally return to the United States to be rejected by his family and friends. Even if he experienced horror, Bryan pointed out, he survived it and flew safely home.

While some elements of Bryan's generic narrative, such as the atrocity scene, the bar girl, and the limited tour of duty, clearly evolved out of the experience of Vietnam, others, particularly the socially complex platoon and the bonding that takes place within it, had their origins in World War II. In films such as *Sands of Iwo Jima* (1949) or *Bataan* (1943), soldiers from a wide variety of ethnic groups and geographic regions found themselves thrown together. Muscular Swedes from Minnesota hunkered down next to Irish boys from Boston and small-town soda jerks met petty gamblers from the Bronx. The races rarely mixed, but otherwise, the single greatest challenge these men faced next to defeating the enemy was learning to get along with one another.

In conventional postwar Vietnam narratives, issues of class and race replace those of ethnicity, but once again, the members of combat units represent a plethora of social types, bear nicknames reflecting their origins, and learn, under the pressures of combat, to get along. Philip Caputo could well be describing the men of an earlier era when, in *A Rumor of War,* he describes the first platoon he commanded as a young Marine lieutenant. Even though "most of them came from the ragged fringes of the American Dream," he writes, "they were to a man thoroughly American, in their virtues as well as their flaws: idealistic, insolent, generous, direct, violent, and provincial. . . ."

Unlike their predecessors, though, the platoons of Vietnam come together not to serve a higher purpose, but to discover that they lack one. In World War II narratives, front-line soldiers often bond with one another in order to accomplish specific missions. This generation of films frequently features long explanations of tactics and of a particular unit's place in the overall scheme of the war that give meaning to the men's individual sacrifices. Vietnam films, however, frequently portray particular missions, like the war in general, as pointless. Rather than focus on maps and tactics, conventional Vietnam stories focus on the private sensations of combat: the experience of waiting for an ambush or triggering a booby trap. Despite this attention to individual experience, Vietnam narratives also remind their audiences that men in combat share a unique and nearly unbreakable bond. Even if they are not sacrificing themselves for a greater cause, as they were in World War II, they must still survive, and their survival depends on their ability to stick together. What's more, the forces that threaten their unity—incompetent or corrupt leaders, racism, drug use—are often the same forces that threatened Americans' *national* cohesion during the war. The fictional soldiers of postwar novels and films represent not only real historical soldiers, but civilian citizens as well. To that extent, their ability to stick together on the page or on the screen suggests that in the real world too, Americans have always found—and will continue to find—ways to maintain their national unity.

Perhaps no film has brought this point home more forcefully than Oliver Stone's *Platoon* (1986). Richard Corliss echoed the encomia of many critics when he wrote in *Time* that the film exploded "like a frag bomb in the consciousness of America." An instant box-office phenomenon, the film was acclaimed as an accurate representation of combat and, therefore, of the war as a whole. "More than any other film," wrote Corliss, *"Platoon* gives the sense—all five senses—of fighting in Viet Nam." For that reason, no less an authority than David Halberstam, former Southeast Asia correspondent for *The New York Times* and author of *The Best and the Brightest,* declared *Platoon* to be "one of the great war movies of all time. The other Hollywood Viet Nam films have been a rape of history. But *Platoon* is historically and politically accurate. . . . Thirty years from now, people will think of the Viet Nam War as *Platoon."*

Despite Halberstam's claim for the film's unique historical accuracy, *Platoon* hews closely to the rules of C. D. B. Bryan's stereotypical Vietnam War narrative. Like Bryan's generic narrator, Stone's Chris Taylor (Charlie Sheen), the narrator of *Platoon,* replaces a dead soldier, gradually earns his place in a multiracial, multiclass fighting unit, lives through combat, watches comrades die, and witnesses an atrocity. Taylor also plays the role of a World War II recruit. Like the men of *Sands of Iwo Jima,* he volunteers for the army because he believes it is his duty, and on the battlefield he finds himself surrounded by men from across the nation. As he tells his grandmother in a letter home (itself a World War II combat tale convention):

> They come from the end of the line, most of them. Small towns you never heard of—Pulaski, Tennessee; Brandon, Mississippi; Pork Bend, Utah; Wampum, Pennsylvania. . . . Most of 'em got nothing. They're poor. They're the unwanted of our society, yet they're fighting for our society and our freedom and what we call America. . . . They're the best I've ever seen, Grandma, the heart and soul [of America].

With his down-home rhetoric, Taylor could well be describing the men who took on the Germans with Audie Murphy in *To Hell and Back* (1955) or any of a dozen other Hollywood combat units of the era. By recalling the cinematic platoons of an earlier war, Taylor not only trains his viewers to see the men around him in terms of filmic stereotypes, but asks them to accept that the same symbolic forum in which Americans came to grips with World War II remains appropriate for the discussion of Vietnam. As Richard Corliss noted, during Vietnam "we were a nation split between left and right, black and white, hip and square, mothers and fathers, parents and children." In Stone's *Platoon,* these conflicts threaten to cripple the fighting unit much as interethnic struggles once threatened to corrode the unity of the Hollywood platoons of World War II. Yet, having watched the movies of Wayne and Murphy, the viewers can take comfort from the fact that here too heroes should emerge. The rules of the combat film genre remind him that in movies, at least, and perhaps in America as well, communities crack, but they never crumble.

The greatest threat to the unity of Stone's platoon is the moral ambiguity of the American role in the war. With Manichaean efficiency, Stone presents two takes on that role in the figures of two sergeants, the saintly Elias (Willem Dafoe) and the vile Barnes (Tom Berenger). Both sergeants have served several tours in Vietnam and have become combat experts, inspiring loyalty from their men. Kind and compassionate, Elias is a champion of underdogs within the platoon and thus an emblem of American idealism in Vietnam. Barnes, on the other hand, embodies an irrational violence, a ruthless love of unrestrained killing that recalls America's destructive power. He has turned cold, stepped outside civilian moral boundaries, and become a berserker. He dominates the battlefield and his men believe him to be immortal. "Barnes has been shot seven times," says one soldier. "[The] only thing that can kill Barnes is Barnes."

Soon enough, Barnes's berserk behavior tests the moral strength of the men in the platoon. One afternoon, after an ambush, Barnes and Elias lead their men into a village. There, they discover weapons and food stored by the Viet Cong. Enraged by the ambush, the men get set to commit mayhem. Even Taylor turns brutal, shooting at the foot of a one-legged villager and making him dance. Barnes, however, leads the way to horror. When he interrogates an old man who refuses to talk, Barnes shoots his wife dead. He then puts his pistol to the head of the man's granddaughter. At that moment Elias appears. "You ain't a firing squad, you piece of shit!" he shouts, clubbing Barnes with his rifle. For a while they wrestle, but when other officers break up the fight, Barnes hisses, "You're dead, Elias! You're fucking dead!"

From that point on, *Platoon* becomes a drama of berserk rage and its containment. Barnes embodies a poisonous amorality, with Elias as its antidote. The question that drives the second half of the film is whether the antidote will work. Will Barnes kill Elias? Will the atrocity he committed in the village go unpunished? Will the unit ever become an efficient, moral whole?

Within the formalized fiction of *Platoon,* these bits of narrative tension suggest larger historical questions: Were Americans in Vietnam as moral as Elias or as berserk as Barnes? And if they were berserk, will they go unpunished? How can the nation's sense of community and morality be restored?

On the screen, Chris Taylor acts out Stone's answers, unifying the opposing camps within his platoon—and, symbolically, within his nation. On his way out of the village, Taylor stumbles across a rape-in-progress and puts a stop to it, thus helping to mend his unit's fraying morality. Later, when he learns that Barnes has killed Elias, Taylor becomes an even greater force for justice. In the film's final minutes, Taylor and his unit endure an overwhelming midnight assault by North Vietnamese troops. At one point during the attack, the berserk Barnes, perhaps thinking Taylor is an enemy soldier, pins him to the ground and raises a shovel over his head. At that moment a napalm strike blows him off and into the bushes. In the morning Taylor comes to, surrounded by Vietnamese and American bodies. Among them, he spots a groaning Barnes. As Barnes tries to crawl away, Taylor picks up an enemy rifle and shoots him four times.

When the film was released, audiences often erupted in cheers as they watched Barnes die and it is not hard to see why. Taylor has killed a criminal, a father figure who stepped outside the boundaries of morality. In that sense, he acted with the same moral authority as the men who killed the sneaky Japanese and the goose-stepping Nazis of the films of World War II. The fact that this time the hero killed another American matters less than the fact that, like his cinematic forefathers, he has restored justice on the battlefield. "You have to fight evil if you are going to be a good man," said Oliver Stone. "That's why Chris killed Barnes." To the extent that they identified with Taylor, moviegoers could now imagine themselves as members of the same heroic nation that had produced such keepers of social and moral order as John Wayne and Clint Eastwood.

Yet, as Stone pointed out at the time, Taylor had to become more like Barnes, violating both American law and his own moral strictures, in order to shoot him. "Chris came out of the war stained and soiled," said Stone. "He becomes a murderer." By identifying with Taylor and, in part, with Barnes, moviegoers too can imaginatively acknowledge their soldiers' murderous actions in Vietnam, as well as their own feelings of being "stained and soiled." With the killing of Barnes, the moral, upright character of Taylor—and, by implication, that of the viewer as well—has come to contain recollections of berserk violence and controlled righteousness side by side. In the final moments of *Platoon,* as the plaintive tones of Samuel Barber's *Adagio for Strings* begin to swell, Taylor makes the point explicitly:

> I think now looking back we did not fight the enemy. We fought
> ourselves and the enemy was in us. The war is over for me now. But it
> will always be there for the rest of my days, as I'm sure Elias will be,

fighting with Barnes for what Rhah [another soldier] called "the pos-
session of my soul." There are times since I've felt like the child born
of those two fathers.

As therapy for citizens of a formerly haywire nation, Taylor's final
oration is potentially quite effective. Like the hero of a World War II
platoon, Taylor has finally brought the warring parties within his unit
together, albeit as spirits within himself. He thus suggests that post-
Vietnam America can overcome the fragmentation brought about by the
war much as the nation had earlier survived and triumphed in the Second World War. Moreover, by reducing the real experience of combat
with an outside enemy to an internal, psychological phenomenon, he
makes our recollection of the war an occasion for personal transformation. Knowing that we struggle with both idealistic and violent impulses,
he implies, Americans are now free as a nation to *choose* to act, as Taylor
did, in the tradition of Elias rather than Barnes.

As history, however, Taylor's voice-over leaves much to be desired.
By suggesting that American behavior in Vietnam was born of the twin
fathers of idealism and blood lust rather than the incompetent, often
immoral, and sometimes illegal decisions of political and military leaders,
Stone has taken the issue of responsibility off the table. The fact that
many Americans supported their government's policies throughout the
war no longer matters: Vietnam, implies Stone, was the product of
widely shared *emotions,* not individual *choices,* and who can be held responsible for their feelings? What's more, American attacks on the Vietnamese have vanished from memory. After all, says Taylor, "we did not
fight the enemy. We fought ourselves and the enemy was in us." If
Americans hurt only themselves in Vietnam, why should they feel overwhelmed by shame?

According to Taylor, they should not—at least, not any more. As his
helicopter flies away, Taylor assigns the audience a mission. "Those of us
who did make it have an obligation to build again," he says, "to teach to
others what we know and to try with what's left of our lives to find a
goodness and meaning to this life. . . ." Having imaginatively joined
Taylor in killing off Barnes and having thus stripped their memories of
berserk American behavior in Vietnam of much of their shame and guilt,
viewers can return to their daily lives with a commitment to restore the

social and moral fabric of their nation. Like the members of veterans' rap groups, they have faced down their most painful recollections of the war, reassured themselves of the solidity of community and goodness, and turned toward the future.

In the late 1980s, the psychodynamics that informed Stone's *Platoon* informed a number of other films and television programs as well. The Brian De Palma epic *Casualties of War* (1989) presented moviegoers with another combat unit torn apart by an atrocity. As they had in *Platoon,* viewers could identify with both a berserker, played by Sean Penn, and a force for moral order, played by Michael J. Fox. Once again they could cheer as the moral hero put an end to the career of his immoral enemy and proved that the social order could withstand and repel almost any assault. Likewise, the films *Jackknife* (1989) and *Cease Fire* (1985) featured a berserker and a moral hero, though this time they set the symbolic platoon aside and drew their viewers directly into therapy groups. In both films, a Vietnam veteran goes haywire and threatens to shatter the social vessel of his family. Only when a fellow vet pulls him into a rap group (with the viewer close on his heels) does the formerly berserk soldier accept his need for social connection and return to his now restrengthened family.

In the critically acclaimed ABC television series *China Beach* (1988–1990), the family, the rap group, and the military unit merged into a single melodramatic, therapeutic whole. Each week *China Beach* took viewers to a seaside hospital and recreation compound, where a group of nurses, doctors, and enlisted men struggled valiantly to save the wounded while the enemy rained down mortar shells on their position. Yet, like their Korean War predecessors on *M*A*S*H,* the men and women of *China Beach* were as preoccupied with maintaining their relationships with one another as they were with keeping soldiers alive. Characters coupled and uncoupled, cried, giggled, moped, mourned, held each other's hands, or sat on the beach staring out at the sea—just as they might have in a melodrama set in Southern California. Like the bonds between the men of Oliver Stone's platoon, these relationships endured despite constant contact with horror and constant attacks by the enemy.

But, of course, that is their therapeutic mission. Like the men of *Platoon,* the inhabitants of *China Beach* aim to restore social meaning and moral value to acts of horrific violence and suffering that, when they actually occurred in history, often seemed pointless and immoral. In one episode, for instance, a visiting go-go girl holds the hand of a dying soldier who has been burned from head to toe. The next day Lieutenant Colleen McMurphy (Dana Delaney), the show's star nurse, comforts her:

> I saw you last night. You know in your heart you made a difference. . . . You were there. He had a mother, a sister, a girlfriend, and you were there. You gave him a home before he died so far away from it."

The viewer, who watched the man die as well, can take the same comfort. By imaginatively joining the dancer within the *China Beach* "family," the viewer can bring his own memories of the carnage that took place so far away and so long ago to a safe, secure home in the present.

With all the comfort they offer, are such recastings of the past merely aids to amnesia, televised fantasies dreamed up to help Americans forget a war they would rather not have fought? Perhaps. Yet, even as they have eased American guilt, fictions such as *China Beach* or *Platoon* have also made it possible for Americans to recall damning details of the conflict. American soldiers burned to a crisp, Vietnamese civilians murdered for no reason, American soldiers themselves becoming feelingless killers— by packaging these events in such a way as to reduce the psychological threat they pose to their audiences, conventional postwar Vietnam narratives have in fact made it possible for Americans to know something of the horror for which their country was responsible in Vietnam.

What's more, like therapy groups, they have transformed these events from disruptive memories into opportunities for the renewal of social and moral connections. As they identify with the go-go dancer on *China Beach* or with Taylor in *Platoon,* civilians who might once have felt isolated from their fellow citizens, repelled by their army's violence in Southeast Asia, even ashamed of the role they might have played in maintaining that violence, can begin to look on themselves and their country with compassion. Like veterans in therapy, they can see themselves not as members of an emotionally numb group of aggressors, but as empathetic, moral citizens of a community that was once at war and that is now, however awkwardly, at peace.

As they begin to feel at home in the present, however, both civilians and veterans may come to neglect the lessons of the past. As Arthur Egendorf explained in 1975, "We all risk being seduced into believing that our capacity for evil has been permanently exorcised when all that has happened is that we have developed a new strategy for pretending it does not exist." To the extent that they have offered us a way to recall and live with an otherwise unbearably violent history, therapy groups and the most common postwar narratives have reduced the personal and political paralysis that can accompany recollections of Vietnam. But to the degree that they have helped us forget the political decisions that sparked the war, as well as the support millions of citizens gave to those decisions, such therapeutic constructions have also made it easier for us to make the same mistakes again.

CHAPTER SEVEN

LOST FATHERS:

REPAIRING THE BETRAYAL OF YOUNG MEN

ONE AFTERNOON IN THE EARLY 1960S, A HIGH SCHOOL senior named Ron Kovic sat in a dim auditorium, surrounded by the other boys in his class, waiting to be addressed by a pair of Marine recruiters. All his life Kovic had fantasized about becoming a soldier. He had thrilled to Audie Murphy's heroism in *To Hell and Back* and to John Wayne's courage in *Sands of Iwo Jima*. Each weekend he had run out into the woods with his friends from the neighborhood and set mock ambushes, fired toy machine guns, thrown plastic grenades. And when the Marine recruiters appeared, marching smartly down the aisle in crisp blue uniforms and polished shoes, Kovic's heart skipped a beat. As he described the moment in his acclaimed memoir *Born on the Fourth of July,* "It was like all the movies and all the books and all the dreams of becoming a hero come true." At the end of their talk, Kovic got up and walked down the aisle to meet the recruiters. "As I shook their hands and stared up into their eyes," he wrote, "I couldn't help but feel I was shaking hands with John Wayne and Audie Murphy. They told us that day that the Marine Corps built men—body, mind, and spirit. And that we could serve our country like the young president [Kennedy] had asked us to do."

As a teenager who had been handed a road map to manhood, Kovic signed up. Yet, when the Marine Corps sent Kovic to Vietnam, he suffered a profound disillusionment. As a child, he had imagined battlefields where he would find a communion with heroic forebears and on which, as a young man, he had expected to be initiated into a meaningful masculine tradition. What he experienced instead was chaos and disconnection, the breakdown rather than the building of a transgenerational community. In the course of his tour of duty, Kovic saw his unit fire on a group of children they thought were Viet Cong soldiers, and he himself accidentally shot an American corporal. "He'd never figured it would ever happen this way," he explained, describing himself in the third person. "It never did in the movies. There were always the good guys and the bad guys, the cowboys and the Indians. There was always the enemy and the good guys and each of them killed the other." On Kovic's final afternoon in combat, a bullet bit into his shoulder, spun down through his lung, and severed his spinal cord. "All I could feel," he later wrote, "was the worthlessness of dying right here at this moment for nothing."

Some months later, Kovic returned to the United States and, with his hair long and his body paralyzed from the waist down, became an outspoken member of Vietnam Veterans Against the War. At the 1972 Republican Convention, in a scene made famous by Tom Cruise in Oliver Stone's 1989 film of his memoir, Kovic rolled his wheelchair into the aisle to confront President Nixon. When Nixon mounted the podium, Kovic shouted, "Stop the bombing! Stop the war!" until the security men hustled him away. As he did, he presented his own damaged body to the President and, through the assembled reporters and photographers, to the entire American nation as evidence: A President, a pair of Marine recruiters, John Wayne, Audie Murphy—all Kovic's symbolic fathers—had promised him a war that would bring him to manhood, but they had delivered one that had emasculated him instead.

As its now-legendary status suggests, Kovic's protest spoke to the losses of an entire generation of young men. Raised on the heroic ideology of World War II, virtually every boy who came of age in the late 1960s had at some time dreamed of going to war and graduating into manhood. When he faced Nixon, Kovic offered up his broken body as an emblem of the dissolution of that dream and of the contract between young men and their elders. His paralyzed limbs spoke of a crisis in American masculinity spawned by the failure of fathers—both biological and cultural—to offer their sons an honest initiation and to secure them safe passage through it. Teenaged boys went to Vietnam ready to sacrifice their lives in order to convince their elders to admit them to the circle of adult males in "body, mind, and spirit." When the young combatants discovered that the war was no initiation and that no matter how well they performed, their elders would refuse to celebrate their actions, both soldiers and male civilians lost a part of themselves, a part that in the 1980s and 1990s many have gone to extreme lengths to recover.

The recollections of combat veterans make clear the esteem in which many held both their blood fathers and the paternal masculine heroes of American legend. One after another, these men had departed the domestic regions of home and family, regions largely governed by women, hoping to enter, in Vietnam, the twin symbolic landscapes of masculine and national mythology. Many felt obliged to make their fathers proud. "I told my father I was thinking of going to Canada," said one veteran. "I turned to walk out of the room. I saw my father, his head in his hands, sobbing at the kitchen table. I had never seen him cry before. I knew then that I had to go [to Vietnam]." Even those whose own fathers did not approve of their going to war responded to the calls of their cultural fathers. When President Johnson claimed that a fledgling democracy needed American help to keep from being overrun by Communists, many young men offered themselves to the cause. Even after the Tet Offensive of 1968, wrote Charles Anderson, a former Marine, "Most [soldiers] believed their national leaders when they said there was a good reason to go, and most understood the implication in the call— the project might not be exactly pleasant."

Even as they rose to meet the expectations of their blood fathers and of their older male leaders, combat soldiers often imagined themselves taking part in a larger American drama. As Richard Slotkin has pointed out, Americans have looked to armed conflict to confirm their national self-image since the era of the captivity narrative. From the first settlers in New England to the Western pioneers, in a process Slotkin calls "regeneration through violence," Americans have sent men into "wilderness" areas to kill off or imprison their "savage" inhabitants. Each defeat of those savages allowed the nation to grow in size and strength. Such victories also allowed Americans to confirm their national identity as a people more adventurous than their European ancestors and, at the same time, more civilized than the savages they had just eliminated.

When young men went to Vietnam, many imagined that they would undergo their private baptisms of fire on behalf of the nation they had left behind and that they would once again renew Americans' confidence in their national mythology. War, writes William Broyles, "is, for men, at some terrible level the closest thing to what childbirth is for women: the initiation into the power of life and death." It is also, he writes, "the frontier beyond the last settlement." Even as they gained the adult male's "power of life and death," many of the young men who went to Vietnam were expecting to reconquer America's mythological frontier.

Of course, Vietnam bore little resemblance to the Old West, mythological or real. Triple-canopy jungle, booby-trapped mines, an invisible enemy, the inflation of body counts, the wholesale destruction of villages to create "free-fire zones," the building of concentration camps for Vietnamese civilians—all worked to corrode the combat soldier's link to his older male leaders and his masculine forebears. John Durant, a helicopter crew chief in Vietnam, explains the effects of American tactics on his perceptions of the war:

> If you need forty acres for an airstrip or if you suspect an area to be a VC staging ground, you turn the jets and B-52s loose. Then we announce accidental deaths. Or consider the hamlet programs. Basically, it involves rounding up people who don't want to be rounded up. Who gave this country the right to masturbate with other people?

Durant's choice of verbs is telling. Traditionally, initiation ceremonies celebrate a young man's passage into sexual maturity, his right to take a female partner and start a family. Vietnam, however, presented young men not with images of the military penetration of a foreign country and the successful procreation of American myths, but with the specter of violent national onanism. And as they witnessed their country's failure to "couple" with South Vietnam and to produce the victory predicted by their leaders and their myths, young men let go of their faith in those leaders and myths and clung instead simply to the urge to survive. Charles Anderson explains his comrades' growing disillusionment:

> No matter how many patrols they went on, how many air strikes they called, how many rounds they fired at sounds in the night, and no matter how much money they gave to build schools and hospitals, nothing ever got any better. Vietnam stayed as backward and screwed up as it was at the beginning of everyone's tour. The war then became an apolitical and personal project—the struggle to survive.

As they watched their twin struggles to become adult men and to renew American mythology fade into the simple struggle to stay alive, many soldiers began to see themselves as the *anti*heroes of American myth. In his memoir *A Rumor of War,* Philip Caputo has described breaking into villagers' huts on a mission and feeling like "one of those bullying Redcoats who used to barge into American homes during our Revolution." Tim O'Brien compares himself to a "conscripted Nazi" in his memoir *If I Die in a Combat Zone.* Within the precincts of American mythology, of course, Redcoats and Nazi soldiers are not only agents of oppressive empires, but forces of evil against which Americans define themselves as good. Their cultural fathers had promised soldiers that the war in Vietnam would make them heirs to the Minutemen and the heroes of D day; when it did not, men like Caputo and O'Brien feared they had come to resemble their forefathers' *enemies.*

Today not all Vietnam veterans believe that the war was wrong. James Webb, for instance, who commanded a platoon of Marines in Vietnam, earned a fistful of medals, and, like Ron Kovic, left the battlefield on a stretcher, has said that Vietnam was "probably the most moral effort we have ever made. We fought for purely ideological reasons. . . ." Yet veterans like Webb live with a sense of betrayal every bit as strong as that suffered by their antiwar counterparts. In his 1978 novel

Fields of Fire, a story based largely on his own experience, Webb explains that the war offered men an appropriate initiation into the mysteries of life and death, but that those who should have acknowledged the adult status of the soldiers who returned—fathers, politicians, mothers, girl-friends—had failed to do their duty. "It was the fight that mattered, not the cause," says Webb's fictional alter ego, Lieutenant Hodges. "It was the endurance that was important, the will to face certain loss, unknown dangers, unpredictable fates. And if one did it long enough and hard enough, he might happen upon a rewarding nugget. But, in any event, he was *serving,* offering himself on the altar of his culture."

Webb and others like him felt they had fulfilled their half of their culture's initiation contract by offering themselves to be sacrificed. Now, however, their elders and their peers refused to go through with their part of the deal. They declined to recognize the holiness of the young men's acts and so refused not only to admit them into the long line of American male heroes, but often to simply acknowledge them as good men.

Ironically, a number of those who had opposed the war regretted not having sacrificed as veterans had. In 1975, journalist James Fallows wrote an article explaining how he had starved himself to avoid the draft in the spring of 1970. Where he had deliberately slimmed away his masculine musculature, Fallows recalled that "The boys from Chelsea, thick, dark-haired young men, the white proles of Boston," had not even considered altering their masculine bodies or their masculine roles. "It had clearly never occurred to them that there might be a way around the draft," wrote Fallows.

Yet, alongside his traditional upper-class envy of an imagined lower-class virility, Fallows was suffering from a form of survivor guilt. As he explains:

> [W]e happy few [from Harvard] were sped along to Maui or the enter-tainment law firm, or at worst temporarily way-laid in the reserves, while from each of our high schools the less gifted and industrious students were being shipped off as cannon fodder. . . . The question is why, especially in the atmosphere of the late sixties, people with any presumptions to character could have let it go on.

For Fallows, the antiwar protests he and his friends engaged in "never involved substantial risk, nothing more serious than the threat of a night in jail." If they had really wanted to stop the war, he argued, more men of his generation should not merely have dodged the draft, but should have aggressively resisted it.

By the time Fallows dodged the draft, however, the kind of aggressive action he wished he had taken against the war had fallen into widespread disrepute. Aggression meant masculinity, which, according to many, lay at the heart of the conflict. From the beginning, American leaders had conceived of their war-making as a species of masculine display ("I didn't just screw Ho Chi Minh. I cut his pecker off," exclaimed Lyndon Johnson after the bombing of North Vietnam in 1965). But when their displays led to atrocities such as My Lai (an event that Ron Ridenhour, who photographed the massacre, claimed "completely castrated the whole picture of America") or to chaos at home, Americans of all political persuasions began to question not only their leaders' competence, but the tradition of American masculinity within which they acted. Those who could see no logic to Americans' behavior in Vietnam began to suspect, as the feminist journalist Barbara Ehrenreich put it, that "Some masculine demiurge, latent perhaps in all men, had simply run amok."

By the mid-1970s, that suspicion had spread across the political spectrum. During the war, left-wing critics of the government believed, as journalist Benjamin DeMott put it, that members of "The Establishment" suffered from an "intellectual blindness and emotional rigidity," a form of masculinity to be rejected. Pop psychologists soon picked up the left-wing critique, accusing traditional men of being numb, mechanical warriors. "He has armor-plating that is virtually impregnable," wrote Marc Feigen Fasteau in 1974 of a creature he called "the male machine": "His circuits are never scrambled or overrun by irrelevant personal signals. He dominates and outperforms his fellows, although without excessive flashing of lights or clashing of gears." Where, ten years earlier, young men had gone to war hoping to acquire the tight-lipped masculine power of their elders and of their mythological heroes, they now found themselves asked, even by the most conservative of commentators, to aspire to a new emotional presence. In his 1977 book *Understanding the Male Temperament,* Tim LaHaye, a member of the national board of the Moral Majority, explained that

> For the past thirty years, six-foot-four John Wayne has stalked through the American imagination as the embodiment of manhood. . . . He has left not only a trail of broken hearts and jaws everywhere, but millions of fractured male egos which could never quite measure up to the two-fisted, ramrod-backed character who conquered the Old West. The truth of the matter is that no man could measure up to that myth in real life—not even John Wayne.

For Americans of all political stripes, the Vietnam War had broken the link between young men and their elders, between citizens and the largely male "Establishment" that governed them, and between the culture and the male heroes of its myths. In households across the country, fathers and sons found themselves at odds with one another. "My father became an embarrassment to me," wrote Lawrence Wright. "I was no longer proud of his accomplishments or his position in the community— they were merely evidence of his involvement in the establishment." By the same token, Wright's father "saw the [antiwar] protests on the news" and came to view his longhaired son as "one of the nihilistic unwashed barbarians, opposed to progress, naively longing for peace."

Both during and after the war, writers portrayed the breakdown in the American masculine tradition as a rift in the symbolic American family. In David Rabe's 1969 play *Sticks and Bones,* a Vietnam veteran returns to the Norman Rockwell home of his parents Ozzie and Harriet (named for the too-perfect parents of the 1950s sitcom). When he confronts them with what he has seen and done in Vietnam, they induce him to slit his wrists. In one of the most popular television shows of all time, *All in the Family,* Carroll O'Connor's old-style mechanical male, Archie Bunker, squared off against his seventies-sensitive son-in-law, Rob Reiner's Meathead, for twelve consecutive seasons (1971–1983). Both Ozzie and Archie, like Lawrence Wright's real father, belonged to the generation that won World War II, the generation that more than any other in recent memory had lived out the masculine prescriptions of American mythology. Yet, far from being heroic elders, they were presented as emotional cripples whose macho inflexibility had made one, Rabe's Ozzie, a killer and the other, Archie, a bigoted clown.

By the 1980s, Americans felt the devaluation of their symbolic fathers acutely. With Vietnam an initiation gone wrong, both the would-be initiates (the men who fought the war) and their elders (their fathers, their leaders, their matinee idols) had emerged from the conflict discredited. The few who believed that their elders had not misled them in Southeast Asia felt they had neglected them at home, while many of those who avoided the war worried that even if they had been asked to fight in a bad cause, they might be less than men for having stayed home.

In a 1983 article for *Esquire,* Christopher Buckley, neoconservative son of archconservative commentator William F. Buckley, described how he had escaped the draft by claiming a history of severe asthma and how, ever since, he feared he had missed out on something. "I didn't suffer with [the soldiers who went to Vietnam]," he wrote. "I didn't watch my buddies getting wiped out next to me. . . . I haven't served my country. I've never faced life or death. I'm an incomplete person." The Vietnam veterans he knows, on the other hand, have "a spiritual sinew that I ascribe to their experience in the war. I don't think I'll ever have what they have, the aura of *I have been weighed on the scales and have not been found wanting,* and . . . I will always feel the lack of it and will try to compensate for it, sometimes in good, other times in ludicrous ways [italics in the original]."

Buckley would not be alone. Throughout the 1980s and into the 1990s, American men began to conjure up new forms of successful initiation and to recover in fantasy what they had lost—or thought they had missed—in reality. They flocked to films in which young men underwent successful transformations into heroes (more often of the rescuing than the vengeful variety). They applauded as young men forgave unfeeling, mechanical father figures for their loss of emotion and their violence in the past. They cheered as those father figures in turn recovered their ability to feel. In tandem with the on-screen heroes of masculine action pics, men on both the left and right of the political spectrum began to act out in fantasy the initiations they failed to receive in Vietnam. In the process, they tried to redeem the "masculine demiurge" that so many felt had run amok in Vietnam and to restore older men to positions of authority and trust.

Few films have dramatized this attempt to rehabilitate the American masculine tradition more effectively than George Lucas's *Star Wars* trilogy. In the first film, *Star Wars* (1977), Luke Skywalker's (Mark Hamill) dark father, Darth Vader (body, David Prowse; voice, James Earl Jones), embodies the metaphor of the "male machine." He hides his face behind a mask, he wears some kind of control panel on his chest, he breathes with a now-famous iron lung regularity. He feels little except anger and the sensations that come to him through the Force—both of which he turns repeatedly to evil purposes.

His son, on the other hand, who does not yet know his parentage, has begun to become a feeling man. After finding the aunt and uncle with whom he grew up killed and their house burned to the ground, Luke begins to take lessons in feeling from the Jedi master Obi-Wan Kenobe (Alec Guinness). His training mirrors what many soldiers hoped to receive in Vietnam. Like them, Luke has left home to take on a mission that a cultural father has declared all-important. But where the Vietnam soldier's mission often decayed into an exercise in self-preservation, Luke's evolves into a potent expression of his now-adult masculinity. Having successfully learned to feel the "Force" and to trust his feelings, Luke "penetrates" the Death Star's defenses, flies up through a long canal, and shoots his bomb down a narrow opening into the heart of Empire's machine. "I got it! I got it!" he shouts as the Death Star undergoes an orgasmic explosion.

Unfortunately, Darth Vader escapes the blast. The next two *Star Wars* films—*The Empire Strikes Back* (1980) and *Return of the Jedi* (1983)—see Luke and his father fight face-to-face. In *The Empire Strikes Back,* Vader retains his cruelty and lops off Luke's hand. But in *Return of the Jedi,* Vader has changed. Obi-Wan Kenobe warns Luke that Vader is "more machine now than man, twisted and evil." But when Luke confronts him, he feels "the good" in Vader. He refuses to kill him, thus triggering an elaborate death sequence in which Vader is forced to rescue Luke and to be mortally wounded doing it. In the film's final moments, Luke removes his father's mask and sees a gentle, childlike visage within. With his last breaths, Vader acknowledges that he never lost the last bits of good within himself. After he dies, Luke burns his body on funeral pyre as if he were a fallen Viking hero.

With Vader's funeral, the rupture in the relations between young men and old brought about by the Vietnam War has been healed—at least symbolically. After he has cremated Vader's body, Luke sees a vision of his three surrogate fathers in white robes: his two teachers, Obi-Wan Kenobe and Yoda, and his uncle from the first *Star Wars* film. He also takes his own place as a father figure. In the course of the third film, he has learned that his erstwhile sweetheart, Princess Leia (Carrie Fisher), is actually his sister. As a keeper of the Force and of the memory of the good in his father, he will have to teach her the Jedi traditions (which are now a family legacy) much as Obi-Wan and Yoda taught him. Thereby he will be able to prove, as his own father and as American leaders during Vietnam did not, that a warrior-father can be highly sensitive *and* highly moral.

Through this symbolic recreation of our past, Luke's success in battle has also restored the audience's link to their national myths. In Southeast Asia, Americans had seen their soldiers kill and die to support a series of corrupt and oppressive South Vietnamese regimes. Now, in the Tropics of George Lucas's future world, they identified with young men who fought to overturn such regimes. In *Return of the Jedi,* the lightly armed rebels gather in a dense jungle and attack the heavily fortified, high-tech bases of the Imperial troops much as the Viet Cong once attacked American firebases in Vietnam—or, for that matter, as American Minutemen once attacked the fixed formations of the British. Like Rambo, they have laid a perverse claim to the prowess of America's former enemies. At the same time, these battle scenes allow moviegoers to recast their memories of the Vietnam conflict in the shape of earlier, more acceptable victories. As John Hellman has pointed out, Darth Vader is "an image of the dark past of Europe, wearing Nazi helmet and medieval robe." By taking on the Empire, Luke and his comrades remind their audiences that Americans had once taken on the Redcoats of England and the Nazis of Germany and had defeated both.

As it melds Luke's own coming-of-age story into the tale of America's national coming-of-age as a world power, the *Star Wars* trilogy validates the logic with which many Americans went to war in Southeast Asia. The conflict in Vietnam, said American leaders, was the direct descendant of the American Revolution and World War II, in that Americans faced a foe bent on oppressing a people who would be free. As such, it offered the nation a chance to see if a new generation of young men had inherited the masculine prowess needed to defeat such a force. In the *Star Wars* trilogy, George Lucas supplies a similar drama, but this time the film begins with the assumption with which the Vietnam War ended—that it is not the enemy, but our own male elders, who have fallen into lockstep with the forces of evil. When he forces his father to rescue him and thus to reveal the goodness in his heart, Luke offers his audience a vision of their own leaders as highly moral rescuers. At the same time, he reassures them that Vietnam was but a glitch in the graph: With Luke's triumph, the line of Jedi succession—and, by extension, the masculine American tradition of individual and national heroism in defense of freedom—remains unbroken.

The themes of paternal rescue and redemption at the heart of the *Star Wars* series run through many of the most popular films of the 1980s and 1990s. In *Rambo III* (1988), John Rambo goes to war in Afghanistan to rescue Colonel Trautman, his square-jawed former commanding officer in Vietnam and a man who, in *First Blood* (1982), had tried to trick Rambo into getting himself locked away in jail. In *Indiana Jones and the Last Crusade* (1989), the heroic archaeologist Indiana Jones (Harrison Ford) snatches his father (Sean Connery) from the clutches of the Nazis. In *Back to the Future* (1985), Marty McFly (Michael J. Fox) returns to the past to make it possible for his father to first rescue and then marry his mother. In *Terminator 2: Judgment Day* (1991), the Terminator (Arnold Schwarzenegger), a nearly unstoppable mechanical killer in the first film in the series *(The Terminator,* 1984), has been reprogrammed by the rebel leader he first tried to kill to go back into the past, to get to know him as a boy, and to become his loving, trustworthy surrogate father. In each of these father-son epics, it is the love of a good son that transforms an inadequate father into a complete human being. The proof of that love is the son's willingness to offer himself up in some sort of battle on behalf of his father. In the reality of the Vietnam War, such offerings caused rifts between fathers and sons; in the world of the movies, they repair them.

Many men, however, have sought out a more than simply cinematic restoration of their links to the American masculine tradition. Throughout the 1980s and 1990s, men have staged mock initiations, coming-of-age rites often jury-built from the scrap wood of the Vietnam War, initiations through which they can assert their adult masculinity and take their place beside the male heroes of American mythology. In his book *Warrior Dreams,* William Gibson describes three sites for such initiations: paintball game fields, combat shooting schools, and paramilitary conventions. As Gibson points out, all three cater to an anxious generation of men, one "lacking confidence in the government and the economy, troubled by changing relations between the sexes, uncertain of their identity or future." Coming of age during and immediately after the Vietnam War, these men, like Christopher Buckley, had missed out on a conflict that many of them viewed as a chance to prove their masculinity. Cut off from the American tradition of masculinity, these men began to play at combat in the hopes of restoring themselves to what they imagined was their rightful place in the long line of aggressive American males.

In paintball, at least, that combat was not supposed to resemble the fighting in Vietnam. Modeled on capture-the-flag and officially called the National Survival Game, paintball was created in 1981 by two men, one a veteran of a Long-Range Reconnaissance Patrol group in Vietnam and the other a scriptwriter for early Arnold Schwarzenegger movies. The rules were fairly simple: Two teams, each armed with paint-firing rifles with which to "kill" their opponents, would try to steal the other team's flag. In a 1987 manual, one early rule-maker wrote, "There will be no machine guns on Game fields. No tanks. No helicopters. And the Game will always be played in the spirit in which it was conceived. In a spirit of fun and play. There will be no Viet Cong villages, no mock mutilations. No bogus wars."

But things didn't work out that way. In the Mojave Desert, a Los Angeles policeman named Denis Bulowski built an extremely popular playing field called Sat Cong Village. Over the bamboo "village" he flew the National Liberation Front flag, the banner of the Viet Cong; *Sat Cong* means "Kill Communists" in Vietnamese and was a phrase much used in Vietnam. In order to make play more realistic at Sat Cong Village and elsewhere, a company called Corliss Delay, Inc., created a replica of the Vietnam-era Claymore antipersonnel mine, the Playmore P.D.S. Tripwire-Activated Paintmine. In order to increase the realism still further, players often fought in bits and pieces of American military uniforms. "The basic idea," wrote one paintball fan, "is to look military, but not regular military. You're a specialist, a dangerous individual. . . .

With the right patches and equipment, you'll leave them guessing as to whether or not you really were a SEAL [e.g., a Navy commando]."

A SEAL in Vietnam, that is. While paintball fields were designed with other battlefields in mind as well, especially those of Central America, the wellspring of the game was the war in Vietnam. A referee at Sat Cong Village told Gibson that "maybe 5 percent of the players had seen action." The rest, said another employee, were "people who wanted to be in a war; people who didn't get the chance." For most of those people, the war they missed was Vietnam. "I would have loved fighting in Vietnam, fighting to keep everybody free, fighting to keep the Communists out," one man told Gibson at a convention held by *Soldier of Fortune* magazine. "I wanted to be a sniper. I'm a pretty good shot when I want to be. I like to shoot and I own forty guns, including M-16s. Guns stand for freedom. That's how our country was born." By playing paintball, these Walter Mittys could not only satisfy their fantasies about going to war—they could take up the larger American fight for freedom. They could act out the violence that in earlier wars had helped Americans regenerate their national self-image. On the playing field, they could become living links between the muscular spirits of heroes like the Minutemen of Massachusetts and the real, defeated men of Vietnam.

Since its creation, paintball has become enormously popular. In 1988, one survey revealed there were over one thousand "paramilitary playing fields" in America. Over two million men had fought on them at least once and one million fought at least four times a year. Yet, for many of these men, paintball fields are only local sites at which to participate in what Gibson calls a nationwide phenomenon—"paramilitary culture," a fascination with guns, military regalia, and preparation for an unnamed, upcoming Armageddon. If they want to see the heart of that culture, men must make a pilgrimage to paramilitary Mecca: the annual convention of *Soldier of Fortune* magazine in Las Vegas, Nevada.

Like those who play paintball, the thousand or so men who attend the *Soldier of Fortune* convention are rarely combat veterans. Convention organizers, however, like the designers of paintball game fields, go out of their way to grant these men the initiation many feel they have missed. With an attention to the details of their customers' fantasies that would turn the owners of Disneyland green with envy, the executives of *Soldier of Fortune* annually convert their rented corner of Las Vegas into an imitation war zone. In the conventions he attended, Gibson recalls that as soon as they arrived at the Sahara Hotel and Casino, conventioneers had to sign a document that released *Soldier of Fortune* "from any legal responsibility in the event of death or dismemberment." For the next four days, most attendees would move from workshop to workshop within the conference wearing camouflage fatigues. Even time itself had been changed—the *Soldier of Fortune* staff had replaced the peacetime distinctions of A.M. and P.M. and scheduled all events according to the standard twenty-four-hour military clock (in which 8:00 A.M. is referred to as "0800 hours" and so on).

Within this fantasy war zone, the men came face-to-face with real veterans—symbolically, fathers who had survived the initiation of combat. When they attended talks on how to disable a Soviet tank or on how to infiltrate and wipe out a camp full of Third World rebels, they met men who had actually killed. These men, writes Gibson, were "blessed with a special aura" in which their audience could share simply by sitting and listening.

For the most committed of Gibson's paramilitary warriors, such a symbolic link to the men of Vietnam and to the original heroes of American mythology was insufficient. These men wanted weapons training. In the late 1970s and 1980s, Gibson explains, a number of combat shooting schools were founded to meet their needs, about five of which "established national and international reputations." Gibson chose to attend the American Pistol Institute (also known as Gunsite Ranch) in Pauldin, Arizona, a well-known institution at which all enemies are referred to as "Gooks." There, after showing him the basics of pistol control, his instructors sent him through "narrow, craggy ravines filled with metal humanoid targets called 'poppers' and houses stocked with human figures painted on plywood." Gradually, Gibson writes, he realized that:

> Gunsite was taking men through an initiation. . . . It was not by chance that I regressed into a naked little boy. . . . In this state, the initiate surrenders his resistance to the tribal elders; their authority is confirmed by the rite: *Since the masters survived this same ordeal in the past, they must know what to do* [italics in the original]. The initiate finally realizes that he must absorb their instructions in order to sum-

mon up the force necessary to defeat the remaining monsters and safely pass through the dark tunnel.

On his final day at the school, Gibson passed through the darkness of his initiation and into the light of his instructors' approval. As he entered a mock-combat environment called the "Play House," in which targets would snap up and attack him, Gibson recalls, "I was hungry for the unseen adversaries. I knew they were out there. I wanted to kill them." Once inside the Play House, he writes, "My mind and body worked together, remembering moves without consciously trying, dancing in one seamless flow. I had become the *armed man*—a reborn warrior [italics in the original]." His instructors, proud of his accomplishments, awarded him a certificate that named him a Marksman First Class.

It was of such certificates, of course, that boys like Ron Kovic once dreamed. As he shot his way through the Play House, Gibson acted out the war that thousands of young men expected to find in Vietnam. Through violence, he tested himself and earned the approbation of his ritual fathers. He did not suffer wounds, see friends die, endure betrayals by his superiors, or find himself rejected at the end of his journey. On the contrary, he found himself admitted into a clan of honorable older men.

In his explorations of places like Gunsite Ranch and the paintball game fields, Gibson also worked his way into a deeply paranoid right-wing subculture that, at its most moderate, has supported President Reagan's interventions in South America with cash and surplus weapons and that, at its most extreme, has given birth to homegrown bomb-wielding terrorists, such as those who attacked the Federal Building in Oklahoma City on April 19, 1995. But that subculture is not the only one given to putting its members through rituals that resemble combat. The longing for initiation that Gibson traced in the paramilitary world has afflicted men across the political spectrum and so has the habit of staging warlike ceremonies of masculine inclusion. In 1982, for instance, only a few years before Gibson attended his first *Soldier of Fortune* convention, Robert Bly, an antiwar poet and guru to a burgeoning men's movement, delivered a talk called "The Vietnam War and the Erosion of Male Confidence" to a gathering of scholars, veterans, and ex-politicians. "When men lose their confidence in older men," Bly asked, "what happens then? When older men betray younger men, and lie to them, in government and in the field, what happens then to male values? What happens to a society in which the males do not trust each other? What kind of society is that?"

Like Gibson, Bly believes that many factors have contributed to the decline of male confidence over the last few decades—the industrial revolution's success at drawing fathers away from their farms and their sons and into other people's factories; the dissolution of faith in a body of myths; the atomized organization of suburban life. But few, says Bly, have done more damage to men than "the attacks launched against men by the separatist part of the women's movement and the Vietnam War." As Bly explains:

> The waste and anguish of the Vietnam War made men question what an adult male really is. And the women's movement encouraged men to actually look at women, forcing them to become conscious of certain things that the '50s male tended to avoid. . . . Some men began to see their own feminine side and pay attention to it. That process continues to this day.

In Bly's view, however, the feminizing of American men that took place in the Vietnam era has deprived many of an essential masculine spirit. "Here we have a finely tuned young man," he says, "ecologically superior to his father, sympathetic to the whole harmony of the universe, yet he himself has no energy to offer."

Bly's critique echoes the laments of men like James Fallows and Christopher Buckley. Like them, Bly took a stand against the war while it was going on and, like them, he seems to fear that those who opposed the conflict had come to lack a certain "spiritual sinew." In the early 1980s, along with several Jungian psychotherapists and other men's activists, he began to develop a set of rituals designed to help all men find that sinew in themselves. These rituals soon formed the heart of what Bly and his colleagues called the "mythopoetic" men's movement— "mythopoetic" because its leaders drew on ancient fairy tales and myths to help men understand their current predicaments. Through initiation rites of their own devising, the leaders of the movement hoped to reconnect men to the aggressive parts of their personalities they had lost during the Vietnam War, as well as to older men and to a broad masculine tradition.

The trouble was, Vietnam had discredited both masculine aggression in general and the American masculine tradition in particular. If they hoped to remain true to the pacifist principles most had espoused in the 1960s, the theorists of the mythopoetic men's movement had to find a way to reclaim their masculine "energy" without invoking the damage it had caused in Vietnam. The solution they came up with was a mythical beast, a not-so-gentle giant who lived in the thickets of ancient fairy tales, whom they called the "Wild Man" or, in Bly's book of the same name, Iron John. In an article for *Changing Men* magazine, Christopher Burant explained that:

> The Wild Man is not a Warrior gone berserk, not another deranged muscleman with a cache of automatic weapons. He also is not another highly skilled technician with no tender human relationship to another person. Rather, he is a deep, soulful being, close to animals and forest life, whom we repressed long ago in our movement toward refined city life.

In other words, the Wild Man is neither Rambo nor General William Westmoreland. Among participants in the men's movement, discussions of the Wild Man almost invariably dig up the ghosts of Vietnam—if only to try to bury them more deeply. In a column for *Playboy* magazine, the former Marine and Vietnam combat veteran Asa Baber wrote that all men can "be in touch with the Cro-Magnon man who lives . . . deep inside our hearts" and that they should not be afraid that his presence will turn them into atrocity-makers:

> It is vital to remember that this man is not a savage. In no way is he an uncontrolled killer or evil oppressor. He is primordial but not barbaric, aboriginal but not vicious. He represents what is best in the spirit of manhood.

Of course, Baber is referring to the spirit of *American* manhood. Despite their claims to have identified a universal element of the male psyche, men's movement theorists have often borrowed their notions of the Wild Man at least in part from American mythology. When Baber describes a man who is "primordial" and "aboriginal," but not "vicious" or "barbaric," he recalls not only a Cro-Magnon stereotype, but Daniel Boone and Davy Crockett—men who took what they needed from the wilderness but who never, at least according to myth, became entirely wild themselves. American novels and films have long teemed with such "soulful beings and their closeness to animals and forest life." From Natty Bumppo, the woodsman-hero of James Fenimore Cooper's *Leatherstocking Tales,* to Kevin Costner's renegade Civil War soldier in *Dances With Wolves* (1990), the leading men of American tall tales have displayed a unique affinity for nature and for the ragged fringes of civilization. Only there, the story goes, can they fully express themselves as men.

During the Vietnam War, young men went to Southeast Asia expecting to become those leading men. In its wake, thousands of American males have taken to the woods in the hope of finding their own roles in the American masculine myth. In weekend retreats variously called "Wildman Gatherings" or "Journeys into the Male Wilderness," or in weekend seminars entitled "Recovering the Deep Masculine" or, in one case, "The New Warrior Training Adventure," men have undertaken rituals designed to help them feel the carefully modulated aggression of the mythological Wild Man within themselves.

As is true of those who attend *Soldier of Fortune* gatherings in Las Vegas, more of these men belong to the Vietnam generation than any other. In 1984, Michael Schiffman found that the median age at a men's meeting in Oak Glen, California, was thirty-five and that 48 percent of the men were between thirty and forty-three years old. In 1992, Lorraine H. Bray studied 130 men in two men's groups in Seattle, Washington, and found that 46 percent were between the ages of thirty-six and forty-five, while 20 percent were between the ages of twenty-six and thirty-five, and 25 percent were between forty-six and sixty. Both Schiffman and Bray reported that the vast majority of men in the groups they studied were white and college-educated, while Bray also noted that the majority of the men she studied were employed in full-time jobs and heterosexual. Neither study measured the presence of combat veterans.

Regardless of their particular link to the fighting, however, many of the men involved in the mythopoetic men's movement see themselves as part of a generation wounded by the war. "You could call it cultural post-traumatic stress syndrome or a generation standing in a fire," writes movement mythologist and storyteller Michael Meade. "The fires of war are ritual fires. Once they are set, they can only be put out by healing rituals of an equal intensity."

In order to achieve that intensity, those rituals have paralleled many of the rites of war. In his article entitled "What Happens at a Mythopoetic Men's Weekend?", Shepherd Bliss, a facilitator of such events, explains that men come together hoping to get in touch with the "deep masculine" within themselves, a masculinity that is not "shallow, negative, or abusive" but "bold and sensitive, vigorous and gentle." Much as young men once joined the military to add their own link to the intergenerational chain of American masculinity, Bliss suggests that men volunteer for these weekends in order to "restore the male community." Like new recruits, they will encounter older, more experienced men, come to trust them, and, through that trust, take their own places in a larger masculine tradition.

The mechanics of men's weekends are carefully arranged to encourage this process. As Bliss explains, mythopoetic men's workshops are usually held in a rural or wilderness area far away from women and children. "When the men arrive for the weekend," he writes, "it is important that they have contact only with men and begin to orient feelings and experiences exclusively toward men during these days." Once cut off from their families, the men at these retreats join new, all-male families. Not unlike the average combat squad, these groups are composed of four to eight men recruited from the weekend's general population. Unlike many Vietnam-era units, however, these groups work under the supervision of highly competent and caring officers. As Bliss explains, "The leaders [of the weekends] come well prepared to exercise power, take initiative, help ensure the safety of the weekend for all, and be flexible."

Once they have been made members of well-fathered families, the men at Bliss's weekends enter a wilderness of ritual in search of a masculinity invisible to the untrained eye. They drum, tell stories, read their own and others' poetry, and, in their units, create dramas which they will stage for the group as a whole—all in order to enter an altered state of mind essential to uncovering the "deep masculine." "We want the men to leave solar consciousness and give themselves to lunar awareness," says Bliss. While he never defines either state, Bliss seems to hope to draw his men away from the rational restriction of their emotions and toward an appreciation of their animal selves. "We stimulate the men and seek to move through feelings by heightening them rather than avoiding them," writes Bliss. "We rely on the release or discharge of feelings more than having insight into them." It is, of course, the discharge of feelings, albeit violent ones, that the drill sergeant seeks when he asks his charges, "What's the spirit of the bayonet?" And it is only by sidestepping any rational insights into those feelings that his men can answer, "To kill! To kill!"

Clearly neither Bliss nor the mythopoetic men's movement as a whole is trying to inculcate the habit of violence-on-demand in the men who come to their workshops. On the contrary, writes Bliss, "the masculinity we affirm is vital, robust, zany, unpredictable, and spontaneous." Yet, as an initiation, the kind of weekend Bliss describes does resemble both boot camp and an idealized form of combat. As men like Ron Kovic had hoped to in Vietnam, the men at Bliss's weekends find themselves watched over by caring elders, allow themselves to experience feelings prohibited in ordinary, "civilian" life, and emerge with the approval of their leaders and a strengthened sense of their own masculinity. Like William Gibson at Gunsite Ranch, they become "reborn" men, warriorlike in their ability to tap the deep streams of their "lunar awareness." And like Gibson, they find themselves welcomed into a community of adult males. In a closing ceremony not unlike the one in which Gibson received his marksmanship certificate, the men at Bliss's weekends gather together, clasp each other's hands, and look into one another's eyes. Like soldiers returning from battle, they confirm the bond they have established in the wilderness and depart for home.

But, of course, they are not soldiers. Most have never seen a weapon aimed at another man, let alone fired one themselves. Where soldiers in Vietnam chased an often invisible enemy who was, in reality, trying to kill them, the men of the mythopoetic men's movement are chasing their own psychological shadows. "The new hero," writes movement theorist Sam Keen, "must reclaim and redirect the energies and virtues of the warrior psyche—fierceness, fortitude, daring, courage, cunning, the strategic use of power—that were once used in defense of tribe and nation."

But reclaim them to what end? Redirect them to what new action? Few in the mythopoetic men's movement ever say. Like Luke Skywalker—or, for that matter, like the men who devote their weekends to *Soldier of Fortune* conferences or paintball—these men seek to know their cultural fathers and to absorb their warrior attributes. But where Luke hopes to save the galaxy from an evil empire and where the pseudowarriors of paramilitary culture dream they are preparing to rescue their countrymen from some upcoming Armageddon, these men hope mostly to save themselves from their own private psychological pain. "A warrior," explains one popular movement manual, "knows the *real* war is within [italics in the original]."

Such a preoccupation with the internal experience of individuals has done little to repair the American masculine tradition. Even as the members of the mythopoetic men's movement don masks in the woods and even as their counterparts in paramilitary culture don their camouflage, the wounds their rituals seek to heal remain open, raw, and firmly fixed in history. In the spring of 1995, Robert McNamara, Secretary of Defense under Presidents Kennedy and Johnson and a man who was as responsible as any except perhaps Johnson himself for the American plunge into Vietnam, published *In Retrospect: The Tragedy and Lessons of Vietnam*. In this long-awaited recollection of his years in government, McNamara described how, by the end of 1965, he had begun to doubt that the war could be won. He recalled a May 19, 1967, memo in which he told Lyndon Johnson that the Vietnam War presented "the picture of the world's greatest superpower killing or seriously injuring 1,000 noncombatants a week, while trying to pound a tiny backward nation into submission on an issue whose merits are hotly disputed." McNamara went on to explain how, by the time he left the Johnson Administration in early 1968, he had turned completely against the war he had supported so vigorously only three years before. "We were wrong, terribly wrong," he wrote in what appeared to be a public apology.

In the weeks after the book's publication, McNamara went on a speaking tour. As he addressed audiences across the United States, it gradually became apparent that what McNamara was offering was not so much a heartfelt apology as a chillingly rational and much-belated admission of error. When a host on a radio talk show asked him why he would not apologize directly for supporting the war and for failing to speak out against it when he knew it was wrong, McNamara responded with an icy appeal to reason of the kind for which he was so famous during the war: "I believe the greatest contribution I can make is to examine our mistakes," he said. "Redemption. Apology. That's not the important issue. The important issue is *why* we were wrong and how we can avoid those mistakes in the future." Like former President Nixon in his dotage, McNamara seemed to hope that the public would forget the errors of his earlier days and see in him the sober senior statesman he saw in himself.

Perhaps Americans should not have expected more from one of the principal architects of a war of attrition. But many did. Far from binding the wounds of the war, McNamara's strangely stunted confession revealed that many Americans remain locked in a rage sparked by his wartime betrayals and by his refusal to stay quiet now. Those who opposed the war resented the fact that, despite his antiwar views, McNamara remained silent during the continued prosecution of the conflict by the Nixon Administration. Those who believed that Americans could have won the war with enough support at home deplored his assertions to the contrary. And veterans, the young men who had survived the killing and dying McNamara had once promoted, suffered from his reminder that they witnessed and inflicted violence to no meaningful end at all. For all the attempts American men had made in the 1980s to initiate themselves and to redeem their fathers, for all the movies and war games and therapeutic rituals, Americans in the mid-1990s largely remained bitter. Few had forgiven men like McNamara and many remained cut off from the masculine tradition he represented. David Halberstam, author of *The Best and the Brightest* and a reporter who, like McNamara, had experienced a turnaround in his views on the war during the fighting, spoke for many when he called McNamara "a man so contorted and so deep in his own unique self-delusion and self-division that he still doesn't know who he is and what he did at that time."

If Robert McNamara is the best our culture has to offer in the way of father figures, surely we should rage along with Halberstam. Cloaked in the authority of his former positions as Secretary of Defense and head of the World Bank, masked by his own determination to wear a stoic face in public, Robert McNamara is America's living, breathing real-world counterpart to the cinematic caricature of Darth Vader. And yet, is there no way that we Americans can, like Luke, push our anger aside and accept him as our own? Is there no way to grieve for the creature he became and, at the same time, for the violent acts so many Americans committed at the behest of leaders like him? What can we do, short of running through the woods in masks and worn-out uniforms, to reassure ourselves that we won't get fooled again?

"I am a member of a generation of men who were born with a deep father longing," wrote George Taylor, a men's movement activist. "I long to experience the great, ancient masculine forces in the universe." If we are ever to satisfy our longing for honest, emotionally present cultural fathers, then we must stop searching for the source of their masculine power in the ancient universe of myth and fantasy. We must recognize that we have never been helpless children—not during the Vietnam era and not today. As powerful as America's masculine mythology may be, in the political realm at least, we remain the people who set the mantle of that mythology on our leaders' shoulders. Solid majorities voted in the presidents whom Robert McNamara served. During the period of his antiwar silence, millions of Americans voted to elect and reelect a President who continued to fight the war McNamara had come to oppose. We must take responsibility for the fact that to the degree we are a democratic society, we grant our leaders much of their paternal authority.

In short, we must acknowledge that, in part, Robert McNamara is our own creation. Only then will we be able to find the kind of fathers we crave and to accept those who fail us.

CHAPTER EIGHT

HEALING AS HISTORY:

THE VIETNAM
VETERANS MEMORIAL

ON DECEMBER 22, 1967, ONLY FIVE MONTHS AFTER arriving in Vietnam, Brian Winhover jumped down off his tank, took a few steps, and sat down to have lunch. Moments later his closest friend, a man he had served with since the start of boot camp, jumped off the tank as well, landing just where Winhover had. This time, though, a mine that had been buried in the dirt exploded. "There was nothing left of him," says Winhover. "His scalp. That's what was in the coffin. He would have been an MIA if I hadn't seen him blown up."

After his friend was killed, Winhover became an expert soldier. He rose from gun loader to tank commander. He completed a total of three tours of duty, two more than the Army required. Having earned a reputation for being able to sniff out and avoid Vietnamese ambushes, he became someone the men around him looked up to, the kind of man who in another war might have been called a hero. But at the same time he turned numb. "You had no feelings," he explains. "I was *not* a human being. You turned. You had to turn to survive. There was no love. Nothing. Revenge. That was my motivation. Revenge."

Twenty-five years later Winhover is living with what he couldn't feel in Vietnam. "I don't think there's been one day since I've been back that I've had peace," he says. "I have no peace. It's there. It's always there. There isn't a day that you don't see shit happening in your inner mind. I relive [my friend's] death, *all* this death, all the time."

For the last several years, Winhover has tried to deal with those memories by attending the Veterans Improvement Program (VIP), a counseling program for veterans with post-traumatic stress disorder run by the Department of Veterans Affairs in Boston, Massachusetts. In May 1992, he and seven other veterans from VIP, along with three therapists, drove to the Vietnam Veterans Memorial in Washington, D.C. They checked into the rooms at a local Army base where they were staying, got a few hours sleep, and went to the Memorial at three o'clock in the morning. As Kurt Ocher, once an engineer and gunner on a riverboat, puts it, "We wanted to deal with the wall, not the crowd at the wall."

When they arrived, no one else was there. Floodlights set into the ground along the wall gently lit the black granite and the names of the dead. As Winhover and the other veterans walked onto the Memorial grounds, the twenty years that had passed since the end of the war seemed to disappear. The names on the wall seemed to come alive and for some, the visit to the wall became a night patrol in Vietnam. "It was all of us," says Ocher. "I had the very strong feeling that I could have changed places with any of [the names]." As Winhover began to walk down the wall, he surrounded himself with his memories. "I was into the wall," he says, "I was part of the wall. It was just me and the guys." He saw the name of the friend who had died on December 22, 1967, and he spoke, not to the name, but to the friend, as if he were standing there. "It should have been me," he said.

For Winhover, the Memorial was a three-dimensional model of his own divided psyche. When he saw his friend killed, his pain was so extraordinary that he set both his feelings and the memory of the event aside, in a separate, self-enclosed part of himself. Back home, Winhover's memories of Vietnam had a life of their own. In nightmares and flash-backs, they decided when to return, when to make Winhover relive an experience. He might be riding in an elevator when he would suddenly recall the claustrophobic interior of a tank and drop to the floor, terrified. He might be standing in line at the supermarket, feel a bump from behind, and, without thinking, turn and kick the person behind him full force. At the Memorial, though, Winhover was able to gain some control over his memories. The wall became a borderline between the present and the past not unlike the one in his mind, but this time, Winhover could choose to cross into the past and stand with his comrades: "I was part of the wall," he said. "It was just me and the guys." At the wall, Winhover chose how close to come to his memories, how to be with them, and how to leave them behind.

Nor was Winhover's experience unique. Over the years, thousands of veterans have used the wall to revisit parts of themselves. Dr. Terence Keane, Chief of Psychology at the Veterans Affairs Medical Center in Boston and a specialist in the study of trauma, explains that for many veterans, "going to the wall becomes a metaphor for confronting the events that caused their deepest pain." As they revisit the combat zone in their minds, they reexperience the misery it brought them and this time they face the pain not as naive eighteen-year-olds, but as men with forty years of living behind them. "They can confront those memories and with all the new life experiences they've had," says Keane, "they can begin to construct new meanings" for what they went through.

But they can't construct those meanings alone. James Munroe, one of the leaders of the trip to the Memorial, explains that "trauma is absorbed by a community rather than an individual." After combat, he says, "You don't trust the world anymore. You have to go back and rebuild the basic concept of what a community is." In other words, he suggests, veterans who have long suffered flashbacks not only have to revisit and gain control over their memories of the past; they also have to reconnect themselves emotionally to people in the present.

When they visited the wall before dawn, says Munroe, the veterans were alone with one another and their grief. But the next afternoon, when they returned, the Memorial was crowded with tourists and schoolchildren. When they saw masses of people where there had been no one before, he explains, the veterans discovered "they weren't the only ones who cared about this wall." Edward Ravitch saw some children leaving something at the statue of the three infantrymen that overlooks the wall. "They moved me—they were respectful," he says. When he walked up to them, one of them asked if he was a veteran and he told them he was. "One of them says, 'Welcome home.' They said they loved me and I should be proud." Down by the wall, Winhover saw an older man walking toward him. "The guy touched his forehead," says Winhover. "We both started crying. It was a sacred moment. He knew my pain and I knew his. He definitely lost a son in Vietnam. I didn't talk to him. It was just a moment of feeling."

In the middle of the night, the veterans of VIP had revisited their memories; in the daylight, they stood in the presence of the names of the dead and talked to the living. As they drove back to Boston, many took comfort from a newfound confidence in their ability to confront the past, if not to erase its effects on their lives today. "There's always this hope that okay, after you face [the wall and your memories], things will be wonderful again," says Kurt Ocher. But as powerful as it was, the Memorial had sparked no complete and sudden healings. Instead, as Ocher puts it, the visit "eliminated the fear for me of whether I could manage what it would provoke as far as memories and feelings." For the men of VIP, the visit to the wall had not lessened the need to endure painful recollections. Nevertheless, the trip made many feel that as painful as they were, their recollections could in fact *be* endured.

In the ten years since its dedication, the Memorial has offered thousands of veterans a place in which to come to such a realization. At the same time, it has presented their private rituals of recovery as public spectacles. After earlier wars, the process of healing veterans from combat was confined to hospital wards and the cement-block drinking rooms of VFW halls. But at the Vietnam Veterans Memorial, men like Winhover and Ravitch weep openly on what amounts to the national front lawn. While, in the late 1970s, the American public avoided all mention of the Vietnam War and shunned the men who fought it, fifteen years later, the Vietnam Veterans Memorial has become one of the most visited monuments in all of statue-studded Washington, D.C. More than a million and a half people file by the wall each year. So far they have left over 25,000 objects—letters, poems, and mementos of the dead such as flak jackets, boots, and photographs—enough to fill a special warehouse in Maryland. In the early 1980s, three full-sized replicas of the wall traveled from town to town across America. In more recent years, its image has appeared in TV ads for cotton (a small child touches the wall while a smoothly blended studio chorus sings, "The touch, the feel, the fabric of our lives. . . ."), in movies (most recently a remake of *Born Yesterday* starring Don Johnson), and, thanks to the wall's tenth anniversary, on the cover of *Life* magazine.

As images of the wall and grieving veterans have flowed out from the Mall and into the culture at large, veterans' private processes of recovering from the experience of combat have become entangled with a national need to make sense of the war. When they first conceived it, the veterans and designers who created the wall intended it to heal and honor a wounded generation of soldiers. But even before its completion, veterans and civilians alike were using its construction as an occasion to ask how the Vietnam War should be remembered. In that sense, the Memorial was never exclusively a nonpoliticized site for individual healing. On the contrary, since its conception, the Memorial has been a place where the traumatized veteran's search for integration, his need to bring the past and present together into a coherent and useful story, has overlapped with the national need to incorporate the Vietnam War into the set of legends and myths that give America its identity. Even today at the Memorial, public and private stories intermingle, interbreed, and as they do, the work that veterans must do to heal themselves both echoes and spawns agreements about the meaning of the war among Americans at large. These agreements in turn often set aside questions of who started the war, and why, and how it was conducted, in favor of an amoral rhetoric of recovery. Having cleared the decks of the rancor that characterized debate on Vietnam in the late 1960s and early 1970s, that rhetoric ultimately offers civilian Americans a way to absolve themselves of responsibility for the war.

In the beginning, though, according to its founder, former infantryman Jan Scruggs, the Memorial sprung up as a solution to the problems posed by private psychological trauma. One evening in March 1979, Scruggs went to see *The Deer Hunter*. Winner of five Academy Awards (including Best Picture), *The Deer Hunter* tells the story of three hunting buddies who enlist in the Army, go to Vietnam, and get captured by the North Vietnamese. In *To Heal a Nation,* his third-person memoir of how he recognized the need for the Memorial and led the campaign for its construction, Scruggs described what happened after he got home from the theater:

That night, Scruggs couldn't sleep. At 3:00 A.M. he was alone in the
kitchen with a bottle of whiskey. Mortar rounds hit. Twelve men were
unloading an ammunition truck. An explosion. Scruggs came running.
By instinct, he pulled the first-aid bandage from his trousers. Organs
and pieces of bodies were scattered on the ground. They belonged to
his friends. He had only one bandage. He stood and screamed for help.

The flashbacks ended, but the faces continued to pile up in front
of him. The names, he thought. The names. No one remembers their
names.

"I'm going to build a memorial to all the guys who served in
Vietnam," Scruggs told his wife the next morning. "It'll have the
names of everyone killed."

Much as Brian Winhover did when he saw his friend killed, Scruggs
suffered a psychological trauma and, with it, a split in his memory. The
part of his mind that names, that consciously recalls, had been cut off
from the knowledge of his comrades' violent deaths. Unable to deliberately recollect his friends, he knows them only by means of a flashback.
Scruggs suddenly believes he's back in Vietnam. He feels it, smells it so
completely that even when the sensation of actually living in the past
dissolves, "the faces continued to pile up in front of him." Frozen and
mute, they seem to inhabit an untouchable place in Scruggs's mind, to
lie as far beyond the reach of language as the actual dead lie beyond his
ability to bring them back to life. And yet, if he is to stop being tormented by the unasked-for visitations of these images, Scruggs knows he
has to find a way to bring them into the part of his memory which can
put words to things. He has to "make sense" of them by bringing them
back out of the region of uncontrollable imagery, giving them names,
and working those names into a story.

Yet, as he described his desire to remember and commemorate,
Scruggs let a piece of his past slip by. In 1970, when he saw the ammunition truck attacked, Scruggs was a combat infantryman whose job it was
to search for and destroy the enemy. In his memory, he isn't even armed.
Instead, he's a kind of frustrated medic, a would-be healer overwhelmed
by events. The war is exploding all around him, while his friends are
collapsing in the face of an invisible enemy. Scruggs pulls "the first-aid
bandage from his trousers," but what good is a single strand of gauze

when "Organs and pieces of bodies [are] scattered on the ground"? Scruggs can do nothing except howl for help. He has become an animal, isolated, incapable of reason, acting only from "instinct." And his instinct is to aid, rather than injure. Despite all his Army training to respond to force with force, Scruggs reacts to the enemy attack by reaching for a piece of gauze. In his story, Scruggs is a victim of violence, a man who wants to help but can't. His role as an aggressor, as an infantryman in an invading army, has gone unspoken.

In this his story resembles the movie that triggered his flashback. Even though it is a "war" movie, *The Deer Hunter* includes relatively few combat scenes and focuses instead on images of imprisonment. Having captured the three American hunting buddies, the Vietnamese hold them in semi-submerged cages and force them to play Russian roulette. The Vietnamese are sadists, descendants of the wicked Japanese of World War II propaganda flicks. The Americans, who have apparently come to Vietnam on the symbolic equivalent of a hunting trip, fall into their clutches as innocent victims. The film does nothing to suggest that the Americans might have entered their country as aggressors or that, from a Vietnamese point of view, they might deserve incarceration. Like Scruggs's story, the film portrays its Americans as helpless objects of Vietnamese depredation.

In contrast to many later Vietnam films, the movie also presents Americans as failed rescuers. In one of the film's few depictions of actual fighting, the deer hunter of the title guns down a North Vietnamese soldier. Moments before, the Vietnamese had lobbed a grenade into a bunker where he knew an unarmed mother and her children were cowering. Clearly, the deer hunter would have saved them if he had gotten there a moment earlier. Later in the movie, after two of the buddies escape their captors and return to the States, the third stays to make his living playing Russian roulette in the alleys of Saigon. The deer hunter goes back to Vietnam to try to save his friend, even offers his life for his friend's at the roulette table, only to watch his friend blow his brains out in front of forty or fifty gleeful Vietnamese gamblers. Like Scruggs, the deer hunter discovers that he is powerless to save his friend, that he has no gauze to staunch his wound and so can only hold him as he dies.

In both *The Deer Hunter* and Scruggs's flashback, soldiers suffer and die through no fault of Americans back home. Failed rescuers, they have been surrounded by Vietnamese and decimated. Unwilling or unable to ask what responsibility civilian Americans, their government, or their officers might have had for the loss of these soldiers, both Scruggs's story and *The Deer Hunter* focus our attention on the need to remember the dead. In *The Deer Hunter*'s final scene, a group of friends gathers to mourn the roulette player. Scruggs finishes his story with a commitment "to build a memorial to all the guys who served in Vietnam" that lists "the names of everyone killed." In both cases, the personal process of recalling and grieving for the dead seems to transcend, but has in fact obviated, the need to question why they died.

As planning for the Memorial got under way, Scruggs worked hard to keep the monument's focus on helping veterans heal and to avoid letting the project become bogged down in debates about the meaning of the war. In April 1979, a few weeks after he saw *The Deer Hunter,* he and Bob Doubek, a lawyer and Air Force veteran, formed the Vietnam Veterans Memorial Fund in order to raise money and come up with a design for the Memorial. Membership was open to all comers, but at the start the Fund members were mostly veterans and a few of their wives. According to Scruggs, they worked together every day for several years to commemorate the service of Vietnam veterans and yet they avoided talking about what that service might have meant:

> They never discussed their personal views about what the Vietnam War meant, whether it should have been fought, whether proper tactics were used, what they thought of the antiwar movement, or why America lost. They knew that the war had been too complex, and had gone on for too long, for their views to be unanimous. There was no need to replay the passions of the 1960s and early 1970s.

In short, there was no need to remember why and how the war had been fought. On the contrary, according to Scruggs, the Vietnam Veterans Memorial Fund operated on the principle that "Vietnam veterans could be honored without commenting on America's Vietnam policy; the warrior could be separated from the war."

In part, the members of the Fund had to separate the warrior from the war if they were going to get anything built. By 1980, debates about the meaning of Vietnam were no longer boiling over into the streets, but the old lines between hawks and doves were still strong enough to keep many people from giving money to the Fund. Scruggs and Doubek believed that "the old and powerful antiwar movement . . . would seek to destroy anything that memorialized America's Vietnam policy." But when they put the name of Senator George McGovern, a famous dove and an early, ardent supporter of the Memorial, on a fund-raising letter already signed by the likes of Gerald Ford, Nancy Reagan, and William Westmoreland, hundreds of letters came back with notes appended: "I would have given you money, but this man is why we lost the war." Clearly, the farther the Fund stayed from trying to interpret the war, the better its chances of finding something that everyone could agree to support.

But separating the warrior from the war was more than a search for the lowest common denominator of meaning. It was also a clearing of ancient therapeutic ground. In many primitive cultures, those who have entered the combat zone employ special rituals to cross back into civilian society. Among the Orokaiva of Papua New Guinea, for instance, a warrior who has killed may not drink pure water, eat stewed taro root, or engage in sexual intercourse for several days. He must then be "thoroughly and ritually bitten by a certain kind of ant" and be "fed the steaming stew" before he can leave his seclusion. A hundred and fifty years ago, when the men of the Plains Indians would return from battle, they would give the women of the tribe the scalps they had taken. The women would then welcome them home by carrying the scalps in a special dance. In twentieth century America, the most visible of these ceremonies is the ticker-tape parade. When they marched down Broadway after the First World War, doughboys who had only recently endured a rain of artillery and mortar rounds found themselves showered with confetti. Crowds cheered for men who not long before had listened to the cries of the wounded and the dying. Even as they celebrated the exploits of a conquering army, post-World War I parades reminded their participants that the danger had passed, that they had reentered a world where the worst thing that could fall out of the sky was little bits of paper.

For the veterans of Vietnam, there were no ticker-tape parades. Not only had America lost the war, but thanks to the military's rotation system, most soldiers had returned home one at a time. What's more, as scholar Peter Ehrenhaus has written, "Those who were killed and those who returned were the embodiment of a national moral character in crisis; regardless of how one defined those failures, [the veterans] were its personification. How could Americans celebrate that which they abhorred and disdained in themselves? For the Vietnam veteran, the message was simple: 'You have failed yourself and that country which can be no better than the inner fiber of you, its people.'"

But even if they would never be cheered as members of a victorious military and even if their sense of personal self-worth had become entangled with a national sense of shame, Vietnam veterans still needed to be returned to the world of civilian safety that greeted doughboys on Broadway. By consciously separating the Vietnam warrior from the Vietnam War, Scruggs and the members of the Fund were doing what American society as a whole refused to do. They were announcing that they were no longer soldiers, that their war was over, that they had left the combat zone and come home. Their Memorial would express the finality of their return much as parades had when they welcomed their fathers.

At the same time, as they declared that it was not their service but the war that was wrong, they offered American civilians a way to set aside the notion that there was something wrong with American society that had led to the Vietnam War. Civilians could now say to themselves that if Scruggs and other American soldiers had gone overseas intending to help the Vietnamese and had been brutalized by the combat they saw there, then perhaps America as a whole had undergone an analogous experience. Maybe, like its soldiers, America had been sucked into a conflict it didn't understand. True, once there, its army had behaved cruelly. But perhaps, like many individual veterans, the country as a whole had gone to war on behalf of the idea of freedom and only then been driven to extremes of violence. And if that was true, then was the America of today really so different from the America of legend, the country that first went to war to free itself from the king of England or later sent its soldiers overseas to free Europe from Hitler?

Even if the Memorial Fund's separation of the warrior from the war did not directly support a renewal of traditional patriotism, it opened the door to a process by which a new language of psychological recovery could replace the old rhetoric of victory and loss. In May 1981, a jury of architects, sculptors, and designers sorted through 1,421 designs submitted in a national competition and chose the wall of names created by Maya Ying Lin, a twenty-one-year-old undergraduate at Yale. Having been born in 1959, the year of America's first casualties in Vietnam, and having been only nine years old during the Tet Offensive, Lin could hardly help but see veterans outside the politics of the conflict. She knew no one who had fought or died in Vietnam. As she later told reporters, she had never thought much about the controversies surrounding the war. She had come up with her design for the Memorial in a class on funerary architecture at Yale. She had studied a monument to the dead of World War I's Somme offensive in Thiepval, France—a great arch inscribed with 73,000 names that Lin later called "a journey from violence to serenity"—and had tried to create an equally healing memorial of her own. In 1982, she explained that "The [wall] was built as a very psychological memorial. It's not meant to be cheerful or happy, but to bring out in people the realization of loss and a cathartic healing process. A lot of people were really afraid of that emotion; it was something we had glossed over."

In order to spark catharsis, Lin dug into the ground. Her design called for a black V-shaped wall to be carved into the green lawn of the Mall between the State Department and the Washington Monument. The Memorial would be invisible from any distance. It would be so carefully wedded to the earth and the grass and the trees of the Mall that if a visitor wasn't careful, he could tumble into it by accident. It would list the names of the dead in the order they were killed from the center of the V out the length of one arm and back along the other to the center again and, in its polished black stone, it would reflect the faces of visitors and, on a clear day, the image of the Washington Monument as well. As she later explained, Lin "had an impulse to cut open the earth . . . an initial violence that in time would heal. . . . It was as if the black-brown earth were polished and made into an interface between the sunny world and the quiet, dark world beyond."

For veterans, that interface would come to mark the boundary between their memories and their present lives. "I wanted to return the vets to the time-frame of the war," said Lin, "and in the process, I wanted them to see their own reflection in the names." At the same time, she said, "I didn't want a static object that people would just look at, but something they could relate to as on a journey, or passage, that would bring each to his own conclusions." For combat veterans, the wall itself would become a doorway through which veterans could reenter their pasts, their memories, even as they stood firmly in the here and now. As they touched the names and crossed over, in their imaginations at least, to the other side of the wall, they could engage in the psychological business of mourning, of naming the dead and honoring their losses.

At the press conference called to announce the choice of Lin's design, Jan Scruggs told reporters that "The Memorial says exactly what we wanted to say about [the] Vietnam [War]—absolutely nothing." Scruggs believed the wall was completely apolitical, that it offered no comment on the war but only healing for its survivors. Others vehemently disagreed. James Webb, the former Marine, author of *Fields of Fire,* and, under Ronald Reagan, Secretary of the Navy, wrote that "The memorial will occupy a permanence in the national mind-set, with an even greater power than history itself. History can be reevaluated. New facts can be discovered, leading to different interpretations. But a piece of art remains, as a testimony to a particular moment in history, and we are under a solemn obligation to get that moment down as correctly as possible."

In the fall of 1981, Webb met with Tom Carhart, who had served in the 101st Airborne and had commanded Viet Cong informers and Navy SEALs in the Mekong Delta. When he saw Lin's design, he called it a "black gash of shame and sorrow." On national television Carhart explained that he thought Vietnam veterans had been cheated: "In a city of soaring white monuments, we get a black ditch in the ground," he said. Once again, he suggested, Vietnam veterans had been aced out of the recognition that their fathers and grandfathers had received for fighting in earlier wars. Once again they had been told that their service should remain out of sight, underground, in darkness. Together with Ross Perot, the Texas billionaire who had funded the design competition, Webb and Carhart pushed to get the Memorial sent back to the drawing board. After months of negotiation and with the help of Ronald Reagan's Secretary of the Interior, James Watt, they succeeded in having a realistic statue of three combat infantrymen and a large American flag added to the design.

"In a funny sense," wrote Maya Lin after tempers had cooled, "the [addition of the statue and flag] brings the memorial closer to the truth. What is also memorialized is that people still cannot resolve that war, nor can they separate the issues, the politics, from it." As much as she had tried to design a strictly therapeutic monument, Lin found that, in the early 1980s, personal healing and historical interpretation could not be pulled apart. For many Americans, the warrior could not, as Jan Scruggs had hoped, "be separated from the war." On the contrary, ex-soldiers and civilians alike saw the Memorial Scruggs had intended to honor veterans as a black granite symbol for the entire Vietnam War. Some called its V-shaped wall a peace sign. Others saw it as a vagina set to match the phallic Washington Monument (a sculptural articulation of the belief that American soldiers in Vietnam "got screwed by Washington"). Some perceived the wall as a pointless, mechanical list of the dead that suggested that the war itself had no meaning. Others saw the Memorial as a black canyon of death, a figure for a war into which an unwary nation had accidentally fallen. For some veterans, the fact that the wall was nearly imperceptible to casual passersby echoed the sense they had of being invisible to the nation while they served in Vietnam.

Today, ten years after its dedication, the Memorial continues to offer visitors those specific interpretations of the war, but it also presents them with a more complex metaphorical experience. As they enter the park and walk down along the wall, visitors are invited to undertake their own versions of the veteran's "journey from violence to serenity." As they run their fingers across the names on the wall, they can imagine, if not remember, the lives behind them. They can cross over into an imagined past, much the way a Brian Winhover or Kurt Ocher can reenter the Vietnam of their memories, to feel a terrible sadness for the lives lost in the war and they can return, hearts eased, to the calm, cathedral-like atmosphere of the Memorial in the present. At the same time, as they make their way through the Memorial, visitors can read a coherent story of the conflict in Vietnam. Even as it provides a healing journey, the monument offers visitors a three-dimensional history of the war.

Visitors can enter the Memorial along either wing of its V-shaped walls, but regardless of which direction they choose, they eventually encounter Carhart and Webb's statue (*Three Servicemen* by Frederick Hart) and flag. Set at the head of the footpath that runs through the Memorial, the bronze soldiers look off toward the wall, tired and surprised, as if they were returning from a patrol and finding their base overrun. The sixty-foot flagpole is ringed by the seals of the five armed services and the words: THIS FLAG REPRESENTS THE SERVICE RENDERED TO OUR COUNTRY BY THE VETERANS OF THE VIETNAM WAR. THE FLAG AFFIRMS THE PRINCIPLES OF FREEDOM FOR WHICH THEY FOUGHT AND THEIR PRIDE IN HAVING SERVED UNDER DIFFICULT CIRCUMSTANCES. Whether visitors are just beginning or just completing their tours of the wall, the flag frames their experience, suggesting that the deaths recorded in the black granite were not private affairs, but sacrifices to the flag. The banner and its plaque remind visitors that the Vietnam Veterans Memorial is a monument to a national historic event as well as to the individual dead. They suggest that the "principles of freedom" for which many soldiers thought they were fighting—rather than an outsized fear of communism or an urge to keep Third World countries economically aligned with the United States— were in fact the principles for which the nation went to war.

At the wall itself, patriotism gives way to the experience of uncontrollable death. As visitors begin to walk along the monument, the black granite wall and the names of the dead begin to rise beside them—first to their ankles, then to their waists, and finally to their eyes. Along the wall, as in the war itself, the death toll seems to grow of its own accord, rising until the rows of names seem to blur, become a quagmire. Visitors reach the point at which the names slip over their heads, and still they go down, becoming ever more helpless before the sheer number of the dead, until they stand at the apex, the crux of the V, looking up at a wall of names ten feet tall. Above the point where the names of the first and last Americans killed in Vietnam meet, there is an inscription: IN HONOR OF THE MEN AND WOMEN OF THE ARMED FORCES OF THE UNITED STATES WHO SERVED IN THE VIETNAM WAR. THE NAMES OF THOSE WHO GAVE THEIR LIVES AND OF THOSE WHO REMAIN MISSING ARE INSCRIBED IN THE ORDER THEY WERE TAKEN FROM US.

Here the wall offers its visitors a chance to hear an echo of the helplessness many Vietnam veterans once felt in combat. At the center of the Memorial, a visitor stands surrounded by the names of the dead much as Jan Scruggs once stood ringed by the bodies of his comrades. The names are as mute in their way as the faces that once haunted Scruggs. There is nothing a visitor can do to save these men, nothing a visitor can do to bring them back. And in the same way that when

Scruggs describes the deaths of his comrades, he neglects to mention his role as an aggressor, the inscription on the wall suggests that the visitor—and American civilians in general—need not look too closely at their roles in these men's deaths. The dead, says the inscription, "were taken from us." They were not sent to their deaths by confused politicians, patriotic draft boards, or fathers eager to see their sons become men. They were simply taken away, as if by a random act of God.

In walking down to the center of the wall, visitors imitate America's own progress from the confident patriotism of the Eisenhower and Kennedy years to the nadir of the 1968 Tet Offensive. As they watch the names mount beside them, they seem to be reliving America's escalation of the war. More and more American boys get sent to Vietnam and die, and at the crease of the V, where the names tower over their heads, they meet an image of the moment of maximum American troop commitment in Southeast Asia. Now, as they turn to walk along the wall's far wing, the names begin to fall away, just as American soldiers were once withdrawn. Suddenly they can see over the wall to the grass of the Mall. Like America after Tet, they can slowly disengage themselves from the war. The names reach up to their shoulders, then to their waists, then their knees, until, like the last helicopter pilots to fly out of Saigon, they have left the war behind and below them.

As visitors walk away across the open Mall, the architecture of the Memorial suggests they may take with them the belief that in Vietnam Americans were simply in over their heads, that the war snuck up on them, that its effects were beyond their control. As visitors remember the sufferings and losses of American soldiers, they may forget that Americans started the war and pursued it long after their dreams of victory had evaporated. As they look at the more than 58,000 names on the wall, they may lose sight of the fact that, when their last Huey helicopter lifted off from Saigon in 1975, Americans left more than two million Vietnamese dead behind them. As they step quietly across the grass and into the maples overlooking the wall, they may forget that Americans dropped twenty million gallons of herbicide on Vietnam and destroyed five million acres of its forest. Having walked through a model of the war's progress and having found at the center of that model nothing but an overwhelming number of American dead, visitors can cling to the sorrowful knowledge that many "were taken from us" and never ask,

"By whom? For what purpose?" The Memorial has asked them to mourn the dead and celebrate the healing of the living. If visitors ask why these men had to die, the Memorial answers only that the dead, like generations of American soldiers before them, "were taken from us" as they fought for "principles of freedom" under "difficult circumstances."

In November 1982, at the Memorial's dedication, thousands of Americans demonstrated that they were ready to embrace both the monument's healing power and its historical vagaries. Between November 10 and 14, more than 100,000 veterans descended on Washington, D.C.; on the morning of November 13, 15,000 of them paraded down Constitution Avenue to the Memorial. Sandwiched between various floats and a colonial fife and drum corps, the veterans marched in old fatigues and three-piece suits, keeping cadence. From the sidelines, spectators shouted, "Thank you!" and "Welcome home!" Some of the veterans sang *The Battle Hymn of the Republic* and *America the Beautiful*. Others wore buttons reading: "I'D DO IT AGAIN." A few veterans carried angry signs: "WE KILLED, WE BLED, WE DIED FOR WORSE THAN NOTHING"; "57,000 KILLED IN VAIN. SHAME, HORROR, DECEIT, TREACHERY"; "NO MORE WARS. NO MORE LIES." Many others refused to march and simply watched the parade go by. By and large, though, the dedication was not a time to remember anger or antiwar protests, but a time to shake off shame. "I could almost hear the chains clinking as they fell off us," said one veteran. "How do you explain the feelings when you embrace a brother and you feel your heart beat against his heart?" asked another. An editorial writer for the Quincy, Massachusetts, *Patriot Ledger* put it this way:

> Never mind the often-discussed public policy "lessons" of the war. These will be recorded in history books—and kept alive in public debate. What the history books do not record, and what politicians almost always ignore, is the human sacrifice of Americans who served in Vietnam. Dedication of the Memorial closes the chapter of denial. It could end years of bitterness. It should be a balm for wounds that were too long in healing.

For the *Patriot Ledger* writer, the veterans' regained pride, their sense of unity and their newfound lack of shame, should serve as models for the nation as a whole. What helps heal veterans, the writer believes, will help heal America.

In the last decade, this conflation of veteran, civilian, and country has continued to seep out from the Memorial and into American culture. In 1985, for example, Bobbie Ann Mason published her novel *In Country*. An instant bestseller and later a movie, *In Country* tells the story of Samantha Hughes, a teenager whose father was killed in Vietnam. As Sam tries to learn more about her father, she undergoes combat flashbacks (even though she was never in a war zone). In order to drive the flashbacks away, she makes a pilgrimage to the Vietnam Veterans Memorial. In the novel's final scene, she finds her own name—Sam A. Hughes—carved on the wall. "How odd it feels," writes Mason on Sam's behalf, "as though all the names in America have been used to decorate this wall." Like the *Patriot Ledger* writer, Mason proffers veterans as symbolic figures and suggests that the broken memories so many of them suffer belong to civilians and to America as a nation. As the copy on the front cover of the 1989 edition puts it, neatly summarizing the message of the book, what matters now is that "In the heartland of a nation . . . In the mind of a young girl . . . In the memory of a soldier . . . In the soul of America . . . The healing has begun."

By suggesting that soldiers, civilians, and "the soul of America" share the same disease, Mason echoes the inscription at the apex of the wall. Just as the dead were "taken from us" in Vietnam, as if neither we nor the dead themselves were agents in the matter, so the war has spread its suffering throughout American society, as if it were a sickness Americans had done nothing to catch. There is no room for debate, nowhere to point the finger of blame: "The healing has begun."

Having replaced debate about the war, the rhetoric of recovery has so reduced the toxicity of the Vietnam War that it can now be safely woven into the traditional stories Americans have told about themselves. On July 6, 1987, for example, to celebrate the publication of a book of photographs of the Memorial, *Newsweek* magazine devoted nearly half its pages to a feature story entitled "Heroes, Past and Present." The story opens with pictures of veterans and children at the wall and a text that explains that "This special section is a two-part celebration of heroes, those who died in the war and those who are among us now." At the wall, says the text, "We can see our sons and daughters and honor them, knowing finally that they are us." After the pages devoted to the wall, the magazine offers fifty-one portraits of "Everyday Heroes"—policemen, volunteers who work with the poor, founders of support groups. Of both the "Everyday Heroes" and Vietnam veterans, the text says: "The people celebrated here have dedicated and sometimes sacrificed their lives to the rest of us. By doing so, they have shown us the possibilities in ourselves."

With this story, Jan Scruggs's dream of himself as a would-be healer surrounded by gore has come full circle. In *Newsweek,* Vietnam veterans carry no weapons and look as if they never did. Instead, they embrace one another, cry, touch the wall. As the article compares them to civilians who have pulled babies from the wreckage of trains or set up food centers for the homeless, they too become rescuers, men who have made sacrifices and who, far from being objects of scorn, have become examples for the nation.

But if our veterans really are us, if their story is the nation's story, what was Vietnam? *Newsweek* suggests a comforting allegory: Once young and innocent, like its soldiers, America went to Southeast Asia to rescue a democracy, to fight for "principles of freedom"; the rescue failed and America became a victim of the conflict, but the sacrifices it made, like those of its soldiers, were noble. And this story accords well with the popular tales of America's participation in earlier, so-called "good" wars. In *Newsweek,* the Vietnam War's complexities have disappeared from discussion. Only images of veterans healing at the wall remain. The war's sharp edges have been sanded down and the conflict, now smoothed into a traditional tale of national altruism, has been slipped safely into the library of American myths.

CHAPTER NINE

SCAR TISSUE:

NARRATIVE FRAGMENTATION AND THE MEMORY OF TRAUMA

DESPITE THE WAYS IN WHICH THE VIETNAM VETERANS Memorial has encouraged us to mourn our dead soldiers and to gloss over the nature of the conflict in which they died, the war still presents Americans with an agonizing set of questions. If we accept the historical evidence that in Southeast Asia our country committed acts of self-serving aggression rather than unsuccessful acts of rescue, then we must each examine our individual relationship to those acts. Did we serve in the combat zone, at the war's ground zero? Or did we hover at the edges of protest marches, not sure quite what or even whether to shout? Our answers to these questions will determine the psychological risks we run by confronting the facts of the past. As the experiences of traumatized veterans suggest, the more entangled one became in the violence of the war and the less one did to stop it, whether on the battlefield or here at home, the more psychologically threatening an appraisal of that violence becomes today.

At the same time, if we view American actions in Southeast Asia as unwarranted and brutal, we also put at risk many of the most fundamental assumptions we hold in common, as citizens, regardless of the role we each played in the war. If Americans' motives and actions were less than benevolent in Southeast Asia, can we continue to claim that our nation is a force for good in the world? If in the future we believe that we have to take military action overseas, particularly on behalf of an ally, will we be able to take that action knowing that many of us were once convinced that we had acted on behalf of a true partner, rather than a client state, in Vietnam?

The questions mount and, as they do, so too does the temptation to despair. If we accept that as citizens of the nation that sent them to war, we each bear some responsibility, however small, for the crimes our countrymen committed in Southeast Asia, then we run the risk of thinking not only that we turned away from or supported or committed evil acts, but that somehow we ourselves *are* evil. Traumatized veterans know this danger well. Varnado Simpson, for example, who killed some twenty-five people during the My Lai massacre, sat for years in his living room in Jackson, Mississippi, the shades drawn, thinking of suicide:

> How can you forgive? I can't forgive myself for the things—even though it was something that I was told to do. But how can I forget that—or forgive? It's easy for you to say: Well, you go ahead with your life. But how can you go ahead with your life when this is holding you back? I can't put my mind to anything. . . . Yes, I'm ashamed, I'm sorry, I'm guilty. But I did it. You know. What else can I tell you? It happened.

The memories of Varnado Simpson may seem to belong to an entirely different world, to mark an entirely different order of horror, than the recollections of those who never saw combat. Yet, even today, a quarter of a century after My Lai, Americans who reach toward a full apprehension of what happened in Vietnam, who try to assign some emotional and intellectual meaning to the war, must approach precisely the knowledge that torments Simpson. They have to face the fact that millions of people who were, before Americans invaded their country, no direct threat to the United States, died needlessly.

At the same time, they cannot afford to lose hope. They can not, as Simpson has, confine themselves to their rooms and refuse to take further action. The world has changed enormously since the start of the Vietnam War. The Soviet empire that in large part sparked American fears of a global Communist menace has crumbled. The Southeast Asian nations that presidents from Eisenhower to Nixon feared might topple like dominoes into the hands of the Communists have instead committed themselves to capitalist expansion and the pursuit of profit. Even Communist Vietnam has lately revved its economic engines. Under a government policy of *doi moi* ("renovation" or "new way") established at the end of 1986, it has loosened internal restrictions on commerce and sought out trade links with such capitalist powerhouses as Japan, Taiwan, Singapore, and even its former enemy, the United States.

This new world presents Americans with a dilemma. If, like Varnado Simpson, we absorb and dwell on the full horror of our country's behavior in Vietnam, we may become crippled. We may so fear repeating the mistakes we made twenty and thirty years ago that we fail to take necessary steps to defend our legitimate geopolitical and economic interests overseas. On the other hand, if we completely ignore the horror of the war, we may well reenact it. If we continue to imagine that, despite the war's ignoble outcome, our country entered the conflict with largely noble intentions, we may also continue to send our soldiers into conflicts that have less to do with protecting America's material security than with defending what we imagine to be our moral prominence in the world. In short, if we are to succeed in adapting to the political challenges of the future, we must somehow strike a balance between our need to recall and our need to ease the emotional impact of what happened in Southeast Asia.

This same struggle confronts our traumatized combat veterans every day. For these men, the knowledge of what took place during the war often remains almost unbearable. As Kurt Ocher, a former riverboat gunner, explains, "The volume of suffering [in the Vietnam War] is so massive, you really can't hold it in your mind." If they could somehow know the entirety of their histories in Vietnam at one moment, men like Ocher would likely cease to be able to function. They would lose their jobs, their marriages would dissolve, their children would drift away.

Rather than confront the totality of the violence they survived in

Vietnam, men like Ocher have parceled out their recollections into several competing stories of the past. Once an active member of Vietnam Veterans Against the War (VVAW) and still a man who condemns the war as pointless and immoral, Ocher nevertheless explains that "the notion that it was for nothing is intolerable. The idea that you were scarred and your friends were butchered for just absolutely nothing is more than anyone can bear. Even me." Worse still, says Ocher, is the notion that Americans in Vietnam died while taking part in an immoral national mission. "The minute I think we were doing the wrong thing [in Vietnam], I go from being a fighting man to being a butcher," he explains. "And there is a fine line—if any—between the two in the first place."

Was Ocher a fighting man or a butcher? Did his service have meaning or did his friends die for no reason? Ocher cannot be entirely sure. It is precisely this uncertainty, however, that allows him to move forward in his life today. By breaking up his recollections, by refusing to allow them into consciousness all at once, Ocher has drastically reduced the frequency with which he is overwhelmed by his combat history. He has retained the ability to acknowledge the moral and emotional complexities of his combat roles, but he has also gained the ability to function in new and successful ways: An empathetic father and husband, Ocher in no way resembles the butcher he fears he became in Vietnam.

In the years since the Vietnam War, the fragmentation that marks Ocher's recollection of his time in combat has also come to mark our collective responses to the conflict as a whole. Like Ocher, we have asked ourselves whether Americans in Vietnam were fighting men or butchers and what, if anything, their killing and dying might have meant. And like Ocher, we have apportioned our answers to these questions, along with our suffering and our sense of shame, among a number of competing and at times overlapping narratives. We have told ourselves stories of rescue and revenge, of therapy and initiation, of mourning and recovery and over the years, these narratives have spread like a network of scars across our national discourse. Found in junior high school textbooks and presidential speeches, popular movies and private conversations, these stories have closed and partially concealed the wounds left by the war in our national self-image. Part fact, part fiction, they have allowed us to simultaneously remember and forget, and thus they have made it possible for us to move forward—however haltingly—as a nation.

Few stories have appealed to more Americans than those that recast the war as a tragedy. In the late 1980s, Harry McPherson, Special Counsel to the President from 1965 to 1969 and thus a subcontractor to the architects of the war, expressed the tragic view succinctly: Vietnam, he explained, taught us that "powerful nations may stumble, though their intentions are good, and that tragedy and failure are often the lot of humanity, even of the citizens of a great and favored nation such as ours." McPherson's diction and logic recall the high-flown rhetoric of ancient Greek drama. At the heart of classical Greek tragedy lies the notion that men and women, no matter how noble, stand helpless before their fates. When Oedipus killed a wealthy man at a crossroads and later, when he took a former queen to bed, he had no idea that he was killing his father and sleeping with his mother—even though he had long known that it would be his fate to do so. When the oracle at Delphi revealed that the presence of the king's murderer in Thebes had caused a plague to fall over the city, Oedipus sought the murderer relentlessly. Despite prophecies to the contrary, he remained confident of his innocence until his own investigations proved his guilt. In Greek terms, it was precisely this combination of ignorance and hubris that made Oedipus' actions tragic. Despite the fact that he was a good man (albeit overproud), a man driven neither by violent impulses nor lust, Oedipus could not avoid committing the crimes his fate required. Like Oedipus, McPherson implies, Americans in Vietnam acted with the best of intentions, if also with a bit too much self-confidence. The United States was a "great and favored nation." If it failed in its mission, it did so only because it could not escape certain fates that have always been "the lot of humanity."

By framing the war as a tragedy, Americans like McPherson have accomplished several difficult psychological tasks. They have acknowledged, albeit obliquely, that what their country did in Southeast Asia caused extraordinary harm. They have also recognized the fact that, from presidents to foot soldiers, many Americans who went to Vietnam did so on behalf of what they perceived to be a noble national mission. Like the heroes of the ancient plays, many did what they thought was right, only to discover that they had committed horrible wrongs. At the same time, by assigning responsibility for their actions to forces outside their control, the tragedy theorists have managed to sidestep feelings of guilt and to reassert the validity of many of their prewar assumptions. If we do not believe that we brought about our own downfall in Vietnam, then we can continue to believe that we are a uniquely powerful nation favored by God; that we are a force for good in the world; that, though we may fail to *achieve* good, it will not be because we have not *sought* to do good.

Even the *form* of the story reassures us. Taken as a whole, the Vietnam War was far too complex and emotionally strenuous to fit into the highly stylized cathartic mold of tragedy. The war was never simply the story of a noble nation who saw its good intentions undone by a horrible and unavoidable fate. But by whittling away at the facts of the war, by pushing here and pulling there, and finally reshaping the history to match this streamlined modern version of the ancient narrative structure, those who call the war a tragedy have given us the comforting illusion that the war's violence and mayhem can be safely contained. Even as they face events that threaten to break out of the frames they have set around their experience, events that threaten to overturn their assumptions about themselves, their government, and their nation, those who take the tragic view assert that at least one prewar frame—the narrative architecture of classical tragedy—remains inviolable.

To the extent that they have preserved certain fundamental prewar assumptions, those who promote the tragic view have also preserved the ability to take certain kinds of political and military action. When George Bush sent troops to rescue starving Somalis or even to defend Kuwaiti oil sheiks, for example, he based his decisions on the view that America remained a uniquely "great and favored nation"—the view promoted by tragedy narratives. In addition, his vision of a new world order depended on his confidence in America's right and might—a confidence that dated back to his experiences in World War II and that, without the aid of tragedy narratives, might have been difficult to sustain in the wake of Vietnam. Throughout his presidency, Bush derived much of his ability to rally the public behind him from the faith both he and they shared in America's moral leadership. Having simultaneously pointed Americans toward and insulated them from the full horror of their moral and military failures in Southeast Asia, popular recastings of the Vietnam War as a tragedy helped make that faith possible.

Of course the tragic interpretation has not been the only one to preserve Americans' prewar assumptions. In a story line that parallels that of the tragedy narrative, many Americans have come to view the war as a noble enterprise whose successful outcome was undermined by the perfidy of politicians, the press, or antiwar protestors. To the promulgators of this betrayal theory, the leaders of South Vietnam were not puppets of the United States, but the legitimate leaders of a democratic state struggling for independence. That state had been attacked by local Communists and by its Communist "neighbor," North Vietnam, and would not survive without help from the United States. "The South Vietnamese ally was caught up in a civil war," explains Peter Braestrup, a war "abetted by outsiders from North Vietnam." Or as G. Gordon Liddy, former Watergate conspirator and vocal proponent of the betrayal theory, explains it, the Vietnam War "was not a 'civil war.' It was aggression by one state, valid politically and having ethnically different people, against another such state."

Men like Braestrup and Liddy tend to ignore the fact that South Vietnam was not so much a state created in Vietnam by the Vietnamese as a state created in Geneva, largely by French, American, British, Soviet, and Chinese negotiators. At the end of World War II, its defeated Japanese occupiers had returned a unified Vietnam to its previous colonial master, France. For the next nine years, Ho Chi Minh and his army, the Viet Minh, fought a guerrilla war to oust the French and their Saigon-based puppet government. After defeating the French at the Battle of Dien Bien Phu in 1954, the Viet Minh controlled most of northern and southern Vietnam politically and militarily. Yet, for Cold War reasons of their own, both their Communist allies and the Western allies of the French pressured the Viet Minh into agreeing to temporarily divide the country in half and to hold elections for a unified government two years later, in July 1956. When the time for elections came, the descendant of the French puppet government, now funded and advised by Americans, refused to participate.

In that sense, South Vietnam was never "valid politically," nor are its inhabitants "ethnically different" from those in the North. By making these claims, however, betrayal theorists can cast themselves in the roles of loyal friend and rescuer. They can maintain the assumption that American intentions abroad were then—and therefore remain—good.

Like proponents of the notion that the war was a tragedy, they can assert, even in the face of historical evidence to the contrary, that their prewar assumptive world remains intact.

At the same time, like the tragedy theorists, those who promote the betrayal interpretation do acknowledge, however obliquely, certain truths about the war. In the years of the conflict, American politicians *were* perfidious, many in the press *did not* support their President's policies, and those who protested the war *did* help bring it to an end. Moreover, like the tragedy narrative, the betrayal theory has also helped justify certain political and military actions. During the invasion of Grenada and later, during the Gulf War, for instance, the military feared that journalists might undermine the mission at hand as betrayal theorists suggested they had once subverted American efforts in Vietnam. The generals severely limited reporters' access to the battlefield and, as a result, found themselves able to act with unprecedented freedom—and substantial public support—in both conflicts.

For some on the left, the generals' evident willingness to take advantage of their newfound freedom, their delight in handing out snapshots of wholesome Marine homecomings and videotapes of precision bombing runs to information-starved reporters, exemplified a fundamental moral flaw in American culture, a flaw few have been able to accept. "What most of us can't deal with—can't even begin to imagine," wrote W. D. Erhart, a poet and Vietnam veteran, "is the vision of the U.S. as a force of evil in the world every bit as malignant as that archvillain the Soviet Union. Such a notion runs against the very fabric of self-perception. It is too hideous to imagine."

As Erhart suggests, the contemplation of American immorality in Vietnam can lead to despair—a despair from which those who cling to the tragic and betrayal views have fled. "Back in 1969," as Tim O'Brien writes, "the wreckage was all around us. . . . Wreckage was the rule. Brutality was S.O.P. Scalded children, pistol-whipped women, burning hootches, free-fire zones, body counts, indiscriminate bombing and harassment fire, villages in ash, M-60 machine guns hosing down dark green tree lines and any human life behind them." Who can recall such wreckage without shame?

In the years since the end of the war, however, some on the left have become so entranced by the harm Americans did in Southeast Asia that they have begun to assume that American intervention abroad can *only* do harm. They have tended to play down and even to deny the fact that there may be times when it is necessary for a country to go to war outside its borders in order to preserve the lives of its citizens, to maintain its own economic or material well-being, or to ensure its continued existence as a state. When thousands marched to protest the start of the Persian Gulf War—a war that restored not only the Kuwaiti monarchy to power, but the flow of Kuwaiti oil to America—more than a few carried signs reading: NO MORE VIETNAMS.

Given that many of their most vocal promoters served the government or the military during the Vietnam War and given that leaders have since used them to underwrite military action, it is tempting to view the tragic and betrayal interpretations of the conflict merely as revanchist fairy tales. Likewise, given the astonishing amount of suffering Americans inflicted on the Vietnamese, as well as the citizens of Cambodia and Laos, and given the rarity with which Americans have acknowledged their responsibility for that suffering, it is tempting to assign a fundamental immorality not only to our conduct of the war, but to those who still believe that we were right to wage it. From both the right and the left, it is tempting to condemn those whose recollections of the conflict do not match our own.

And yet, even as we debate the legacy of the war, even as we struggle to recognize its lessons and to apply them, perhaps we can see that, like scar tissue, our conflicting narratives of the war are also the inevitable products of a social process of recovery from traumatic events. As the psychologist Ronnie Janoff-Bulman has written, "the reconstruction of a viable, nonthreatening assumptive world . . . constitutes the core coping task" of survivors of trauma. By shaping our experience into commonly accepted, if often contradictory, stories, we have found ways to reconstruct our faith in ourselves and to mitigate the psychological threats posed by our knowledge of the war. These stories rarely cling to the facts of the conflict. More often, like scars, they grow up over raw and painful recollections of the war, the symmetry of their narrative forms obscuring the bloody history out of which they came to life. But loyalty to the hard facts is not the issue: As Janoff-Bulman points out, healing from trauma merely requires the creation of a *viable* assumptive world. In other words, in order to become a basis for individual or

national action, our stories don't have to be entirely true—they just have
to make sense.

It should not surprise us that they often make that sense by borrow-
ing the assumptions and narrative forms of the prewar past. Psychologists
have long known that when presented with information that challenges
their fundamental beliefs, most people tend to alter the content of the
information at hand rather than the shape of their beliefs. In one study,
for instance, a group of college students watched a videotape of a woman
dining with her husband. When interviewed later, those students who
had been told she was a librarian recalled that she was wearing glasses and
owned classical records. Those who had been told she was a waitress
remembered that she drank beer and owned a television.

Like those who have rewritten the history of the Vietnam War, most
people cling to what they thought they knew and to the ways they knew
it not only despite, but *because of* the damaging nature of any evidence to
the contrary. As a number of psychologists have pointed out, our core
beliefs not only help us define our identities—they also serve as practical
guides to behavior. To let go of our most basic assumptions can be both
enormously painful and terribly disruptive to our daily lives, even in the
case of the most seemingly self-destructive beliefs. A highly successful
scientist in one psychological study, for example, had long thought of
himself as a "complete failure." Accordingly, he twisted each new
achievement into evidence of his insufficiency. It seems likely, however,
that those perceived failures in turn drove him to new accomplishments.
In that sense, by forcing his perceptions of his career into the confines of
his self-image, he not only preserved his self-image, but increased his
success.

In the wake of the conflict in Southeast Asia, it is as much a collective form of this expedient cognitive conservatism as the individual urge
for self-exculpation that has given us our most common rewritings of the
war. In the over-muscled adventures of heroes like Rambo or the Terminator, we have not only symbolically rescripted our roles in Vietnam,
recreating ourselves as muscular and moral rescuers, but we have reaf-
firmed our faith that our mythological past can continue to serve as a
guide to action in the present. Likewise, by acting out rituals of initiation
in the woods or on firing ranges, we have not only found a way to
disown the emotionally remote generals and politicians who led America

into Vietnam and to reclaim our places as the feeling sons of ancient frontiersmen, but we have asserted that the frontier ethos itself remains a valid cognitive framework through which to view the world.

Of course, even in the face of our longings for such mythological continuity, we retain the obligation to try to get the facts of our history right. At the same time, we must find the courage to acknowledge that no matter how hard we work to recover the past, we will never entirely succeed in knowing how wrong we went in Vietnam or in reassuring ourselves that we won't go just as wrong again. The notion of healing, at least in its popular conception, often invokes hopes of self-improvement or at least a return to normalcy. But in the wake of the war in Vietnam, we have had to face the fact that our sufferings have not made us a better people and that, so far at least, we have been unable to recover the ideological coherence and sense of purpose that marked the prewar years.

Like Kurt Ocher, Americans today inhabit a post-traumatic world of fragmented, conflicting narratives, each true to a degree and each in part false. Yet it is precisely their fragmentary, conflicting nature that allows us to turn toward the future. To succeed in recognizing the full horror of the Vietnam War and of America's role in it, to actually hold it in our minds, would leave us crippled individually and as a nation. If we are to take effective action in the years ahead, we must allow the psychological wounds of the past to close. At the same time, if we are to avoid repeating the mistakes of the past, we must also continue to run our fingers along the scars.

NOTES

CHAPTER 1

PRIVATE TRAUMA AND PUBLIC MEMORY

p. 4 "They finger bracelets . . .": These bracelets were first produced
in 1970 and worn by the likes of Richard Nixon, George McGovern,
General William Westmoreland, Cher and Sonny Bono, and Bob Hope.
In his comprehensive study of the POW-MIA phenomenon, *M.I.A., or,
Mythmaking in America,* H. Bruce Franklin explains that "By the time of
the January 1973 Paris Peace Agreement, between four million and ten
million Americans were wearing POW-MIA bracelets. The influence on
the national imagination cannot be calculated. Each person who wore a
bracelet vowed never to remove it until his or her POW-MIA was either
found to be dead or returned home from Vietnamese prison camp"
(Franklin, *M.I.A.,* p. 57).
p. 6 "a limited incursion . . .": Quoted in Gloria Emerson, *Winners
and Losers: Battles, Retreats, Gains, Losses, and Ruins from the Vietnam War,*
p. 330. My account of Dewey Canyon III depends largely on hers.
p. 6 "We are here to ask . . .": Quoted in Emerson, *Winners and Losers,*
pp. 331–32.
p. 7 "I met Roger Hulbein . . .": Roger Hulbein is not this veteran's
real name. All other details of his story, including his use of the nick-

name "Sarge," are accurate. Since the majority of combat veterans I interviewed requested anonymity, I have assigned pseudonyms to all of them. The names of veterans I did not interview are real.

p. 8 "What veteran would stain . . .": Less than a decade after the defeat of Germany and Japan, the same rhetoric silenced the veterans of the Korean War. In the summer of 1992, I met a former Army Ranger who had fought in Korea for three years. "I can't understand these Vietnam guys," he said. "They're always crying. When we came home, we kept it to ourselves and did what we had to do." For this veteran, to do anything less than keep one's upper lip stiff and one's mouth shut was to be a crybaby. Even so, he had suffered from the same delayed stress reactions that haunt many Vietnam veterans. A few months after returning home, he woke up in bed and saw that he was strangling his wife. To this day, his children fear his flashbacks. When they want to wake him up, they won't touch him. Instead, they throw things at him until he responds.

p. 8 "Americans had dropped . . .": Figures on bombing tonnage come from William L. Griffen and John Marciano, *Lessons of the Vietnam War: A Critical Examination of School Texts and an Interpretive Comparative History Utilizing* The Pentagon Papers *and other Documents,* p. 49. Figures on defoliation come from H. Bruce Franklin, "Teaching Vietnam Today: Who Won, and Why?", *The Chronicle of Higher Education,* November 4, 1981, p. 64.

p. 9 "In memoirs and oral histories . . .": See, for instance, John Ketwig, . . . *And a Hard Rain Fell;* Robert Mason, *Chickenhawk;* Mark Baker, *Nam: The Vietnam War in the Words of the Men and Women Who Fought There;* and Al Santoli, *Everything We Had.*

p. 11 "His M-16 still points . . .": This photograph was taken in September 1965, north of Qui Nhon, by Martin Stuart Fox (UPI/Bettmann Archive); reprinted in Marilyn B. Young, *The Vietnam Wars 1945–1990,* pp. 242–43.

p. 11 "Most American soldiers in Viet-Nam . . .": Eric Norden, "American Atrocities in Vietnam," *Liberation,* February 1966, p. 20.

p. 12 "Psychiatrist Mardi Horowitz . . .": Mardi Horowitz, *Stress Response Syndromes,* pp. 99–101. Horowitz is a psychiatrist and one of the foremost theorists on human responses to stress. I'm essentially summarizing his argument from Chapter 6. Perhaps the most succinct description of traumatic memory and the psychological profession's attempts to categorize it can be found in Dr. Judith Herman's *Trauma and Recovery.*

p. 14 "For that reason, established veterans organizations . . .": David E. Bonior, Steven M. Champlin, and Timothy S. Kolly, *The Vietnam Veteran: A History of Neglect,* pp. 99–118.

p. 15 "Today America can again . . .": Gerald Ford, "Excerpts from Ford Address at Tulane," *The New York Times,* April 24, 1975; quoted in Peter Ehrenhaus, "Commemorating the Unwon War: On *Not* Remembering Vietnam," *Journal of Communication* (Vol. 39, No. 1, Winter 1989), p. 102.

p. 15 "On the same day . . .": Ehrenhaus, "Commemorating the Unwon War," pp. 100–6. In his article, Ehrenhaus tells the story of the Tomb of the Unknown and relates it to Ford's rhetoric at the end of the war.

p. 15 "It is time we recognized . . .": Ronald Reagan, speech to the Veterans of Foreign Wars Convention, Chicago, Illinois, August 18, 1980; quoted by Lou Cannon, in *Reagan,* p. 271.

p. 15 "Morning in America.": Reagan campaign video, 1984.

CHAPTER 2

THE HORROR, THE HORROR: THE VIETNAM
WAR AS INDIVIDUAL AND CULTURAL TRAUMA

p. 17 "I learned how to function . . .": Mason, *Chickenhawk,* pp. 109–10.

p. 18 "more than a million and a half Americans . . .": Lawrence M. Baskir and William A. Strauss, *Chance and Circumstance: The Draft, the War, and the Vietnam Generation,* p. 5. Baskir and Strauss report that of the approximately 8,615,000 men who served in the military during the Vietnam era, 1,600,000 saw combat in Southeast Asia, 550,000 served in Vietnam but did not see combat, and 6,465,000 never went to Vietnam. They also estimate that their figures have a 0.5 percent margin of error. Given the nature of the fighting in Vietnam, soldiers in noncombat specialties often witnessed or participated in violent actions. Thus, it is hard to identify and enumerate "combat veterans" with precision.

p. 18 "as many as 40 percent . . .": Charles Kadushin, Ghislaine Boulanger, and John Martin, *Long-Term Stress Reactions: Some Causes, Consequences, and Naturally Occurring Support Systems,* Volume IV of Egendorf, et al., *Legacies of Vietnam: Comparative Adjustment of Veterans and Their Peers,* p. 521. One of the most comprehensive studies of veterans' reactions to Vietnam ever completed, the *Legacies of Vietnam* study showed that 40 percent of respondents who had seen heavy combat and 31 percent of respondents who had served in Vietnam had developed a "war-related stress reaction" by the end of 1979, the year in which the study was completed.

In the *National Vietnam Veterans Readjustment Study* (NVVRS), a nationwide study of veterans mandated by Congress and conducted between 1984 and 1988, researchers found that of the 3.14 million men and women who served in Vietnam, 829,000 (approximately 26 percent), still displayed significant symptoms of post-traumatic stress disorder in 1988. 479,000 (or 15.2 percent of) male theater veterans had full-blown PTSD, as did 610 (or 8.5 percent of) female theater veterans. The study also showed that more than 960,000 (or 30.6 percent of) male theater veterans and more than 1,900 (or 26.9 percent of) female theater veterans had the full-blown disorder at some point in their lives. As the researchers point out, about half the men and a third of the women who ever had PTSD still had it in 1988 (see Richard A. Kulka, William E. Schlenger, John A. Fairbank, Richard L. Hough, B. Kathleen Jordan, Charles R. Marmar, and Daniel S. Weiss, *Trauma and the Vietnam War Generation: Report of Findings from the National Vietnam Veterans Readjustment Study,* pp. v and xxvii–xxviii).

As their report explained, NVVRS researchers found that "those who were most heavily involved in the war are those for whom readjustment was, and continues to be, most difficult" (Kulka, et al., p. xxviii). Citing data from the NVVRS, psychiatrist Judith Herman has pointed out that the severity of veterans' PTSD symptoms depends largely on their exposure to combat. Fifteen years after the withdrawal of American forces from Vietnam, she writes, 36 percent of those veterans exposed to "heavy" combat could still be diagnosed with full-blown PTSD. The same could be said of only 9 percent of veterans "with low or moderate combat exposure," 4 percent of veterans who were not sent to Vietnam, and 1 percent of the civilian population (see Herman, *Trauma and Recovery,* p. 57).

p. 18 "Simultaneously drawn to and repelled by . . .": First formally accepted as a diagnosis by the American Psychiatric Association in 1980, post–traumatic stress disorder afflicts those who have "experienced, witnessed, or [been] confronted with an event or events that involved actual or threatened death or serious injury, or a threat to the physical integrity of self or others." The illness "is characterized by the reexperiencing of an extremely traumatic event accompanied by symptoms of increased arousal and by avoidance of stimuli associated with the trauma" (American Psychiatric Association, *Diagnostic and Statistical Manual of Mental Disorders,* Fourth Edition, pp. 427–28 and 393). For a discussion of the evolution of the diagnosis and its political implications, see Chapter 3.

p. 18 "Psychologists tell us . . .": See, for instance, James Munroe, Jonathan Shay, Lisa Fisher, Christine Makary, Kathryn Rapperport, and Rose Zimering, "Preventing Compassion Fatigue: A Team Treatment Model," in Charles R. Figley, ed., *Compassion Fatigue: Coping with Secondary Traumatic Stress Disorder in Those Who Treat the Traumatized.*

p. 19 "America had a mission . . .": Lawrence Wright, *In the New World: Growing Up with America from the Sixties to the Eighties,* p. 109.

p. 19 "History and our own achievements . . .": Quoted in Arthur M. Schlesinger, Jr., *The Crisis of Confidence: Ideas, Power, and Violence in America,* p. 175.

p. 19 "In the forties and fifties . . .": Quoted in Michael Bilton and Kevin Sim, *Four Hours in My Lai,* p. 27.

p. 20 "This Nation [sic] was founded . . .": *Congressional Record,* February 16, 1966; quoted in Marcus G. Raskin and Bernard B. Fall, eds., *The Viet-Nam Reader: Articles and Documents on American Foreign Policy and the Viet-Nam Crisis,* Revised Edition, p. 386.

p. 20 "It is very hard to plant corn . . .": Quoted in Richard Slotkin, *Gunfighter Nation: The Myth of the Frontier in Twentieth-Century America,* p. 495.

p. 20 "Wagon-Train GIs . . .": *New York Daily News,* February 26, 1968; quoted in Daniel C. Hallin, *The "Uncensored War": The Media and Vietnam,* p. 11.

p. 21 "John Wayne was always . . .": Wright, *In the New World,* pp. 136–37.

p. 22 "In October of the same year . . .": Neil Sheehan, *The New York Times,* October 9, 1966; quoted in Bilton and Sim, *Four Hours in My Lai,* p. 36.

p. 22 "main concern in off-duty hours . . .": Quoted in Christian G. Appy, *Working-Class War: American Combat Soldiers and Vietnam,* p. 174.

p. 22 "Before 1968, American civilians . . .": To get an idea of how unreal the fighting in Vietnam seemed to many in 1965, consider the opening to Frank McGee's documentary for NBC entitled *Vietnam: December 1965.* According to Don Oberdorfer, "The show opened with McGee standing in front of the Main Station Recruiting Center in Chicago speaking of the young men who reported for duty there, and then shifted to GIs in the Ia Drang Valley, while McGee's voice told of the men who had died there. Then the titles of the program were shown and a network announcer's voice said: 'In another special report, NBC News presents *Vietnam: December 1965,* a definitive report of the war in Vietnam and the reactions in the United States, brought to you by Dial, the most effective deodorant soap you can buy. Aren't you glad you use Dial? Don't you wish everybody did? And by new Magic Spray Sizing, made to help you iron the shortcut way, new Magic Spray Sizing; and by Armour Star canned meats, the good meat meals that come in a can. Now, here is NBC News correspondent Frank McGee' " (Don Oberdorfer, *TET!,* p. 272).

Five years later enough men had come home in aluminum coffins to make the image of meat in a can far less appetizing.

p. 22 "It didn't take long . . .": Luke Jensen, quoted in Appy, *Working-Class War,* p. 116.

p. 22 "We might have been . . .": Rob Riggan, *Free Fire Zone* (New York: Ballantine, 1984, p. 4); quoted in Appy, *Working-Class War,* p. 122.

p. 23 "We had just left Hawaii . . .": Quoted in Bilton and Sim, *Four Hours in My Lai,* p. 62.

p. 23 "They dress differently . . .": Peter V. Fossel, quoted by Philip Scribner Balboni in "What Every Vietnam Veteran Knows: Mylai Was Not an Isolated Incident," *The New Republic,* Vol. 163, No. 25, December 19, 1970, p. 13.

p. 24 "If . . . the children held up two fingers . . .": See Appy, *Working-Class War,* p. 132.

p. 24 "Those kids, raised during years of killing . . .": John Durant, quoted in Murray Polner, *No Victory Parades: The Return of the Vietnam Veteran,* p. 52.

p. 24 "Chance. Pure chance . . .": Philip Caputo, *A Rumor of War,* p. 266.

p. 24 "When you're in that setting . . .": Quoted in Norma Wikler, "Hidden Injuries of War," in Charles R. Figley and Seymour Leventman, eds., *Strangers at Home: Vietnam Veterans Since the War,* p. 90.

p. 25 "Instead, they melted . . .": In Vietnam, unlike Korea or Europe, the enemy set the time and place for over 80 percent of all combat engagements.

p. 25 "The foot soldier has a special feeling . . .": Caputo, *A Rumor of War,* p. 273.

p. 25 "You couldn't pinpoint who . . .": Quoted in Bilton and Sim, *Four Hours in My Lai,* p. 39.

p. 25 "Nothing is what it seems . . .": Quoted in Jonathan Shay, *Achilles in Vietnam: Combat Trauma and the Undoing of Character,* p. 170.

p. 26 "Where they had expected . . .": This was not true of all combat soldiers. In fact, for many, the opportunity to fly a helicopter or walk point for a platoon offered them more responsibility than they had ever had in civilian life. Doing the job well offered an occasion for pride. Yet, their pride in their competence offered few of even these men the feeling of being able to control, as John Wayne could, their destinies.

p. 26 "The dependence of a modern soldier . . .": Shay, draft for *Achilles in Vietnam,* p. 73.

p. 26 "He would send . . .": Officers and men rarely shared the same risks in Vietnam. As Edward Luttwak wrote in *The Pentagon and the Art of War: The Question of Military Reform* (p. 34): "In Vietnam . . . officers above the most junior rank were . . . abundant and mostly found in well-protected bases. . . . During the Second World War, the Army ground forces had a full colonel for every 672 enlisted men; in Vietnam (1971) there was a colonel for every 163 enlisted men. In the Second World War, 77 colonels died in combat, one for every 2,206 men thus killed; throughout the Vietnam war, from 1961 till 1972, only 8 colonels were killed in action, one for every 3,407 men."

p. 27 "Unarmed women and children . . .": When they left the field, officers often took care to make sure their "achievements" were recognized. In 1969, for instance, 50 of the 57 generals returning from Vietnam were awarded Air Medals (once awarded only for extraordinary service, but now granted simply for completing a set number of air missions in a "war zone"). Twenty-six received either the Silver Star, the Distinguished Flying Cross, or the Bronze Star. Of the approximately 345,000 enlisted men who returned to America that year, only 30,000— about one in ten—received medals of any kind (James William Gibson, *The Perfect War*, pp. 117–18).

p. 27 "Daylight came . . .": Shay, *Achilles in Vietnam*, pp. 3–4 and 171.

p. 28 "Despite the intense cohesion . . .": In the Army, the standard tour of duty was twelve months; in the Marines, thirteen. Commissioned officers above the rank of lieutenant in both services ordinarily spent half that time in a combat area and half in the rear. In World War II, enlisted men by and large entered and left the combat zone as a unit and had the length of their service determined by the military exigencies of the situation rather than any fixed rotation agreement.

p. 28 "In this kind of war . . .": Don McCullin, *Unreasonable Behaviour: An Autobiography*, p. 105.

p. 28 "I couldn't believe . . .": Quoted in Shay, *Achilles in Vietnam*, p. 31.

p. 29 "According to one well-known study . . .": According to Egendorf, et al., *Legacies of Vietnam*, a nationwide study conducted for the Veterans Administration between 1977 and 1979, 9 percent of all combat troops committed acts of abusive violence, while 30 percent witnessed such acts. In their analysis of the *Legacies of Vietnam* data, Ellen Frey-Wouters and Robert Laufer explain that the abusive acts most frequently mentioned by veterans were "torture of prisoners, including pushing them from helicopters; physical mistreatment of civilians; use of napalm, white phosphorus, or cluster bombs on villages; death or maiming by booby trap; and mutilation of bodies." Americans were not responsible for all such events: Frey-Wouters and Laufer point out that 31 percent of their respondents reported seeing acts of abusive violence by Viet Cong or North Vietnamese Army troops, while 13 percent reported acts committed by South Vietnamese or South Korean troops. 78

percent of respondents, however, reported "cases in which U.S. regulars were involved." Frey-Wouters and Laufer also note that their percentages "do not sum to 100 percent since over a third of those exposed mentioned more than one episode" (Ellen Frey-Wouters and Robert Laufer, *Legacy of a War: The American Soldier in Vietnam,* p. 410). By the late 1960s, American troops had begun cutting ears off enemy corpses so frequently that General William Westmoreland had to issue a directive, later widely ignored, forbidding the practice (Myra MacPherson, *Long Time Passing: Vietnam and the Haunted Generation,* p. 492).

p. 29 "You know, when I think . . .": Quoted by Robert Lifton, in Erwin Knoll and Judith Nies McFadden, eds., *War Crimes and the American Conscience,* p. 110.

p. 29 "I have to admit . . .": Baker, *Nam,* pp. 163–64.

p. 30 "I felt like a big bolt of lightning . . .": Jerry Samuels, quoted in Balboni, "What Every Vietnam Veteran Knows," p. 15.

p. 30 "These acts . . . make you think there is no God . . .": Quoted in Frey-Wouters and Laufer, *Legacy of a War,* p. 11.

p. 31 "been repeatedly faced with . . .": Quoted in Appy, *Working-Class War,* p. 20.

p. 31 "With 1968, a new phase is starting . . .": Quoted in Bilton and Sim, *Four Hours in My Lai,* p. 25.

p. 32 "The victory that was about to complete . . .": Slotkin, *Gunfighter Nation,* p. 578.

p. 32 "National leaders had declared . . .": Todd Gitlin, *The Sixties: Years of Hope, Days of Rage,* p. 299.

p. 32 "Television networks that had formerly been reluctant . . .": "A faithful television viewer, watching the evening news five nights a week, would have seen film of civilian casualties and urban destruction in South Vietnam an average of 3.9 times a week during the Tet period (January 31 to March 31), more than four times the overall average of 0.85 times a week. Films of military casualties jumped from 2.4 to 6.8 times a week. Tet was the first sustained period during which it could be said that the war appeared on television as a really brutal affair" (Hallin, *The "Uncensored War,"* p. 171).

p. 32 "tethered bullocks . . .": David Douglas Duncan, "Khe Sanh," *Life,* February 23, 1968, p. 21.

p. 32 "Later *Life* ran . . .": *Life,* March 8, 1968.

p. 33 "But in the United States . . .": On February 16, 1968, for example, North Vietnamese regulars found themselves on the cover of *Life* magazine. Under the words "A Remarkable Day in Hué: The Enemy Lets Me Take His Picture," two young soldiers, handsome in their clean green uniforms, strong with their AK-47s, turn toward the camera. They are everything that the South Vietnamese and their American allies during Tet are not: clean, calm, organized, and in charge.

p. 33 "The failure of half a million American soldiers . . .": Schlesinger, *The Crisis of Confidence*, p. xi.

p. 33 "the fate of Hué demonstrated . . .": *Life*, March 8, 1968, p. 26.

p. 34 "A powerful lesson . . .": Benjamin DeMott, "The Way It Is: Some Notes on What We Feel," *Surviving the 70's*, p. 27.

p. 34 "the destruction of the fundamental institutions . . .": James Fletcher, "The Politics of Emptiness," *The National Review*, February 13, 1968, p. 151.

p. 35 "And the war itself . . .": For a thorough discussion of how reporting on Vietnam changed after Tet, see Hallin, *The "Uncensored War,"* pp. 171–80.

p. 35 "Great streamers of acrid smoke . . .": *Time*, April 12, 1968, p. 17.

p. 35 "immediately prompted, at home and abroad . . .": Editorial, *Time*, June 14, 1968, p. 15.

p. 36 "200 million Americans . . ." and "It would be . . . wrong . . .": Ibid.

p. 36 "The country had gone wrong . . .": Wright, *In the New World*, pp. 146–47.

p. 36 "a flat rejection . . .": DeMott, "The Way It Is: Some Notes on What We Feel," *Surviving the 70's*, p. 28.

p. 36 "Neither wanted to be . . .": It is important to remember that at the time, many Americans saw the assassinations of King and Kennedy as the flip side of the Vietnam coin. Writing about the assassinations less than a year later, historian Arthur Schlesinger likened "[t]he terrible things we do to our own people" to "the terrible things we do to other people [i.e., the Vietnamese]." Those who murdered at home, wrote Schlesinger, had been "stamped by our society with an instinct for hatred and a compulsion toward violence." Yet it was those same impulses, he thought, that drove the Vietnam War: "For the zeal with which we have pursued an irrational war—a war which makes so little sense in the classical terms of foreign policy—suggests internal impulses of hatred and violence demanding outlet and shaping our foreign policy to their ends" (Schlesinger, *The Crisis of Confidence,* p. 9).

p. 37 "[S]o disturbing is today's civil commotion . . .": Hugh Davis Graham and Ted Robert Gurr, Introduction, in National Commission on the Causes and Prevention of Violence, *Violence in America,* eight volumes, esp. Graham and Gurr, eds., *Historical and Comparative Perspectives,* Vol. 2, Part I, p. xiii; quoted in Slotkin, *Gunfighter Nation,* p. 555.

p. 37 "life is not solid and predictable . . .": Schlesinger, *The Crisis of Confidence,* p. 50.

p. 37 "[O]ur nation is in a state of incipient fragmentation . . .": Ibid., pp. 239 and 240–41.

p. 38 "In a live interview . . .": Why CBS executives chose that particular night to broadcast the Meadlo interview remains a mystery. CBS had broadcast Ron Haeberle's famous snapshots of the massacre four nights earlier. Before putting Meadlo on the air, the network had to make a series of arrangements with Meadlo and his representatives. I suspect that in order to capitalize on public interest in the massacre, the network simply showed the interview as soon after displaying Haeberle's photographs as it could. For more details, see Bilton and Sim, *Four Hours in My Lai,* pp. 260–61.

p. 38 "Lieutenant Calley started pushing them off . . .": Paul Meadlo, interview on CBS-TV, November 24, 1969; quoted in William G. Effros, compiler, *Quotations Vietnam: 1945–1970,* pp. 153–54.

p. 38 "WALLACE: You're married?" to "MEADLO: I just lay there thinking about it . . .": Quoted in Bilton and Sim, *Four Hours in My Lai,* p. 262.

p. 39 "In the weeks ahead, Pinkville would come to be known . . .": The village that military planners referred to as My Lai-4 and which most Americans know simply as My Lai, was known by its inhabitants as Xom Lang, a subhamlet of the hamlet of Tu Cung within the village of Song My and the province of Quang Ngai. See Appy, *Working-Class War,* p. 273.

p. 39 "Americans would learn . . .": At the same time, Bravo Company was massacring between 50 and 90 civilians in Co Luy, a hamlet a few miles away. The exact number of deaths in My Lai remains unknown. A military investigation led by Lieutenant-General William Peers gave what it called a "conservative" estimate of between 175 and 200 civilian deaths. A second military investigation, conducted by the Criminal Investigation Division, suggested that Charlie Company had killed 347 civilians. Two American civilians, reporter Seymour Hersh and international law specialist Richard Falk, each of whom conducted extensive investigations of the massacre, believe that between 450 and 500 villagers were killed. See Appy, *Working-Class War,* pp. 274–75.

p. 40 "They were later congratulated . . .": For the most complete account of the massacre and its aftermath, see Bilton and Sim, *Four Hours in My Lai.*

p. 40 "Several weeks after Meadlo appeared . . .": *Life,* December 5, 1969, pp. 36–45.

p. 40 "Having been a Marine . . .": *Life,* December 19, 1969, p. 46.

p. 40 "Yes, it *is* terrible . . .": Ibid., p. 46.

p. 40 "One feels a need . . .": Ibid., p. 47.

p. 41 "A typical cross section of American youth . . .": Quoted in Bilton and Sim, *Four Hours in My Lai,* p. 3.

p. 41 "We sense—all of us . . .": Jonathan Schell, "The Talk of the Town: Notes and Comment," *The New Yorker,* December 20, 1969, p. 27.

p. 41 "the mask off the war . . ." and "a national policy on trial . . .": George McGovern, speaking on CBS's *Face the Nation,* November 30, 1969.

p. 41 "I can't believe an American serviceman . . .": Quoted by Edward M. Opton, Jr., in Knoll and McFadden, eds., *War Crimes and the American Conscience,* p. 121.

p. 41 "they were horrified . . .": Seymour Hersh, *My Lai 4: A Report on the Massacre and Its Aftermath,* p. 153.

p. 42 "What obviously happened at My Lai . . .": Quoted in Bilton and Sim, *Four Hours in My Lai,* p. 364.

p. 42 "The most pertinent truth . . .": Editorial, "My Lai: An American Tragedy," *Time,* December 5, 1969, p. 26.

p. 42 "Thanks to 'the presence of evil in the world' . . .": An interesting variation of the "evil in the world" method of displacing responsibility is the notion that, as 65 percent of the public claimed in a December 1969 Harris poll, "incidents such as this are bound to happen in war."

Once again, it is the abstract force of "war," rather than the decisions of individual soldiers and their officers, which causes incidents to "happen" (Harris poll, conducted December 1969; published in *Time,* January 12, 1970, pp. 12–13).

p. 42 "amoral vacuum out there . . .": Joan Didion, "A Problem of Making Connections," *Life,* December 5, 1969, p. 34.

p. 43 "Americans as a national group . . .": Robert Lifton, in Knoll and McFadden, eds., *War Crimes and the American Conscience,* pp. 107–8.

CHAPTER 3

BRINGING IT ALL BACK HOME: THE VIETNAM
WAR AS MENTAL ILLNESS

p. 45 "People are drained . . .": Quoted in "Fed Up and Turned Off," *Time,* April 14, 1975, p. 22.

p. 45 "Recriminations over 'who lost Vietnam' . . .": Ibid., p. 22.

p. 45 "There cannot be an infinite cycle of protests . . .": Ibid., p. 27.

p. 46 "Television and film producers . . .": As a group, Vietnam veterans were not particularly maladjusted. In 1974, a comprehensive survey of 906 veterans in Illinois showed that while 60 percent of the combat veterans were suffering symptoms of psychological distress, fewer than a third of noncombat veterans could say the same (Figley and Leventman, eds., *Strangers at Home,* p. 171). "Our general conclusion," wrote the psychologists in charge, "is that these men are apparently coping well in mainstream America" (p. 178). Anecdotal reports from men who worked with veterans supported their findings. "Most of the guys are married, or back to school or work," said one Veterans Administration counselor in 1971. "They've done their job and now they want to get on with their lives" (quoted in Murray Polner, "Back from Vietnam: The Sense of Isolation," *The Nation,* September 20, 1971, p. 234).

p. 46 "if I acted according to what I have seen on television . . .": Robert Brewin, "TV's Newest Villain: The Vietnam Veteran," *TV Guide,* July 19, 1975, p. 4; quoted in M. Duncan Stanton and Charles R. Figley, "Treating the Vietnam Veteran Within the Family System," in

Charles R. Figley, ed., *Stress Disorders Among Vietnam Veterans: Theory, Research and Treatment,* p. 281.

p. 46 "Prone to weeping . . .": For a stock, if particularly clumsy, example, see Eugene O'Neill's 1918 one-act play *Shell Shock,* in which a traumatized veteran chain-smokes, fidgets, and ultimately screams out in agony—but *not* in rage—in his college club (Eugene O'Neill, *Complete Plays, 1913–1920,* pp. 655–72). For a further discussion of the role shell shock came to play in the modern imagination, see Modris Eksteins, *Rites of Spring: The Great War and the Birth of the Modern Age,* especially Chapter 4, "Rites of War," and Chapter 5, "Reason in Madness."

p. 47 "By minimizing the symptoms . . .": As Thomas Doherty notes in his superb study of World War II films, *Projections of War: Hollywood, American Culture, and World War II,* there were several movies made during and after World War II that did depict combat-induced mental illness. In 1943, *The Fallen Sparrow* presented a Spanish Civil War veteran "tormented by flashbacks of torture" in "a thin allegory for the anticipated influx of afflicted GIs" (p. 200). In 1944, *I'll Be Seeing You* depicted a "burnt-out combat veteran on sick leave" (p. 11). In 1947, *Crossfire* portrayed a returning vet consumed by hatred of Jews. Perhaps the most accurate portrayal of combat-induced stress disorders came in a documentary the War Department commissioned director John Huston to make. Entitled *Let There Be Light* (1946), the film focused on men with combat stress disorders and the psychiatrists treating them. As Doherty explains, though, "the anguish and trauma of Huston's visibly shattered witnesses seem well beyond the restorative powers of polite and concerned surgeons, shrinks, or any other war-bred expert. With too much revealed and too little resolved, it was deemed a violation of the patients' privacy by the War Department and withheld from public screening" for more than thirty years (p. 201). After the Korean War, *The Manchurian Candidate* (1962) expressed American anxieties about the mental health of its veterans by portraying a number of them as brainwashed. Nevertheless, these films are the exceptions that prove the rule. After both wars, the overwhelming majority of movies focused on the homecomings of psychologically "normal" men who had had "tough" experiences.

p. 47 "Everything was Vietnam in my head . . .": Brian Winhover, interview with the author, May 10, 1994. Subsequent quotations of

Winhover's remarks come from interviews with the author on June 7, 1994; February 28, 1994; and March 15, 1994.

p. 48 "What happened twenty years ago feels like yesterday . . .": Arnie Shaestack, interview with the author, June 3, 1994.

p. 49 "American feelings on the war . . .": In early May 1972, for example, during a North Vietnamese offensive, the editors of *Time* magazine gathered 200 citizens at random and asked them for their views on the state of the nation. "A majority of them," reported *Time,* "are sick of the war in Viet Nam and feel that it is going badly," wrote the editors. "Some 70 percent of the panelists feel the war has taken a turn for the worse, and many fear that U.S. involvement may continue indefinitely" *("Time* Citizens Panel: The Sour, Frustrated, and Volatile Voter," *Time,* May 8, 1972, p. 22). A month later, after Nixon had ordered the mining of Haiphong harbor and intensified the bombing of North Vietnam, another *Time* gathering of 200 citizens revealed that opinion had flipped: "Seven out of ten," wrote the editors, "express a renewed confidence in the President's conduct of the war. Only three of ten give him a vote of no confidence" *("Time* Citizens Panel: The President Buys More Time—and Some Hope—on the War," *Time,* June 12, 1972, p. 16).

p. 49 "could bring him back . . .": Quoted in Theodore H. White, *The Making of the President 1972,* p. 333.

p. 49 "I don't want to feel . . .": Ibid., p. 333.

pp. 49–50 "The Nixon bombing policy . . .": Ibid., p. 116.

p. 50 "Our government would rather burn down schoolhouses . . .": Ibid.

p. 50 "If Americans themselves were not criminals . . .": Ibid.

p. 50 "had been the good boy . . .": Jon Nordheimer, "From Dakto to Detroit: Death of a Troubled Hero," *The New York Times,* May 26, 1971, p. 1.

p. 50 "When it was all over . . .": Ibid., p. 16.

p. 51 "I first hit him . . .": Ibid.

p. 51 "What would happen if . . .": Ibid. As the grocer testified, however, Johnson had not gone on a murderous rampage at home. Rather, he appeared to have forced the manager to help him commit suicide.

p. 51 "the most alienated generation . . .": Patrick Butler, "When Johnnie Comes Marching Home," *America,* March 24, 1973, p. 255.

p. 51 "has no boundaries . . .": "The Violent Veterans," *Time,* March 23, 1972, p. 46.

p. 51 "thinking he had just killed . . .": Ibid., p. 45.

p. 51 "reason and order and hope . . .": Republican Party platform, quoted in Peter N. Carroll, *It Seemed Like Nothing Happened,* pp. 80–81.

p. 52 "There may be emerging . . .": Polner, "Back from Vietnam," p. 233.

p. 53 "[T]he Vietnam veteran serves as a psychological crucible . . .": Robert Lifton, "Surviving in Vietnam," *Commonweal,* February 20, 1970, p. 556.

p. 53 "In the film *Welcome Home, Soldier Boys* . . .": See Renny Christopher's summary and review in Jean-Jacques Malo and Tony Williams, eds., *Vietnam War Films: Over 600 Feature, Made-for-TV, Pilot, and Short Movies, 1939–1992, from the United States, Vietnam, France, Belgium, Australia, Hong Kong, South Africa, Great Britain, and Other Countries,* pp. 472–73. *Welcome Home, Soldier Boys* is currently not available for viewing on video and I have relied on Christopher's review.

p. 56 "can't sleep nights . . .": In this respect, he might well agree with the veteran who told Robert Lifton, "I worked at night because I couldn't stand looking at those nine-to-five people who sent me to Vietnam" (Lifton, "Surviving in Vietnam," p. 556).

p. 57 "He shaves his head . . .": For Scorsese's view of Bickle and his military service, see Richard Goldstein and Mark Jacobson, "Blood and Guts Turn Me On!: Interview with Martin Scorsese," *The Village Voice,* April 5, 1976, p. 69.

p. 58 "there is no catharsis possible . . .": Tom Allen, "A Taxi to Despair," *America,* March 6, 1976, p. 182.

p. 58 "forced the audience to . . . empathetically experience . . .": Julian C. Rice, "Transcendental Pornography and *Taxi Driver,*" *Journal of Popular Film,* Vol. 5, No. 2, 1976, p. 122.

p. 58 "the kind of adrenaline-pumping . . .": Michael Dempsey, *"Taxi Driver," Film Quarterly,* Summer 1976, p. 41.

p. 58 "the cowboy and the terrorist cubistically fused . . .": Rice, "Transcendental Pornography and *Taxi Driver,*" p. 113.

p. 58 "simultaneously, the roles of the conventional hero . . .": Ibid.

p. 58 "Perhaps most surprising . . .": *Variety* magazine's "Big Rental

Films of 1976" lists *Taxi Driver* as the twelfth top-grossing film of the
year, based on "rentals accruing to the distributors." *Variety,* Vol. 285,
No. 9, January 5, 1977, p. 14.

p. 61 "the nation is ready to change . . .": Quoted in " 'We Love You':
New View of the Viet Nam Vet," *Time,* June 11, 1979, p. 21.

p. 61 "to respect, honor . . .": Ibid.

p. 61 "We love you for what you were . . .": Ibid.

p. 61 "require[d] an extra measure . . .": Quoted in Figley and
Leventman, eds., *Strangers at Home,* p. 366.

pp. 61–62 "a psychologically traumatic event . . .": The American
Psychiatric Association, *Diagnostic and Statistical Manual of Mental Disorders,* Third Edition, p. 236.

p. 62 "may be experienced alone . . .": Ibid.

p. 62 "Whereas Murray Polner had seen . . .": In 1987, in a revised
version of the *Diagnostic and Statistical Manual,* psychologists inserted
even more specific language of victimization. Traumatic stressors, they
wrote, could include "a serious threat to one's life or physical integrity; a
serious threat or harm to . . . close relatives or friends; sudden destruction of one's home or community; or seeing another person who has
recently been, or is being, seriously injured or killed." Once again, being
traumatized meant being threatened or seeing a threatening situation. It
did not mean threatening someone else (see *Diagnostic and Statistical Manual of Mental Disorders,* Third Edition—Revised, pp. 247–48).

In 1994, little had changed. The authors of the Fourth Edition of the
Diagnostic and Statistical Manual no longer suggested that the traumatic
stressor had to fall "generally outside the range of usual human experience," but they continued to avoid the issue of perpetration. PTSD
arose, they wrote, "following *exposure* to an extreme traumatic stressor
involving direct personal *experience of* an event that involves actual or
threatened death or serious injury, or threat to one's physical integrity
[my italics]." They also noted that "the person's response to the event
must involve intense fear, helplessness, or horror." While those who
commit acts of violence certainly have a "direct personal experience" of
their actions, not all of those who later develop PTSD respond by feeling
fear, helplessness, or horror at the time. A number of those who killed in
Vietnam exulted in their work. Yet, despite their failure to feel the
diagnostically prescribed emotions while they killed, many of them still

suffer from PTSD today (see *Diagnostic and Statistical Manual of Mental Disorders,* Fourth Edition, pp. 424–29).

p. 62 "The veteran's [psychological] conflicts . . .": Jeffrey A. Jay, "After Vietnam: I. In Pursuit of Scapegoats," *Harper's Magazine,* July 1978, p. 14.

p. 62 "our failure to *deal with our guilt* . . .": Ibid., p. 14.

p. 62 "Although the nation hastens on . . .": Ibid., p. 15.

p. 63 "In fact, as numerous psychological studies have shown, it is exposure to and participation in . . .": See, for example, Robert S. Laufer, Ellen Frey-Wouters, and Mark S. Gallops, "Traumatic Stressors in the Vietnam War and Post-Traumatic Stress Disorder," in Charles R. Figley, ed., *Trauma and Its Wake: The Study and Treatment of Post-Traumatic Stress Disorder,* pp. 73–89. Working with data from the 1981 Veterans Administration report by Egendorf, et al., *Legacies of Vietnam,* the authors emphasize that three experiences most frequently predict the later onset of PTSD: experiencing a threat to one's life and limb, witnessing abusive violence (such as torture or mutilation), and participating in abusive violence. They also studied how veterans' subjective reactions to their experiences have affected their recoveries. They found that "the most consistent subjective war stress predictor of post-traumatic stress symptoms and disorder is the feeling that the deaths of the Vietnamese were justified" (p. 83). Their research showed that soldiers who believed they were right in killing Vietnamese suffered higher rates of intrusive imagery, numbing, and full-blown flashbacks than those who did not. The authors point out that "The persistent relationship between this feeling of justification and the presence of symptoms suggests that avoidance or defense against the trauma of witnessing Vietnamese deaths did not serve as an effective coping strategy after leaving Vietnam" (p. 85). I would also speculate that the failures of such justifications themselves might be traumatic. That is, perhaps these veterans suffer not only from having committed acts of violence, but from their inability to give those acts meaning.

See also Ghislaine Boulanger, "Predisposition to Post-Traumatic Stress Disorder," in Ghislaine Boulanger and Charles Kadushin, eds., *The Vietnam Veteran Redefined: Fact and Fiction;* John P. Wilson, W. Ken Smith, and Suzanne K. Johnson, "A Comparative Analysis of PTSD Among Various Survivor Groups," in Figley, ed., *Trauma and Its Wake;*

William E. Kelly, *Post-Traumatic Stress Disorder and the War Veteran Patient,*
especially p. 111; Kulka, et al., *Trauma and the Vietnam War Generation.*

p. 63 "For too long, we have lived with the 'Vietnam Syndrome' . . .":
Quoted in Bonior, et al., *The Vietnam Veteran,* p. 75. Once elected,
Reagan showed very little concern for Vietnam veterans. He repeatedly
tried to cut funding for Veterans Administration counseling centers established by Congress in 1979 and allowed his Secretary of the Interior,
James Watt, to oppose the construction of the Vietnam Veterans Memorial in Washington, D.C.

pp. 63–64 "The trouble in Vietnam . . .": Louis Harris and Associates,
Myths and Realities: A Study of Attitudes Toward Vietnam Era Veterans, p.
61.

p. 64 "None of us has faced the specter . . .": Peter Marin, "Coming
to Terms with Vietnam: Settling Our Moral Debts," *Harper's Magazine,*
December 1980, p. 42.

p. 64 "It is [veterans'] voices . . .": Ibid., p. 50.

p. 64 "some of them are forced . . .": Ibid., p. 50; "for who else . . .
has it in their power . . .": Ibid., p. 55.

p. 69 "The reasons for the dramatic psychological impact . . .": Senator Alan Cranston, Foreword, in Kulka, et al., *Trauma and the Vietnam
War Generation,* p. vi.

p. 70 "so bloody, so costly . . .": Republican Party platform, quoted in
Carroll, *It Seemed Like Nothing Happened,* pp. 80–81.

CHAPTER 4
REBUILDING THE HERO: FANTASY, AGENCY,
AND THE PORNOGRAPHY OF WAR

p. 71 "his mouth and beard . . .": Red Bear, quoted in Evan S. Connell, *Custer: Son of the Morning Star,* p. 9.

p. 71 "He could give no commands . . .": Richard A. Gabriel, *The
Painful Field: The Psychiatric Dimension of Modern War,* p. 19.

p. 71 "No one knows how long . . .": Ibid.

p. 72 "He had fought in the Civil War . . .": Connell, *Custer,* p. 41.

p. 73 "In earlier, more popular wars . . .": See Susan Moeller, *Shooting War: Photography and the American Experience of Combat.*

p. 73 "Instead, they reminded them . . .": Moeller, *Shooting War,* p. 141.

p. 73 "Is this the sort . . .": Shana Alexander, "The Feminine Eye: What Is the Truth of the Picture?", *Life,* March 1, 1968, p. 9; quoted in Moeller, *Shooting War,* p. 403.

p. 73 "utter mortal fright . . .": *Life,* December 19, 1969, p. 46.

p. 73 "In June 1969 . . .": *Life,* June 27, 1969, pp. 20–32.

p. 73 "Our Nation's Roll of Honor . . .": A regular feature of *The New York Times Mid-Week Pictorial* during the war; quoted in Moeller, *Shooting War,* p. 137. "From Their Hour of Joy . . .": J. Robert Moskin, "From Their Hour of Joy . . . These Went to Duty . . . and Death," *Look,* June 3, 1952, pp. 32–33; quoted in Moeller, *Shooting War,* p. 307.

p. 74 "Three weeks later . . .": Moeller, *Shooting War,* p. 398.

p. 74 "The 'faces' show us . . .": *Life,* July 18, 1969, p. 16A.

p. 74 "I grew up on a diet . . .": Ibid.

p. 74 "Ever since the beginning . . .": Ibid.

p. 75 "When I went over there . . .": Brian Winhover, interview with the author, May 31, 1994. Subsequent quotations of Winhover's remarks in this chapter come from interviews with the author on March 22, 1994, and May 24, 1994.

p. 75 "The war works on you . . .": Larry Heinemann, *Close Quarters,* p. 111; quoted in James William Gibson, *Warrior Dreams: Paramilitary Culture in Post-Vietnam America,* p. 30.

p. 76 "Everybody was cold . . .": Robert Truxton, interview with the author, July 24, 1992.

p. 76 "They didn't touch me . . .": James Ballantine, interview with the author, March 29, 1994. Subsequent quotations of Ballantine's remarks in this chapter come from an interview with the author on March 22, 1994.

p. 76 "This is my rifle . . .": Quoted in Gibson, *The Perfect War,* p. 182. Throughout boot camp, the military worked hard to link combat-readiness to a complete, heterosexual masculinity. As Robert Lifton has pointed out, a recruit in Marine basic training was called "snuffy," "pussy," or "woman" until he graduated. The Marine Corps itself was called "the crotch," while other (and presumably, less capable) branches of the service were called "the sister services." As Lifton explains, "to graduate from contemptible unmanliness—to be confirmed as a Man-Marine sharing the power of the immortal group—one had to absorb an image of women as a lower element" (Robert Jay Lifton, *Home from the War: Vietnam Veterans, Neither Victims Nor Executioners,* pp. 242–43). Naturally, once they arrived on the battlefield, it was not hard for American troops to transform the "lower element" of the enemy into "women."

p. 76 "It was incredible . . .": Michael Herr, *Dispatches,* p. 142.

p. 76 "I started to enjoy it . . .": Quoted in Baker, *Nam,* p. 85. For other examples of this phenomenon, see MacPherson, *Long Time Passing,* p. 269, and Herbert Hendin and Ann Pollinger Haas, *Wounds of War: The Psychological Aftermath of Combat in Vietnam,* p. 137.

p. 76 "The love of war . . .": William Broyles, Jr., "Why Men Love War," *Esquire,* November 1984, p. 61.

p. 77 "I later found the dead man . . .": Ibid.

p. 77 "As anyone who has fired a bazooka . . .": Ibid.

p. 78 "such targets as would have . . .": Gravel, *The Pentagon Papers,* Vol. 3, p. 169; quoted in Young, *The Vietnam Wars,* p. 113.

p. 78 "the *will* of the DRV . . .": Ibid.

p. 78 "means that we succeed in demonstrating . . .": John McNaughton, "Memorandum for General Goodpaster," in Gravel, *The Pentagon Papers,* Vol. 4, p. 292; quoted in Gibson, *The Perfect War,* p. 97.

p. 78 "use selected and carefully graduated military force . . .": Gravel, *The Pentagon Papers,* Vol. 3, p. 169; quoted in Young, *The Vietnam Wars,* p. 113.

p. 78 "After each turn of the military thumb screw . . .": The analogy is Marilyn Young's. "However modern and reasonable it sounded," she writes, "the logic of calibrated pressure was the logic of the rack, articulated in the language of games theory and the accountant's spread sheet" (Young, *The Vietnam Wars,* p. 113).

p. 79 "the slow escalation of the air war . . .": Quoted in Young, *The Vietnam Wars,* p. 141.

p. 79 "very closely. I'm going up her leg . . .": Gravel, *The Pentagon Papers,* Vol. 3, p. 354; quoted in Young, *The Vietnam Wars,* p. 141.

p. 79 "They're just a bunch of shits . . .": Reported by Nixon and quoted in Stanley Karnow, *Vietnam: A History,* p. 652.

p. 79 "I don't want any more of this crap . . .": Quoted in Karnow, *Vietnam*, p. 652.

p. 80 "How do you take . . .": Norman Mailer, "Democracy Has/ Hasn't a Future" (a debate with Nat Hentoff, Herbert Marcuse, and Arthur Schlesinger), *The New York Times Magazine*, May 26, 1968; re-printed in William L. O'Neill, ed., *American Society Since 1945*, p. 266.

p. 80 "Women marched in support of the war . . .": For a picture of such marchers, see Karnow, *Vietnam*, p. 478.

p. 81 "The conflict between . . .": Herman, *Trauma and Recovery*, p. 1.

p. 81 "the story of the trauma . . .": Herman, *Trauma and Recovery*, p. 175. In this, as she notes, Herman is following the work of the famed French analyst Pierre Janet. Normal memory, wrote Janet in 1919, "is an action; essentially it is the action of telling a story. . . . A situation has not been satisfactorily liquidated . . . until we have achieved, not merely an outward reaction through our movements, but also an inward reaction through the words we address to ourselves, through the organi-zation of the recital of the event to others and to ourselves, and through the putting of this recital in its place as one of the chapters in our personal history. . . . Strictly speaking, then, one who retains a fixed idea of a happening cannot be said to have a 'memory' . . . it is only for convenience that we speak of it as a 'traumatic memory.' ": Pierre Janet, *Psychological Healing,* [1919] Vol. 1, trans. E. Paul and C. Paul (New York: Macmillan, 1925), pp. 661–63; quoted in Herman, *Trauma and Recovery*, p. 37.

p. 82 "recollection without affect . . .": Josef Breuer and Sigmund Freud, *Studies on Hysteria* [1893–95], in *Standard Edition of the Complete Psychological Works of Sigmund Freud*, Vol. 2, trans. J. Strachey (London: Hogarth Press, 1955), p. 6; quoted in Herman, *Trauma and Recovery*, p. 177.

p. 82 "Helplessness constitutes the essential insult . . .": Herman, *Trauma and Recovery*, p. 41.

p. 82 "Rape survivors return . . .": Ibid., pp. 39–41.

p. 82 "The revenge fantasy . . .": Ibid., p. 189.

p. 82 "in reassuring the perverse person . . .": Robert J. Stoller, *Perver-sion: The Erotic Form of Hatred,* p. 131.

p. 82 "By way of illustration . . .": Ibid., pp. 63–91.

p. 83 "On that occasion . . .": Ibid., p. 72.

p. 83 "voluptuous feeling . . .": Ibid.

p. 83 "he is fully potent . . .": Ibid.

p. 84 "In 1975, the year Saigon fell . . .": Gibson, *Warrior Dreams,* p. 142.

p. 84 "In 1974, Brown had gotten hold of . . .": Ibid., p. 144.

p. 84 "Some of the responses . . .": *Soldier of Fortune* press release, "Robert K. Brown: Editor/Publisher Biography," p. 9, 1986 *Soldier of Fortune* Convention, Las Vegas, Nevada; quoted in Gibson, *Warrior Dreams,* p. 144.

p. 84 "When it was founded . . .": Gibson, *Warrior Dreams,* pp. 144 and 148.

p. 84 "Nearly every article . . .": Ibid., p. 147.

p. 84 "gave the impression . . .": Ibid., pp. 147–48.

p. 84 "read like intelligence reports . . .": Ibid., p. 148.

p. 85 "these stories attracted such a readership . . .": Ibid., p. 7.

p. 85 "is a lady: gobble, gobble, gobble . . ." Jonathan Cain, *Cherry-Boy Body Bag,* Vol. 4 of *Saigon Commandos,* p. 76.

p. 86 "Stocker moaned with pleasure . . .": Jack Hamilton Teed, *The Killing Zone,* Vol. 1 of *Gunships,* pp. 220–21.

p. 86 "Scenes such as these proliferate . . .": Gibson found between 20 and 120 violent killings per book (Gibson, *Warrior Dreams,* p. 6).

p. 86 "With the slow-motion eye they cast . . .": And, in fact, as Gibson has pointed out, a number of pulp fiction authors cut their teeth writing sexual pornography (Gibson, *Warrior Dreams,* p. 110).

p. 86 "As Robert Stoller has pointed out, the images . . .": Stoller, *Perversion,* p. 131. See also Robert J. Stoller, *Observing the Erotic Imagination,* pp. 29–64.

p. 87 "victorious vixens . . .": *Panty Raid . . . and other stories of TRANSVESTISM & FEMALE IMPERSONATION,* quoted in Stoller, *Perversion,* p. 67.

p. 87 "a gossamer silk . . ." and "Vampire Red . . .": Ibid., p. 69.

p. 87 "he was breathless . . .": Ibid., p. 70.

p. 87 "Postwar pulp novels . . .": Gibson, *Warrior Dreams,* pp. 33–50.

p. 89 "The twenty years since the war . . .": See Gibson, *Warrior Dreams;* Susan Jeffords, *Hard Bodies: Hollywood Masculinity in the Reagan Era;* Linda Dittmar and Gene Michaud, eds., *From Hanoi to Hollywood: The Vietnam War in American Film.*

p. 92 "He can be the scarred survivor . . .": Toward the end of *Rambo: First Blood Part II,* his Russian captors tie Rambo to a metal bed frame that has been wired to an electrical generator. When they crank the generator, the Russians bear an eerie resemblance to Americans in Vietnam performing an act of torture known as "The Bell Telephone Hour." In Vietnam, Americans would wire a prisoner to a field telephone and then crank the phone as if they were making a call. Electricity would shoot through the prisoner's body at whatever intensity and for however long the Americans wanted it to. In *Rambo: First Blood Part II,* Rambo exacts a form of imaginary vengeance on behalf of the Vietnamese when he leaps up, grabs his torturer, throws him down on the bed, and cranks the electricity himself. But, of course, even as he does, he reenacts "The Bell Telephone Hour."

p. 93 "As James William Gibson and others have pointed out . . .": Gibson, *Warrior Dreams,* pp. 10–19. See also Gaylyn Studlar and David Desser, "Never Having to Say You're Sorry: Rambo's Rewriting of the Vietnam War," in Dittmar and Michaud, eds., *From Hanoi to Hollywood,* pp. 101–12.

p. 93 "The home of the brave will never fall . . .": from the song *Peace in Our Life.* Music by Frank Stallone, Peter Schless, and Jerry Goldsmith. Lyrics by Frank Stallone. Sung by Frank Stallone. Copyright Anabasis Music (BM) and Ekajo Productions, Inc., 1985.

p. 93 "Action films starring violent, overmuscled men . . .": As Susan Jeffords has pointed out in *Hard Bodies,* her study of such films, *Rambo: First Blood Part II* brought in $80 million in 1985, *RoboCop* made $23.5 million in 1987, *Lethal Weapon* grossed $29.5 million in 1987 *(Hard Bodies,* p. 197). The nine top-grossing films of the 1980s ranked as follows: *E.T. The Extra-Terrestrial* $187 million, *Return of the Jedi* $162.5 million, *Batman* $150.5 million, *Home Alone* $120 million, *Indiana Jones and the Last Crusade* $115.5 million, *Terminator 2: Judgment Day* $112 million, *Back to the Future* $96 million, *Ghost* $95 million, *Tootsie* $94.6 million, and *Raiders of the Lost Ark* $90.4 million (Jeffords, *Hard Bodies,* pp. 197–98).

p. 93 "is like an addiction . . .": Arnie Shaestack, interview with the author, June 3, 1994.

p. 94 "We're watching somebody . . .": Edward Ravitch, interview with the author, February 22, 1994. Subsequent quotations of Ravitch's remarks in this chapter come from interviews with the author on February 22, 1994, and May 31, 1994.

CHAPTER 5
EMOTIONAL RESCUE: MAKING MEANING
OF LOSS

p. 96 "I'm as in fear of my well-being now . . .": Albert Mahoney, interview with the author, April 12, 1994. Subsequent quotations of Mahoney's remarks in this chapter come from interviews with the author on February 15, 1994; April 5, 1994; and May 24, 1994.

p. 98 "As they sailed across the Atlantic . . .": That fantasy lingered for more than a century. In the late eighteenth century, the first design for the Great Seal of the United States featured an image of the Red Sea drowning the Egyptians as the Israelites stood safely by. Beneath the image came the motto: "Rebellion to Tyrants Is Obedience to God!" (Greg Sieminski, "The Puritan Captivity Narrative and the Politics of the American Revolution," *American Quarterly,* Vol. 42, No. 1 [1990], pp. 35–50; cited in Susan Jeffords, "Rape and the New World Order," *Cultural Critique* 19 [Fall 1991], p. 207).

p. 98 "a City upon a Hill . . .": John Winthrop, "A Modell of Christian Charity," a sermon delivered on board the *Arbella* in 1630, in Perry Miller and Thomas H. Johnson, eds., *The Puritans,* Vol. 1, p. 199.

p. 98 "Known as 'captivity narratives' . . .": For more on captivity narratives, see Larry Lee Carey, *A Study of the Indian Captivity Narrative as a Popular Literary Genre, Circa 1675–1875.*

p. 99 "small and brave nation . . .": Lyndon B. Johnson, "American Policy in Viet-Nam," remarks at Johns Hopkins University, Baltimore, Maryland, April 7, 1965, in Raskin and Fall, eds., *The Viet-Nam Reader,* pp. 344–45. For a more complete discussion of this point, see Slotkin, *Gunfighter Nation,* pp. 495–96.

p. 99 "simple farmers . . . are the targets . . .": Ibid.

p. 100 "In such a war, soldiers soon let go . . .": For a full discussion of this point, see Lloyd B. Lewis, *The Tainted War: Culture and Identity in Vietnam War Narratives,* pp. 109–22.

p. 100 "The hardest thing to come to grips with . . .": Baker, *Nam,* p. 260.

p. 101 "But where soldiers drew . . .": My description and interpretation of Nixon's handling of the POW issue and the public's response to it derives primarily from H. Bruce Franklin's *M.I.A., or, Mythmaking in America,* perhaps the most accurate and complete study of the Vietnam-era POW/MIA question ever written. I gratefully acknowledge my debt to Franklin's work.

p. 101 "In March 1969 . . .": See Franklin, *M.I.A.,* pp. 48–52.

p. 101 "The Communist side . . .": Editorial, "Inhuman Stance on Prisoners," *The New York Times,* May 29, 1969; quoted in Franklin, *M.I.A.,* p. 49.

p. 101 "Despite the facts . . .": Franklin, *M.I.A.,* p. 59; "the barbaric use of our prisoners . . .": Richard Nixon, "Address to the Nation on the Situation in Southeast Asia," April 7, 1971, *Public Papers of the Presidents of the United States: Richard Nixon, 1971* (Washington, D.C.: GPO, 1972), p. 524; quoted in Franklin, *M.I.A.,* p. 61. Also see Franklin, *M.I.A.,* p. 59.

p. 101 "In 1970 alone . . .": Franklin, *M.I.A.,* pp. 52 and 54.

p. 101 "One sits in the corner . . .": "Exhibit to Stir Opinion on P.O.W.'s Open in Capitol," *The New York Times,* June 5, 1970; quoted in Franklin, *M.I.A.,* p. 54.

p. 102 "In the spring of 1970 . . .": Franklin, *M.I.A.,* pp. 55–57.

p. 102 "Led by Gloria Coppin . . .": Ibid., p. 55.

p. 102 "By midsummer 1972, VIVA was selling . . .": Ibid., pp. 56–57.

p. 102 "the objects of a virtual cult . . .": Jonathan Schell, *The Time of Illusion,* p. 231.

p. 102 "America's vision of the war was being transformed . . .": Franklin, *M.I.A.,* p. 54.

p. 103 "The U.S. military's planning . . .": "A Celebration of Men Redeemed," *Time,* February 19, 1973, p. 13.

p. 103 "Crowds swarmed the runways . . .": See "An Emotional, Exuberant Welcome Home," *Time,* February 26, 1973, pp. 12–17.

p. 103 "For the U.S., the war in Viet Nam . . .": "A Celebration of Men Redeemed," p. 13.

p. 104 "I came back with a lot of guilt . . .": Brian Winhover, interview with the author, May 10, 1994. All subsequent quotations of

Winhover's remarks in this chapter come from interviews with the author on March 29, 1994.

p. 104 "There's endless variation . . .": James Munroe, interview with the author, July 31, 1992. All subsequent quotations of Munroe's remarks come from interviews with the author on the same date and on February 25, 1994, and March 4, 1994.

p. 106 "takes you away . . .": Bob Fox, interview with the author, April 12, 1994.

p. 106 "The savior of the underdog . . .": James Ballantine, interview with the author, March 29, 1994.

p. 106 "the revenge fantasy is often a mirror image . . .": Herman, *Trauma and Recovery,* p. 189.

p. 107 "alienated from the centers of power . . .": Louis Harris, *Inside America,* p. 32. Throughout the final years of the war, Harris chronicled the decline in Americans' sense of individual political efficacy. In the years below, between 1966 and 1985, the following percentages of Americans said they felt "alienated from the centers of power":

      1966 = 29 percent
      1969 = 36 percent
      1971 = 40 percent
      1972 = 44 percent
      1976 = 62 percent (all-time high)
      1983 = 62 percent (all-time high)
      1984 = 55 percent
      1985 = 54 percent

(Harris, *Inside America,* p. 32).

p. 107 "what I think doesn't count much anymore . . .": Ibid., p. 35.

p. 107 "left out of the things going on around me . . .": Ibid., p. 36. The actual figure is 48 percent. Harris notes that blacks, the elderly, women, and the poor expressed particularly high levels of alienation.

p. 107 "On November 4, 1979 . . .": Over the next months, the Iranians released a number of those hostages, leaving a total of 52 in captivity for the duration of the crisis.

p. 108 "A once dominant military machine . . .": "Debacle in the Desert," *Time,* May 5, 1980, p. 12.

p. 108 "this latest debacle became another symbol . . .": Haynes John-son, *Sleepwalking Through History: America in the Reagan Years,* p. 36.

p. 108 "to fear that the future [was] over . . .": Roger Rosenblatt, "Out of the Past, Fresh Choices for the Future," *Time,* January 5, 1981, p. 18.

p. 109 "Out of the Past . . .": Ibid., p. 11.

p. 109 "At 6 ft. 1 in., 185 lbs. . . .": Ibid., p. 13.

p. 109 "What we can see in Reagan . . .": Ibid., p. 18.

p. 109 "You and I live in a real world . . .": Ronald Reagan, "We Need a Rebirth in Leadership," nomination acceptance speech at the Republican National Convention, July 17, 1980, in Reagan, *A Time for Choosing: The Speeches of Ronald Reagan 1961–1982,* p. 229.

p. 109 "island of freedom . . .": Ibid., p. 234.

p. 110 "totalitarian forces . . . who seek subversion . . .": Ronald Reagan, "A Crusade for Freedom," speech to the British Parliament, June 8, 1982, in Reagan, *A Time for Choosing,* p. 327.

p. 110 "commit our resources . . .": Ronald Reagan, speaking at a memorial at Camp Lejeune, North Carolina, for 230 servicemen killed in Lebanon; quoted in *Time,* November 14, 1983, p. 20.

p. 110 "In 1982, two out of three people . . .": 1982 figures on El Salvador: ABC/*Washington Post* poll, March 1982; cited in William M. LeoGrande, *Central America and the Polls,* p. 15. 1983 figures on Nicara-gua: ABC/*Washington Post* poll, November 1983; cited in LeoGrande, *Central America and the Polls,* p. 16.

p. 110 "Throughout the Reagan years, the great majority . . .": Ac-cording to pollster Louis Harris *(Inside America,* p. 318), Americans op-posed aid to the Nicaraguan Contras by the following percentages:

    1983 = 66 percent to 23 percent
    1984 = 68 percent to 25 percent
    1985 = 73 percent to 23 percent
    1986 = 60 percent to 30 percent

William LeoGrande has chronicled similar opposition to American poli-cies in El Salvador. "Even though the public generally has accepted the Administration's view that U.S. security interests are endangered by events in the region, and that Cuba and the Soviet Union are engaged in

subversion there," wrote LeoGrande in 1984, "it has continued to oppose virtually every element of Reagan's policy. Substantial majorities
have been against increases in economic aid, military aid, the deployment of U.S. military advisors [in El Salvador], [and] the prospect of
using U.S. troops [in El Salvador]" (LeoGrande, *Central America and the
Polls,* p. 2).

According to Harris *(Inside America,* p. 318), Americans disapproved
of Reagan's "handling of the situation in Central America" by the following percentages:

1983 = 59 percent to 34 percent
1984 = 65 percent to 30 percent
1985 = 63 percent to 32 percent
1986 = 64 percent to 29 percent

p. 110 "Many, if not most, did so because they feared . . .": Throughout the early 1980s, polls suggested that large majorities of the American
public feared that the conflict in El Salvador could become "another
Vietnam" (LeoGrande, *Central America and the Polls,* pp. 16–18). In June
1983, a Gallup poll found that "People who feared another Vietnam
disapproved of Reagan's handling of the central American crisis by a
wide margin (60 percent disapproval, 20 percent approval), whereas people who thought another Vietnam unlikely, generally approved of Reagan's handling of the situation (49 percent approval, 26 percent disapproval)" (LeoGrande, *Central America and the Polls,* p. 18).
p. 111 "was a Soviet–Cuban colony . . .": Ronald Reagan, in a speech
to the nation, October 26, 1983; quoted in Kai P. Schoenhals and Richard A. Melanson, *Revolution and Intervention in Grenada,* p. 151.
p. 111 "spread the virus . . .": Ronald Reagan, remarks in Barbados,
April 8, 1982; quoted in Schoenhals and Melanson, *Revolution and Intervention in Grenada,* p. 133.
p. 111 "rescue mission . . .": Ronald Reagan, during a news conference October 25, 1983; quoted in Schoenhals and Melanson, *Revolution
and Intervention in Grenada,* p. 147.
p. 111 "Grenada's . . . people were helpless . . .": Quoted in
Schoenhals and Melanson, *Revolution and Intervention in Grenada,* p. 149.

p. 111 "Under Bishop, the school's students had long enjoyed . . .": Schoenhals and Melanson, *Revolution and Intervention in Grenada,* p. 80.

p. 111 "personal safety . . .": Quoted in Schoenhals and Melanson, *Revolution and Intervention in Grenada,* p. 85.

p. 111 "Eighty-seven people were dead . . .": U.S. Department of State and U.S. Department of Defense, *Grenada: A Preliminary Report,* p. 1.

p. 111 "We have heard the terms . . .": *Congressional Record,* October 28, 1983 (S14870); quoted in Schoenhals and Melanson, *Revolution and Intervention in Grenada,* p. 155.

p. 112 "Grenada by itself . . .": Norman Podhoretz, "Proper Uses of Power," *The New York Times,* October 30, 1983, p. E19. Support for the invasion was not an exclusively right-wing phenomenon. Even "Liberals Should Be Cheering U.S. Action in Grenada," wrote centrist columnist Morton Kondracke, since the invasion would "warn the Soviets, Cubans, Sandinistas, and other aggressive leftists that the United States has overcome its Vietnam-bred reluctance to use military power to defend its interests and values" *(Chicago Sun-Times,* October 30, 1983; quoted in Schoenhals and Melanson, *Revolution and Intervention in Grenada,* p. 162).

p. 113 "Slapstick, tongue-in-cheek . . .": For a chilling description of real A Team behavior, see Polner, *No Victory Parades,* p. 113.

p. 115 "On the contrary, in the wake of Operation Homecoming . . .": In 1976, for instance, the CIA reported that even though rumors had alleged that some Americans continued to be held after Operation Homecoming, "none could be equated to Americans who had not been accounted for" (quoted in Franklin, *M.I.A.,* p. 114). That same year, a House Select Committee reported that "no Americans are still being held alive as prisoners in Indochina, or elsewhere, as a result of the war" (quoted in Franklin, *M.I.A.,* p. 130).

p. 115 "Henry Kissinger and Richard Nixon, they claimed . . .": Susan Katz Keating, *Prisoners of Hope,* pp. 87–88. This explanation resurfaced in *Rambo: First Blood Part II* when Colonel Trautman told Rambo, "In '72, we were supposed to pay the Cong four and a half billion dollars in war reparations. We reneged. They kept the POWs."

While Nixon had promised (and failed to deliver) war reparations to the Vietnamese, the Vietnamese did not withhold any POWs. They instead offered a consistent and full accounting of the prisoners they had held. It was the American government that obfuscated the issue. During the Nixon Administration, the Departments of State and Defense held the Vietnamese responsible not only for known prisoners of war, but for *all* Americans missing in action—including many that the American government knew had died in combat. In 1973, the Pentagon compounded the confusion by adding to the list of Americans "unaccounted for" it had given the North Vietnamese the names of 1,114 men that it knew had been killed in battle, but whose bodies had not been recovered (Franklin, *M.I.A.*, pp. 97–98; for an exhaustive study of the evidence that Vietnam did not withhold American POWs, see Franklin, *M.I.A.*, Chapters 2, 3, and 4).

p. 115 "The press reported that at war's end . . .": In 1981, *Parade* magazine, perhaps the most widely read Sunday newspaper insert in America, claimed that "When the war ended . . . an additional 113 men, also known to have been held captive in Laos and Vietnam, were not released during 'Operation Homecoming.' " That same year the conservative *The National Review* suggested that more than 1,250 men "were either known or strongly suspected to be prisoners of the Vietnamese or Laotians." A book written for junior and senior high school students claimed that it was "possible 644 men are still alive" and in captivity (Franklin, *M.I.A.*, p. 96).

p. 115 "Responding to public interest in the issue . . .": Franklin, *M.I.A.*, p. 140.

p. 116 "That's my new war . . .": Roger Hulbein, interview with the author, June 15, 1992. All subsequent quotations of Hulbein's remarks in this chapter come from this interview.

p. 117 "vestiges of men . . .": J. C. Pollock, *Mission M.I.A.*, p. 2; "arms and hands . . .": Ibid., p. 25.

p. 117 "Help him, sweet Jesus . . .": Ibid., p. 25.

p. 118 "In August 1991, despite nearly twenty years . . .": Franklin, *M.I.A.*, p. xi.

p. 119 "In the years before Iraq invaded Kuwait . . .": John Mueller, *Policy and Opinion in the Gulf War*, pp. 49–51.

p. 119 "since World War II . . .": Quoted in Mueller, *Policy and Opinion in the Gulf War*, p. 38.

p. 119 "to protect our oil supplies . . .": Mueller, *Policy and Opinion in the Gulf War,* pp. 244–45.

p. 119 "One week later, a similar march . . .": Ibid., p. 59.

p. 119 "While the world waited . . .": George Bush, "The Battle Has Been Joined," speech to the nation, January 16, 1991, in H. M. Amery and W. A. Madhoun, eds., *Shaping the Gulf: In Search of Order, Readings and Documents on the Iraq–Kuwait Crisis,* p. 354.

p. 119 "small and helpless nation . . .": Ibid., p. 353.

p. 119 "We must act so that innocent men and women . . .": Remarks to the Senate Foreign Relations Committee, December 5, 1990, in U.S. Department of State dispatch, December 10, 1990, p. 309.

p. 120 "I have told the American people before . . .": Amery and Madhoun, eds., *Shaping the Gulf,* p. 355.

p. 121 "According to the Defense Intelligence Agency . . .": "How Many Iraqi Soldiers Died?", *Time,* June 17, 1991, p. 26.

p. 121 "I am sure that many of you saw . . .": Speech to a joint session of Congress, March 6, 1991, in Amery and Madhoun, eds., *Shaping the Gulf,* p. 497.

p. 122 "we have finally kicked the Vietnam syndrome . . .": Quoted in Michelle Kendrick, "Kicking the V. Syndrome: CNN's and CBS's Video Narratives of the Persian Gulf War," in Susan Jeffords and Lauren Rabinovitz, eds., *Seeing Through the Media: The Persian Gulf War,* p. 74.

p. 122 "Less than a year and a half later . . .": Mueller, *Policy and Opinion in the Gulf War,* p. 91.

p. 122 "the letdown is the killer . . .": James Ballantine, interview with the author, March 29, 1994.

CHAPTER 6

IN FROM THE JUNGLE: RESTORING
COMMUNITY IN THE WAKE OF MORAL
TRESPASS

p. 123 "In December 1970, in the first of what would soon become hundreds . . .": Arthur Egendorf, "Vietnam Veteran Rap Groups and

Themes of Postwar Life," *Journal of Social Issues,* Vol. 31, No. 4, 1975, p. 111.

p. 124 "professionals [at the meetings] had no special podium . . .": Robert Jay Lifton, "Advocacy and Corruption in the Healing Profession," in Figley, ed., *Stress Disorders Among Vietnam Veterans,* p. 213.

p. 124 "The process . . . feels to us like reverse basic training . . .": Egendorf, "Vietnam Veteran Rap Groups and Themes of Postwar Life," p. 120.

p. 124 "We see ourselves as members . . .": Ibid., p. 114.

p. 126 "Ours is an assembly of shock . . .": Abraham J. Heschel, "The Moral Outrage of Vietnam," in Robert McAfee Brown, Abraham J. Heschel, and Michael Novak, *Vietnam: Crisis of Conscience,* p. 48.

p. 126 "I am personally involved in the torment . . .": Ibid., p. 57.

p. 126 "The groan deepens . . .": Ibid., p. 55.

p. 127 "The world . . . just exploded . . .": Brian Winhover, interview with the author, July 24, 1992. All subsequent quotations of Winhover's remarks in this chapter come from interviews with the author on May 10, 1994, and June 7, 1994.

p. 127 "I raped a girl one time . . .": Quoted in Frey-Wouters and Laufer, *Legacy of a War,* p. 198.

p. 127 "In a Harris poll taken in January 1966 . . .": Louis Harris, *The Anguish of Change,* p. 59.

p. 127 "PILOT: Our five-hundred-pound nape canisters . . ." to "PILOT: What's so bad about nape anyway?": Fred Branfman, "The Era of the Blue Machine," *The Washington Monthly,* July 1971, p. 11; quoted in Lifton, *Home from the War,* p. 359.

p. 128 "Today . . . machines and technology are permitting economy of manpower . . .": General William Westmoreland, speech, date unknown; quoted in Lifton, *Home from the War,* p. 359.

p. 129 "We have smashed the country . . .": Telford Taylor, *Nuremberg and Vietnam: An American Tragedy,* Bantam Books edition, p. 207. All subsequent citations refer to this edition.

p. 129 "Unlike the Germans and Japanese . . .": Veterans themselves constituted the group that most vocally sought such an accounting. Soon after the public revelation of the My Lai massacre, hundreds of veterans came forward to confess that they had committed war crimes. In February 1971, more than 100 veterans met in Detroit, under the auspices of the Vietnam Veterans Against the War (VVAW), to describe their roles in the war. Called the Winter Soldier Investigation, the meetings resembled trials in which the defendants accused themselves of war crimes: One after another, veterans took to the stage and confessed to acts of atrocious, often berserk, violence. At the time, though, they received relatively little publicity. Later that year, as part of the VVAW-sponsored protest Operation Dewey Canyon III, some 50 veterans marched to the Pentagon to turn themselves in as war criminals. The Pentagon turned them away.

Some might argue that the Watergate hearings constituted such a reckoning. While the American Senate did put a President many suspected of war crimes effectively on trial, the Senators charged him only with political—and not military—crimes. When President Ford pardoned Nixon, of course, even those charges ceased to carry any legal weight. By the end of his life, many Americans seemed to have forgotten why they reviled Nixon in the first place and to consider him simply an oddly retiring senior statesman.

p. 130 "a war that is finished . . .": Gerald Ford, "Excerpts from Ford Address at Tulane," *The New York Times,* April 24, 1975; quoted in Ehrenhaus, "Commemorating the Unwon War," p. 102.

p. 130 "In 1975, two months after the fall of Saigon, a Roper opinion poll . . .": Cited in Patrick Hagopian, *The Social Memory of the Vietnam War,* p. 87.

p. 130 "Two years later, a Gallup poll . . .": The precise figure is 72 percent. Ibid.

p. 130 "From that time to the present . . .": See Hagopian, *The Social Memory of the Vietnam War,* p. 87, for a list of polls on this question and their results.

p. 130 "Driven temporarily insane . . .": For a catalog of the causes of berserking, see Shay, *Achilles in Vietnam,* p. 80. See also B. W. Gault, "Some Remarks on Slaughter," *American Journal of Psychiatry,* Vol. 128, 1971, pp. 450–54.

p. 130 "feels like a god . . .": Shay, *Achilles in Vietnam,* p. 84.

p. 130 "All of our virtues . . .": Ibid., p. 86.

p. 130 "I became a fucking animal . . .": Quoted ibid., p. 83.

p. 130 "After firefights, when soldiers sat weeping . . .": Ibid., p. 81.

p. 131 "There is no authority anymore . . .": James Munroe, interview with the author, May 27, 1994.

p. 131 "a counterfeit universe . . .": Lifton, *Home from the War,* p. 167.

p. 131 "Although they come in many shapes and sizes . . .": For a discussion of some of the different types of group therapy employed with Vietnam veterans, see John Russell Smith, "Rap Groups and Group Therapy for Vietnam Veterans," in Stephen M. Sonnenberg, Arthur S. Blank, Jr., and John A. Talbot, eds., *The Trauma of War: Stress and Recovery in Vietnam Veterans.* For a more general discussion of the role of group therapy in the treatment of psychological trauma, see Herman, *Trauma and Recovery,* and Irvin D. Yalom, *The Theory and Practice of Group Psychotherapy.*

p. 131 "These guys perfectly understood . . .": Ken Smith, quoted in Herman, *Trauma and Recovery,* p. 215.

p. 131 "Whenever you tried to be human . . .": Quoted in Lifton, *Home from the War,* p. 268.

p. 132 "the cure for a life diminished . . .": Arthur Egendorf, *Healing from the War: Trauma and Transformation After Vietnam,* p. 108.

p. 133 "Generic Vietnam War Narrative . . .": C. D. B. Bryan, "Barely Suppressed Screams: Getting a Bead on Vietnam War Literature," *Harper's Magazine,* June 1984, p. 68.

p. 133 "charts the gradual deterioration . . .": Ibid., p. 69.

p. 134 "vital, confident . . .": Ibid.

p. 134 "replace a kid . . .": Ibid.

p. 134 "In conventional postwar Vietnam narratives . . .": See Susan Jeffords, *The Remasculinization of America: Gender and the Vietnam War,* pp. 56–59.

p. 134 "most of them came from the ragged fringes . . .": Caputo, *A Rumor of War,* p. 27.

p. 135 "like a frag bomb . . .": Richard Corliss, *"Platoon:* Viet Nam, the Way It Really Was, on Film," *Time,* January 26, 1987, p. 55.

p. 135 "More than any other film . . .": Ibid., p. 56.

p. 135 "one of the great war movies of all time . . .": David Halberstam, quoted in Corliss, *"Platoon,"* p. 57.

p. 136 "They come from the end of the line . . .": I've transcribed this monologue from the film. For a slightly different version, see Oliver Stone, Platoon *and* Salvador: *The Original Screenplays,* p. 32.

p. 136 "we were a nation split . . .": Corliss, *"Platoon,"* p. 55.

p. 137 "[The] only thing that can kill Barnes is Barnes . . .": The soldier's remarks echo Richard Nixon's famous words from his "silent majority" speech of November 3, 1969: "North Vietnam cannot defeat or humiliate the United States. Only Americans can do that." Quoted in Young, *The Vietnam Wars,* p. 242.

p. 138 "You have to fight evil . . .": Oliver Stone, quoted in Corliss, *"Platoon,"* p. 59.

p. 138 "Chris came out of the war stained and soiled . . .": Ibid.

p. 140 "they have faced down their most painful recollections of the war, reassured themselves of the solidity of community and goodness, and turned toward the future . . .": The popularity of that message was such that when *Platoon* was released on home video, Chrysler Motors placed an advertisement at the front of each tape. In it, Chrysler chairman Lee Iococca approached a Jeep in a field of high grass and declaimed:

> This Jeep is a museum piece, a relic of war. Normandy, Anzio, Guadalcanal, Korea, Vietnam. I hope we will never have to build another Jeep for war. This film, *Platoon,* is a memorial. Not to war, but to all the men and women who fought in a time and place nobody really understood, who knew only one thing—they were called—they went. It was the same from the first musket fired at Concord to the rice paddies of the Mekong Delta—they were called and they went. That in the truest sense is the spirit of America. The more we understand it, the more we honor those who kept it alive. I'm Lee Iococca.

Of course, Iococca's remarks not only advertise Chrysler automobiles, but help weld the Vietnam War to the larger body of American myth. Like the generic continuities of *Platoon,* they suggest that even in a war most Americans consider to have been immoral, certain honorable American principles had survived untainted.

p. 141 "I saw you last night . . .": From the *China Beach* episode "Vets," broadcast March 16, 1989.

p. 142 "We all risk being seduced . . .": Egendorf, "Vietnam Veteran Rap Groups and Themes of Postwar Life," p. 124.

CHAPTER 7

LOST FATHERS: REPAIRING THE BETRAYAL OF
YOUNG MEN

p. 143 "It was like all the movies . . .": Ron Kovic, *Born on the Fourth of July*, p. 74.

p. 144 "He'd never figured . . .": Ibid., p. 192.

p. 144 "All I could feel . . .": Ibid., p. 222.

p. 145 "One after another, these men had departed the domestic regions . . .": See James Hellman, *American Myth and the Legacy of Vietnam*, p. 161.

p. 145 "I told my father I was thinking of going to Canada . . .": Quoted in MacPherson, *Long Time Passing*, p. 36.

p. 145 "Most [soldiers] believed their national leaders . . .": Charles R. Anderson, *The Grunts*, p. 232.

p. 145 "From the first settlers in New England . . .": Slotkin, *Gunfighter Nation*, p. 12.

p. 146 "When young men went to Vietnam . . .": For more on this point, see Hellman, *American Myth and the Legacy of Vietnam*, pp. 112–13 and 117. See also Appy, *Working-Class War*, p. 281.

p. 146 "is, for men, at some terrible level . . .": Broyles, "Why Men Love War," p. 61.

p. 146 "the frontier beyond the last settlement . . .": Ibid., p. 58.

p. 146 "Even as they gained the adult male's 'power of life and death' . . .": For more on this point, see Hellman, *American Myth and the Legacy of Vietnam*, p. 161.

p. 146 "If you need forty acres for an airstrip . . .": John Durant, quoted in Polner, *No Victory Parades*, p. 52.

p. 147 "No matter how many patrols . . .": Anderson, *The Grunts*, p. 232.

p. 147 "As they watched their twin struggles . . .": Hellman, *American Myth and the Legacy of Vietnam*, p. 110.

p. 147 "one of those bullying Redcoats . . .": Caputo, *A Rumor of War,* p. 83; quoted in Hellman, *American Myth and the Legacy of Vietnam,* p. 110.

p. 147 "conscripted Nazi . . .": Tim O'Brien, *If I Die in a Combat Zone, Box Me Up and Ship Me Home,* p. 97; quoted in Hellman, *American Myth and the Legacy of Vietnam,* p. 110.

p. 147 "probably the most moral effort . . .": James Webb, quoted in MacPherson, *Long Time Passing,* p. 537.

p. 148 "It was the endurance that was important . . .": James Webb, *Fields of Fire,* p. 28.

p. 148 "The boys from Chelsea . . .": James Fallows, "What Did You Do in the Class War, Daddy?" *The Washington Monthly,* October 1975, p. 7.

p. 148 "It had clearly never occurred to them . . .": Ibid., p. 7.

p. 148 "[W]e happy few . . .": Ibid., p. 9.

p. 149 "never involved substantial risk . . .": Ibid., p. 12.

p. 149 "I didn't just screw Ho Chi Minh . . .": Lyndon Johnson, quoted in Barbara Ehrenreich, *The Hearts of Men,* p. 106.

p. 149 "completely castrated . . .": Ron Ridenhour, quoted in Hersh, *My Lai 4,* p. 105.

p. 149 "Some masculine demiurge . . .": Ehrenreich, *The Hearts of Men,* p. 106.

p. 149 "intellectual blindness and emotional rigidity . . .": DeMott, *Surviving the 70's,* pp. 27–28.

p. 149 "Pop psychologists soon picked up the left-wing critique . . .": For a detailed chronicle of this process, see Ehrenreich, *The Hearts of Men,* Chapter 8, "The Androgynous Drift," and Chapter 9, "The Male Revolt Redeemed."

p. 149 "He has armor-plating . . .": Marc Feigen Fasteau, *The Male Machine* (New York: McGraw-Hill International Book Co., 1974), p. 1; quoted in Ehrenreich, *The Hearts of Men,* p. 123.

p. 150 "For the past thirty years, six-foot-four John Wayne . . .": Tim LaHaye, *Understanding the Male Temperament* (Charlotte, North Carolina: Commission Press, 1977), p. 11; quoted in Ehrenreich, *The Hearts of Men,* p. 164.

p. 150 "My father became an embarrassment to me . . .": Wright, *In the New World,* p. 121.

p. 150 "saw the [antiwar] protests on the news . . .": Ibid., pp. 121–22.
p. 151 "I didn't suffer . . .": Christopher Buckley, "Viet Guilt," *Esquire,* September 1983, p. 72.
p. 151 "a spiritual sinew . . .": Ibid.
p. 152 "After finding the aunt and uncle with whom he grew up killed and their house burned to the ground, Luke begins . . .": Luke's transition also borrows from the experiences of the Viet Cong. In Vietnam, it was American Zippo squads who burned villages to the ground. It was Vietnamese boys who found their parents' corpses and became rebels against a heavily armed imperial force.
p. 153 "an image of the dark past of Europe . . .": Hellman, *American Myth and the Legacy of Vietnam,* p. 170.
p. 154 "The themes of paternal rescue and redemption . . .": For a more thorough discussion of fathers and sons in the films of this period, see Jeffords, *Hard Bodies,* Chapter 8, "Fathers and Sons: Continuity and Revolution in the Reagan Years."
p. 154 "In *Terminator 2: Judgment Day* (1991), the Terminator . . . has been reprogrammed . . .": An interesting Oedipal variation on the more common rescue theme involves sons who kill their out-of-control fathers and absorb their spirits into themselves. In *Apocalypse Now* (1979), Captain Willard confronts a berserk father figure in Colonel Kurtz. Rather than take him away and ferry him downstream (as the hero of Conrad's *Heart of Darkness* does to the character on whom Colonel Kurtz is based), Willard kills him. When he stands at the head of the stairs of Kurtz's temple, Willard has become Kurtz: Covered in blood, carrying Kurtz's memoirs, he watches Kurtz's tribe bow down before him. But where Kurtz turned his power to violence, Willard chooses to head for home. By killing Kurtz, Willard has accepted his barbarity as part of his own character. By choosing not to pursue that barbarity, he has acknowledged, in a way that few could during the actual Vietnam War, that cruelty and gentleness can coexist in the same person. Seven years later, of course, Chris Taylor made a similar acknowledgment at the end of *Platoon* (1986).
p. 155 "lacking confidence in the government . . .": Gibson, *Warrior Dreams,* p. 11.
p. 155 "Modeled on capture-the-flag . . .": Ibid., p. 8.
p. 155 "There will be no machine guns . . .": Lionel Atwill, *The New,*

Official Survival Game Manual (New London, New Hampshire: The National Survival Game, Inc., 1987), p. 155; quoted in Gibson, *Warrior Dreams*, pp. 126–27.

p. 155 "In the Mojave Desert, a Los Angeles policeman . . .": Gibson, *Warrior Dreams*, p. 127.

p. 155 "In order to make play more realistic . . .": Ibid., p. 133.

p. 155 "The basic idea . . . is to look military . . .": Frank Hughes, "Picking Your Paintball Persona," *Action Pursuit Games*, April 1988, pp. 27 and 72; quoted in Gibson, *Warrior Dreams*, pp. 128–29.

p. 156 "maybe 5 percent of the players had seen action . . .": Gibson, *Warrior Dreams*, p. 136.

p. 156 "people who wanted to be in a war . . .": Ibid., p. 136.

p. 156 "I would have loved fighting in Vietnam . . .": Ibid., p. 165.

p. 156 "In 1988, one survey revealed . . .": James William Gibson, interview with Russell Maynard, publisher and editor of *Action Pursuit Games*, Burbank, California, August 17, 1988; cited in Gibson, *Warrior Dreams*, p. 135.

p. 156 "Over two million men had fought . . .": Ibid.

p. 156 "Like those who play paintball . . .": According to Gibson, as many as half the average of 1,000 men whom he saw at the conventions he attended in the mid-1980s had served in the military or were active duty soldiers. Almost all were white males between the ages of twenty and fifty (a span which includes the Vietnam generation), but few had fought in Southeast Asia (Gibson, *Warrior Dreams*, p. 149).

p. 157 "from any legal responsibility . . .": Ibid., p. 149.

p. 157 "Even time itself had been changed . . .": Ibid., p. 149.

p. 157 "blessed with a special aura . . .": Ibid., p. 153.

p. 157 "established national and international reputations . . .": Ibid., p. 170.

p. 157 "Gibson chose to attend . . .": Ibid., p. 186.

p. 157 "narrow, craggy ravines . . .": Ibid., p. 184.

p. 157 "Gunsite was taking men through an initiation . . .": Ibid., pp. 186–87.

p. 158 "I was hungry for the unseen . . .": Ibid., p. 188.

p. 158 "My mind and body worked together . . .": Ibid., p. 189.

p. 158 "When men lose their confidence . . .": Robert Bly, "The Vietnam War and the Erosion of Male Confidence," originally given as a talk at the "Understanding Vietnam" symposium in Salado, Texas, 1982; published in Reese Williams, ed., *Unwinding the Vietnam War: From War into Peace,* p. 167.

p. 159 "the attacks launched against men . . .": Ibid., p. 162.

p. 159 "The waste and anguish . . .": Robert Bly, quoted in Keith Thompson, "What Men Really Want: An Interview with Robert Bly," in Franklin Abbot, ed., *New Men, New Minds,* p. 166.

p. 159 "Here we have a finely tuned young man . . .": Ibid., p. 167.

p. 159 "Through initiation rites of their own devising . . .": The mythopoetic men's movement was not by any means the first men's movement, although it has certainly become the most visible. Since the early 1970s and the rise of feminism, men had been meeting in groups to contend with their changing social roles. Some supported a feminist agenda, while others took an explicitly antifeminist stance. Some hoped to reform divorce laws they thought discriminated against men or help men recover from alcohol and drug addiction. Where these earlier groups tended to focus on specific political issues, however, the mythopoetic men's movement focused from the start on remolding its members' inner masculine selves. Since the early 1980s, the mythopoetic stream of the men's movement has garnered the lion's share of media and popular attention. For a brief history of the men's movement, see Lorraine H. Bray, *A Preliminary Exploration of the Men's Movement: Demographics and Motivating Factors.* See also "What's All This About a Men's Movement?", in Christopher Harding, ed., *Wingspan: Inside the Men's Movement,* pp. xi–xix.

p. 160 "The Wild Man is not a Warrior gone berserk . . .": Christopher Burant, "Of Wild Men and Warriors," originally published in the periodical *Changing Men* (date unknown); reprinted in Harding, ed., *Wingspan,* p. 175.

p. 160 "It is vital to remember . . .": Asa Baber, "Call of the Wild," originally published in *Playboy* (date unknown); reprinted in Harding, ed., *Wingspan,* p. 9.

p. 161 "In 1984, Michael Schiffman found . . .": See Michael Schiffman, "The Men's Movement: An Exploratory Empirical Investigation," in Michael S. Kimmel, *Changing Men: New Directions in Research on Men and Masculinity,* pp. 295–314.

p. 161 "In 1992, Lorraine H. Bray studied . . .": Bray, *A Preliminary Exploration of the Men's Movement.*

p. 162 "The fires of war are ritual fires . . .": Michael J. Meade, *Men and the Water of Life,* p. 206. During the war, Meade allowed himself to be inducted, but thereafter, because of his opposition to the Vietnam War, refused to follow orders and was imprisoned.

p. 162 "deep masculine . . .": Shepherd Bliss, "What Happens at a Mythopoetic Men's Weekend?", in Harding, ed., *Wingspan,* p. 95.

p. 162 "restore the male community . . .": Ibid., p. 95.

p. 162 "When the men arrive for the weekend . . .": Ibid., p. 96.

p. 162 "The leaders [of the weekends] come well prepared . . .": Ibid., p. 98.

p. 163 "We want the men to leave solar consciousness . . .": Ibid., p. 99.

p. 163 "We stimulate the men . . .": Ibid., p. 97.

p. 163 "the masculinity we affirm . . .": Ibid., p. 95.

p. 163 "The new hero must reclaim . . .": Sam Keen, *Fire in the Belly: On Being a Man,* p. 166.

p. 164 "A warrior . . . knows the *real* war . . .": Robert Moore and Douglas Gillette, *The Warrior Within: Accessing the Knight in the Male Psyche,* p. 98.

p. 164 "the picture of the world's greatest superpower . . .": Robert McNamara, quoted in Theodore Draper, "McNamara's Peace," *The New York Review of Books,* May 11, 1995, p. 10.

p. 164 "We were wrong, terribly wrong . . .": Robert McNamara with Brian VanDeMark, *In Retrospect: The Tragedy and Lessons of Vietnam;* excerpted in *Newsweek,* April 17, 1995, p. 45.

p. 165 "Redemption. Apology. That's not the important issue . . .": Robert McNamara, on the talk show *The Connection,* hosted by Christopher Lydon on WBUR, Boston, April 27, 1995.

p. 165 "a man so contorted . . .": David Halberstam, in a review of McNamara's *In Retrospect* published in *The Los Angeles Times* and quoted in Sidney Blumenthal, "McNamara's Peace," in *The New Yorker,* May 8, 1995, p. 66.

p. 166 "I am a member of a generation of men . . .": George Taylor, "The Longing for the Great Father," in Harding, ed., *Wingspan,* p. 15.

CHAPTER 8

HEALING AS HISTORY: THE VIETNAM VETERANS
MEMORIAL

p. 167 "There was nothing left of him . . .": Brian Winhover, interview with the author, July 24, 1992. All subsequent quotations of
Winhover's remarks in this chapter come from this interview.

p. 168 "We wanted to deal with the wall . . .": Kurt Ocher, interview
with the author, July 24, 1992. All subsequent quotations of Ocher's
remarks in this chapter come from this interview.

p. 169 "going to the wall becomes a metaphor . . .": Terence Keane,
interview with the author, June 2, 1992. All subsequent quotations of
Keane's remarks in this chapter come from this interview.

p. 169 "trauma is absorbed by a community . . .": James Munroe, interview with the author, June 8, 1992. All subsequent quotations of
Munroe's remarks in this chapter come from this interview.

p. 169 "They moved me . . .": Edward Ravitch, interview with the
author, July 24, 1992. All subsequent quotations of Ravitch's remarks in
this chapter come from interviews with the author on this date and on
March 22, 1994.

p. 172 "That night, Scruggs couldn't sleep . . .": Jan C. Scruggs and
Joel L. Swerdlow, *To Heal a Nation: The Vietnam Veterans Memorial,* p. 7.

p. 172 "In his memory, he isn't even armed . . .": Scruggs served in
Vietnam from 1969 to 1970. John Wheeler, a West Point graduate and
logistics officer during the war who went on to help Scruggs run the
Vietnam Veterans Memorial Fund, writes in his memoir, *Touched with
Fire:* "[Scruggs] walked his share of hours as point man on patrols." The
point is important because Scruggs's story has taken on the status of a
founding myth. Unlike the private recollections of other veterans,
Scruggs's tale is a profoundly public act. One has to wonder whether
Scruggs simply "forgot" to include the more aggressive elements of his
duty or whether those details were somehow publicly unacceptable,
somehow unspeakable, in 1985.

p. 174 "In *The Deer Hunter*'s final scene . . .": As they mourn, they sing *America the Beautiful*. Some might see this song as ironic, a caustic reminder that during Vietnam it wasn't America but its soldiers who were "beautiful." To me it suggests that by remembering their dead friend, these veterans and civilians are able to restore and retain their patriotism.

p. 174 "They never discussed their personal views . . .": Scruggs and Swerdlow, *To Heal a Nation,* p. 12.

p. 174 "Vietnam veterans could be honored . . .": Ibid., p. 17.

p. 175 "the old and powerful antiwar movement . . .": Ibid., p. 13.

p. 175 "I would have given you money . . .": Ibid., p. 24. Scruggs and Swerdlow also write that in 1979 an article in *Parade* magazine mentioned the Fund and gave its address for donations. One contributor wrote: "We hope that this memorial will stand to honor our veterans, but also will stand as a warning for those old men who even now are trying to drag us into another useless war" (p. 22; the "useless war" probably refers to the civil war in El Salvador). Yet another explained that "those who chose to disgrace their national heritage and now take pride in 'having ended the war in Vietnam' already have their monument—the bodies of the men, women, and children now resting in the bottom of the South China Sea" (p. 22; the writer is referring to the thousands of "boat people" then setting sail from Vietnam and seeking refuge in Hong Kong, Thailand, and elsewhere).

p. 175 "thoroughly and ritually bitten . . .": Sue Mansfield, *The Gestalts of War: An Inquiry into Its Origins and Meanings as a Social Institution,* p. 31.

p. 175 "The women would then welcome them home . . .": Mansfield, *The Gestalts of War,* p. 32.

p. 176 "Those who were killed and those who returned . . .": Ehrenhaus, "Commemorating the Unwon War," p. 100. Ehrenhaus quotes Martha Banta, *Failure and Success in America* (Princeton, New Jersey: Princeton University Press, 1978), p. 304.

p. 177 "The [wall] was built as a very psychological memorial . . .": Maya Lin, quoted in Scruggs and Swerdlow, *To Heal a Nation,* p. 147.

p. 177 "had an impulse to cut open the earth . . .": Maya Ying Lin, quoted in Michael Norman, Introduction, in Sal Lopes, *The Wall: Images and Offerings from the Vietnam Veterans Memorial,* p. 16.

p. 177 "I wanted to return the vets . . .": Maya Ying Lin, quoted in

Elizabeth Hess, "A Tale of Two Memorials," *Art in America* (April 1983), p. 122.

p. 177 "I didn't want a static object . . .": Maya Ying Lin, quoted in Michael Norman, Introduction, in Lopes, *The Wall,* p. 16.

p. 178 "The Memorial says exactly what . . .": Scruggs and Swerdlow, *To Heal a Nation,* p. 69.

p. 178 "The memorial will occupy a permanence . . .": James Webb, quoted in Scruggs and Swerdlow, *To Heal a Nation,* p. 94.

p. 178 "black gash of shame and sorrow . . .": Tom Carhart, quoted in Christopher Buckley, "The Wall," *Esquire* (September 1985), p. 66. Buckley's article is the most in-depth account to date of the struggle to redesign the Memorial.

p. 178 "In a city of soaring white monuments . . .": Tom Carhart, quoted in Buckley, "The Wall," p. 66.

p. 178 "In a funny sense . . .": Maya Ying Lin, quoted in Scruggs and Swerdlow, *To Heal a Nation,* p. 133. The statue of the three soldiers was not the last addition to the Memorial. In 1993, the Vietnam Women's Memorial Project, headed by Diane Carlson Evans, succeeded in placing a highly realistic Vietnam Women's Memorial on the grounds of the Vietnam Veterans Memorial. Set some distance away from the three infantrymen, up on a small hill directly across from the center of the wall and surrounded by a stand of maples, the Women's Memorial depicts three nurses in fatigues, clustered around a pile of sandbags. One cradles a wounded GI, while another scans the sky (presumably for a dust-off helicopter), and a third sits nearby. In keeping with the therapeutic spirit of Maya Lin's design, Evans and the Women's Memorial Project hope to ease the psychological stress of women who served in Vietnam. As a pamphlet put out by the project explains, "many of these women are not aware of the value of their contributions or their right to heal their own emotional wounds. The Vietnam Women's Memorial Project is search-ing for these women. To bring them together. To help them heal. To depict accurately this page of our history." Yet, like the inscription around Webb and Carhart's flagpole, the Women's Memorial's imagery of rescue suggests that the Vietnam War was, in fact, a noble enterprise. As the bronze nurse holds her American soldier, she offers a visual meta-phor through which visitors can understand that in Vietnam *all* Ameri-cans were engaged in a mission to save those who could not save themselves (e.g., the South Vietnamese). Moreover, the monument's terrific realism reinforces its historical message. The accuracy with which the sculptress, Glenna Goodacre, has captured the details of the women's uniforms and hairstyles suggests that the monument accurately depicts not only women in combat, but the entire Vietnam "page of our history." With little subtlety, the monument hints that like our nurses, we too "are not aware" of the value of our contributions and our "right to heal" our emotional wounds.

p. 181 "They were simply taken away . . .": In this the Vietnam Veterans Memorial is very different from the capital's monuments to other veterans. The Marine Corps Memorial, for instance, was erected after World War II. Modeled on the famous photograph of the flag-raising on Iwo Jima, it shows muscular soldiers leaning hard together to raise a flag on top of Mount Surabachi. The Seabees Monument, another Second World War memorial, offers friezes of even more muscular combat engineers building bridges under a hail of bullets. In front of the reliefs, a hulking, bare-chested American grunt holds the hand of a small boy who, in turn, gazes up reverently into the soldier's face. At both the Marine Corps Memorial and the Seabees Monument, a visitor can feel a sense of pride and can learn that in World War II, Americans cooperated, created, aided the weak, and that by shouldering the war together, they raised the Stars and Stripes of American glory high above foreign lands. The big-chested vigor of the men on the Marine Corps Memorial or the Seabees Monument reminds a viewer that America actively—vigorously—waged the Second World War. Looking at the names on the wall, on the other hand, a visitor might think that the Vietnam War was a plague that befell Americans against their wills.

At the same time, the passive quality of the names on the wall is what gives them much of their healing power. The muscular creatures depicted on the Marine Corps Memorial and the Seabees Monument are stereotypes. Their rigid machismo leaves a visitor little room to recall the complex men whose service they commemorate. The names on the wall, on the other hand, are so unadorned that whatever life they have has to come from the visitor. They are so cold that few visitors can help but warm them, whether, like veterans, with their memories or, like those who never saw combat, with their imaginations of lives lost.

p. 181 "In walking down to the center of the wall . . .": Regardless of the direction from which they enter the Memorial, many visitors have such a strong impression that they are walking through a model of the war that they later believe that the center panels they saw listed the names of men killed at the height of the fighting and not, as they actually did, those killed in the war's first and last days.

p. 182 "Between November 10 and 14 . . . .": Scruggs and Swerdlow say there were 150,000 there (p. 146). My account of the weekend derives largely from their work.

p. 182 "I'D DO IT AGAIN . . . .": Scruggs and Swerdlow, *To Heal a Nation,* p. 150.

p. 182 "WE KILLED, WE BLED . . . .": Ibid., p. 150.

p. 182 "I could almost hear the chains . . . .": Ibid., p. 151.

p. 182 "How do you explain the feelings . . . .": Ibid., p. 151.

p. 182 "Never mind the often-discussed public policy . . . .": Editorial, *Patriot Ledger,* quoted in Scruggs and Swerdlow, *To Heal a Nation,* pp. 154–55.

p. 183 "How odd it feels . . . .": Bobbie Ann Mason, *In Country,* p. 351. This and the next citation refer to the 1989 Perennial Library edition.

p. 183 "In the heartland of a nation . . . .": Mason, *In Country,* front jacket copy.

p. 183 "This special section is a two-part celebration . . . .": "Heroes, Past and Present," *Newsweek,* July 6, 1987, p. 54.

p. 183 "We can see our sons and daughters . . . .": Ibid., p. 52.

p. 184 "The people celebrated here . . . .": Ibid., p. 61.

CHAPTER 9

SCAR TISSUE: NARRATIVE FRAGMENTATION
AND THE MEMORY OF TRAUMA

p. 186 "How can you forgive . . . .": Varnado Simpson, quoted in Bilton and Sim, *Four Hours in My Lai,* p. 378.

p. 187 "The volume of suffering . . . is so massive . . . .": Kurt Ocher, interview with the author, July 24, 1992. All subsequent quotations of Ocher's remarks in this chapter come from this interview.

p. 189 "powerful nations may stumble . . .": From a letter to Bill McCloud, quoted in Bill McCloud, *What Should We Tell Our Children About Vietnam?,* p. 87.

p. 191 "The South Vietnamese ally was caught up . . .": From a letter to Bill McCloud reprinted in McCloud, *What Should We Tell Our Children About Vietnam?,* p. 17.

p. 191 "was not a 'civil war' . . .": From a letter to Bill McCloud reprinted in McCloud, *What Should We Tell Our Children About Vietnam?,* p. 75.

p. 191 "When the time for elections came . . .": See Young, *The Vietnam Wars,* pp. 37–59.

p. 192 "What most of us can't deal with . . .": W. D. Erhart, "Preserving American Myth," *Intervention,* Vol. 1, No. 1, Spring 1984; quoted in Kalí Jo Tal, *Bearing Witness: The Literature of Trauma,* p. 116.

p. 192 "Back in 1969 . . . the wreckage was all around us . . .": Tim O'Brien, "The Vietnam in Me," *The New York Times Magazine,* October 2, 1994, p. 53.

p. 193 "the reconstruction of a viable, nonthreatening assumptive world . . .": Ronnie Janoff-Bulman, *Shattered Assumptions: Towards a New Psychology of Trauma,* p. 69.

p. 194 "Psychologists have long known . . .": Ibid., pp. 29–30 and 34.

p. 194 "Those who had been told she was a waitress . . .": C. E. Cohen, "Person Categories and Social Perception: Testing Some Boundaries of the Processing Effects of Prior Knowledge," *Journal of Personality and Social Psychology,* Vol. 40, pp. 441–52, cited in Janoff-Bulman, *Shattered Assumptions,* p. 30.

p. 194 "As a number of psychologists have pointed out, our core beliefs . . .": For a brief summary of recent psychological research on the roles of psychological schemas in information processing, see Janoff-Bulman, *Shattered Assumptions,* Chapter 2, "Cognitive Conservatism and Resistance to Change," pp. 26–45.

p. 194 "In that sense, by forcing his perceptions of his career . . .": A. T. Beck, *Depression: Clinical, Experimental, and Theoretical Aspects* (New York: Harper & Row, 1967), p. 287; quoted in Janoff-Bulman, *Shattered Assumptions,* p. 32.

BIBLIOGRAPHY

Abbot, Franklin, ed. *New Men, New Minds*. Freedom, California: The Crossing Press, 1987.

Adair, Gilbert. *Vietnam on Film: From* The Green Berets *to* Apocalypse Now. New York and London: Proteus Books, 1981.

American Psychiatric Association. *Diagnostic and Statistical Manual of Mental Disorders*, Third Edition. Washington, D.C.: American Psychiatric Association, 1980.

————. *Diagnostic and Statistical Manual of Mental Disorders*, Third Edition—Revised. Washington, D.C.: American Psychiatric Association, 1987.

————. *Diagnostic and Statistical Manual of Mental Disorders*, Fourth Edition. Washington, D.C.: American Psychiatric Association, 1994.

Amery, H. M., and W. A. Madhoun, eds. *Shaping the Gulf: In Search of Order, Readings and Documents on the Iraq–Kuwait Crisis*. London, Canada: Canadian Institute for Policy Research and Analysis, 1992.

Améry, Jean. *At the Mind's Limits*. Trans. Sidney and Stella P. Rosenfeld. Bloomington, Indiana: Indiana University Press, 1980; rpt. New York: Schocken Books, 1986.

Anderegg, Michael, ed. *Inventing Vietnam: The War in Film and Television*. Philadelphia: Temple University Press, 1991.

Anderson, Charles R. *The Grunts*. Novato, California: Presidio Press, 1976; rpt. New York: Berkley Books, 1984.

Anson, Robert Sam. *War News: A Young Reporter in Indochina*. New York: Simon and Schuster, 1989.

Appy, Christian G. *Working-Class War: American Combat Soldiers and Vietnam*. Chapel Hill, North Carolina: University of North Carolina Press, 1993.

Arlen, Michael J. *Living-Room War*. New York: Viking Press, 1966.

————. *The View from Highway 1*. New York: Farrar, Straus, and Giroux, 1976.

Baker, Mark. *Nam: The Vietnam War in the Words of the Men and Women Who Fought There*. New York: William Morrow & Co., 1981.

Baritz, Loren. *Backfire: A History of How American Culture Led Us into Vietnam and Made Us Fight the Way We Did*. New York: William Morrow & Co., 1985.

Basinger, Jeanine. *The World War II Combat Film: Anatomy of a Genre*. New York: Columbia University Press, 1986.

Baskir, Lawrence M., and William A. Strauss. *Chance and Circumstance: The Draft, the War, and the Vietnam Generation*. New York: Vintage Books, 1978.

Bettelheim, Bruno. *The Informed Heart: The Human Condition in Mass Society*. New York: The Free Press, 1960; rpt. London: Thames & Hudson, Ltd., 1961, and London: Paladin, 1970.

————. *Surviving and Other Essays*. New York: Vintage Books, 1980.

Bilton, Michael, and Kevin Sim. *Four Hours in My Lai*. New York: Viking Penguin, 1992.

Bly, Robert. *Iron John: A Book About Men*. Reading, Massachusetts: Addison-Wesley Publishing Co., 1990.

Boesel, David, and Peter H. Rossi, eds. *Cities Under Siege: An Anatomy of the Ghetto Riots, 1964–1968*. New York: Basic Books, 1971.

Bonior, David E., Steven M. Champlin, and Timothy S. Kolly. *The Vietnam Veteran: A History of Neglect*. New York: Praeger, 1984.

Bonner, Raymond. *Weakness and Deceit: U.S. Policy and El Salvador*. New York: Times Books, 1984.

Boulanger, Ghislaine, and Charles Kadushin, eds. *The Vietnam Veteran Redefined: Fact and Fiction*. Hillsdale, New Jersey, and London: Lawrence Erlbaum Associates, 1986.

Braestrup, Peter. *Big Story: How the American Press and Television Reported and Interpreted the Crisis of Tet 1968 in Vietnam and Washington,*

Abridged Edition. New Haven, Connecticut, and London: Yale University Press, 1983.

Bray, Lorraine H. *A Preliminary Exploration of the Men's Movement: Demographics and Motivating Factors.* Master's Thesis. Edmonton, Canada: University of Alberta, 1992.

Brown, Robert McAfee, Abraham J. Heschel, and Michael Novak. *Vietnam: Crisis of Conscience.* New York: Association Press, Behrman House, and Herder and Herder, 1967.

Bryan, C. D. B. *Friendly Fire.* New York: G. P. Putnam's Sons, 1976; rpt. New York: Bantam Books, 1977.

Buchanan, Jack. *M.I.A. Hunter.* New York: Berkley Books, 1985.

Buckley, Kevin. *Panama: The Whole Story.* New York: Simon and Schuster, 1991.

Cain, Jonathan. *Boonie-Rat Body Burning,* Vol. 5 of *Saigon Commandos.* New York: Zebra Books, Kensington Publishing Corp., 1981.

————. *Cherry-Boy Body Bag,* Vol. 4 of *Saigon Commandos.* New York: Zebra Books, Kensington Publishing Corp., 1981.

Camp, Norman M., Robert H. Stretch, and William C. Marshall. *Stress, Strain, and Vietnam: An Annotated Bibliography of Two Decades of Psychiatric and Social Sciences Literature Reflecting the Effect of the War on the American Soldier.* New York and London: Greenwood Press, 1988.

Cannon, Lou. *Reagan.* New York: G. P. Putnam's Sons, 1982.

Capps, Walter H. *The Unfinished War: Vietnam and the American Conscience,* Second Edition. Boston: Beacon Press, 1983.

————, ed. *A Vietnam Reader.* New York: Routledge, 1991.

Caputo, Philip. *A Rumor of War.* New York: Ballantine Books, 1977.

Carey, Larry Lee. *A Study of the Indian Captivity Narrative as a Popular Literary Genre, Circa 1675–1875.* Doctoral Dissertation. East Lansing, Michigan: Michigan State University, 1978.

Carroll, Peter N. *It Seemed Like Nothing Happened.* New York: Holt, Rinehart and Winston, 1982.

Chandler, Robert. *Public Opinion.* New York: R. R. Bowker Company, 1972.

Cincinnatus. *Self-Destruction: The Disintegration and Decay of the United States Army During the Vietnam Era.* New York: W. W. Norton & Co., 1981.

Clancy, Tom. *Without Remorse*. New York: G. P. Putnam's Sons, 1993.

Connell, Evan S. *Custer: Son of the Morning Star*. New York: Harper & Row, 1984.

Conrad, Joseph. *The Heart of Darkness*. Edinburgh: W. Blackwood, 1899.

Corbit, Irene Elizabeth. *Veterans' Nightmares: Trauma, Treatment, Truce*. Doctoral Dissertation. Houston, Texas: Union Graduate School, 1985.

Corson, William R. *The Betrayal*. New York: W. W. Norton & Co., 1968.

DeBenedetti, Charles, and Charles Chatfield. *An American Ordeal: The Antiwar Movement of the Vietnam Era*. Syracuse, New York: Syracuse University Press, 1990.

DeForest, Orrin, and David Chanoff. *Slow Burn: The Rise and Bitter Fall of American Intelligence in Vietnam*. New York: Simon and Schuster, 1990.

Del Vecchio, John M. *The 13th Valley*. New York: Bantam Books, 1982.

DeMott, Benjamin. *Supergrow: Essays and Reports on Imagination in America*. New York: E. P. Dutton & Co., 1969.

————. *Surviving the 70's*. New York: E. P. Dutton & Co., 1971.

Des Pres, Terrence. *The Survivor: An Anatomy of Life in the Death Camps*. New York and Oxford: Oxford University Press, 1976.

————. *Writing into the World: Essays 1973–1987*. New York: Viking Penguin, 1991.

Dittmar, Linda, and Gene Michaud, eds. *From Hanoi to Hollywood: The Vietnam War in American Film*. New Brunswick, New Jersey, and London: Rutgers University Press, 1990.

Doherty, Thomas. *Projections of War: Hollywood, American Culture, and World War II*. New York: Columbia University Press, 1993.

Donovan, Robert J., and Ray Scherer. *Unsilent Revolution: Television News and American Public Life, 1948–1991*. New York and Cambridge, England: Cambridge University Press, 1992.

Downs, Frederick, Jr. *Aftermath*. New York: W. W. Norton & Co., 1984; rpt. Berkley Books, 1985.

————. *The Killing Zone*. New York: W. W. Norton & Co., 1978.

Edelman, Bernard, ed. *Dear America: Letters Home from Vietnam*. New York: Pocket Books, 1986.

Effros, William G., comp., *Quotations Vietnam: 1945–1970*. New York: Random House, 1970.

Egendorf, Arthur. *Healing from the War: Trauma and Transformation After Vietnam*. Boston: Houghton Mifflin, 1985.

—————, Charles Kadushin, Robert S. Laufer, George Rothbart, and Lee Sloan. *Legacies of Vietnam: Comparative Adjustment of Veterans and Their Peers*. Washington, D.C.: Government Printing Office, 1981.

Ehrenreich, Barbara. *The Hearts of Men*. New York: Anchor Press, 1983.

Eksteins, Modris. *Rites of Spring: The Great War and the Birth of the Modern Age*. Toronto, Canada: Lester & Orpen Dennys, Ltd., 1990.

Emerson, Gloria. *Winners and Losers: Battles, Retreats, Gains, Losses, and Ruins from the Vietnam War*. New York: Random House, 1976; rpt. New York: Viking Penguin, 1985.

Engelhardt, Tom. *The End of Victory Culture: Cold War America and the Disillusioning of a Generation*. New York: Basic Books, 1995.

Erikson, Kai. *Everything in Its Path: Destruction of Community in the Buffalo Creek Flood*. New York: Simon and Schuster, 1976.

—————. *A New Species of Trouble: Explorations in Disaster, Trauma, and Community*. New York: W. W. Norton & Co., 1994.

Falk, Richard A., Gabriel Kolko, and Robert Jay Lifton, eds. *Crimes of War: A Legal, Political-Documentary, and Psychological Inquiry into the Responsibility of Leaders, Citizens, and Soldiers for Criminal Acts in War*. New York: Random House, 1971.

Farber, David. *Chicago '68*. Chicago and London: University of Chicago Press, 1988.

Figley, Charles R. *Helping Traumatized Families*. San Francisco: Jossey-Bass Publishers, 1989.

—————. *Stress Disorders Among Vietnam Veterans: Theory, Research and Treatment*. New York: Brunner/Mazel. 1978.

—————. *Trauma and Its Wake: The Study and Treatment of Post-Traumatic Stress Disorder*. New York: Brunner/Mazel, 1985.

—————. *Trauma and Its Wake: Volume II, Traumatic Stress Theory, Research and Intervention*. New York: Brunner/Mazel, 1986.

—————, ed. *Compassion Fatigue: Coping with Secondary Traumatic Stress Disorder in Those Who Treat the Traumatized*. New York: Brunner/Mazel, 1995.

———— and Seymour Leventman, eds. *Strangers at Home: Vietnam Veterans Since the War*. New York: Praeger, 1980.

Fitzgerald, Frances. *Fire in the Lake: The Vietnamese and the Americans in Vietnam*. New York: Random House, 1972.

Foner, Philip S., ed. *The Black Panthers Speak*. Philadelphia: J. B. Lippincott Company, 1970.

Ford, Gerald R. *A Time to Heal: The Autobiography of Gerald R. Ford*. New York: Harper & Row and the Reader's Digest Association, Inc.

Franklin, H. Bruce. *M.I.A., or, Mythmaking in America*. Brooklyn, New York: Lawrence Hill Books, 1992.

Frey-Wouters, Ellen, and Robert S. Laufer. *Legacy of a War: The American Soldier in Vietnam*. Armonk, New York: M. E. Sharpe, Inc., 1986.

Fussell, Paul. *The Great War and Modern Memory*. New York and Oxford: Oxford University Press, 1976.

Gabriel, Richard A. *The Painful Field: The Psychiatric Dimension of Modern War*. New York and London: Greenwood Press, 1988.

Gallup, George H. *The Gallup Poll: Public Opinion 1935–1971*. New York: Random House, 1972.

Gibson, James William. *The Perfect War*. Boston: Atlantic Monthly Press, 1986; rpt. New York: Vintage Books, 1988.

————. *Warrior Dreams: Paramilitary Culture in Post-Vietnam America*. New York: Hill and Wang, 1994.

Gilbert, Marc Jason, ed. *The Vietnam War: Teaching Approaches and Resources*. New York and London: Greenwood Press, 1991.

Gilman, Owen W., Jr., and Lorrie Smith, eds. *America Rediscovered: Critical Essays on Literature and Film of the Vietnam War*. New York and London: Garland Publishing, 1990.

Gitlin, Todd. *Inside Prime Time*. New York: Pantheon Books, 1983.

————. *The Sixties: Years of Hope, Days of Rage*. New York: Bantam Books, 1989.

Glasser, Ronald J. *365 Days*. New York: George Braziller, 1971.

Goldman, Peter, and Tony Fuller. *Charlie Company: What Vietnam Did to Us*. New York: William Morrow & Co., 1983.

Gordon, William A. *The Fourth of May: Killings and Coverups at Kent State*. Buffalo, New York: Prometheus Books, 1990.

Gravel, Mike. *The Pentagon Papers: The Defense Department History of United States Decisionmaking on Vietnam.* 5 Vols. Boston: Beacon Press, 1971.

Gray, J. Glenn. *The Warriors.* New York: Harcourt Brace Jovanovich, 1959; rpt. New York: Harper & Row, 1970.

Gray, John S. *Custer's Last Campaign: Mitch Boyer and the Little Bighorn Reconstructed.* Lincoln, Nebraska, and London: University of Nebraska Press, 1991.

Greene, Bob. *Homecoming: When the Soldiers Returned from Vietnam.* New York: Ballantine Books, 1990.

Greene, Graham. *The Quiet American.* London: W. Heinemann, 1955.

Griffen, William L., and John Marciano. *Lessons of the Vietnam War: A Critical Examination of School Texts and an Interpretive Comparative History Utilizing* The Pentagon Papers *and Other Documents.* Originally published as *Teaching the Vietnam War.* New York: Allanheld, Osmun & Co., 1979; rpt. Totowa, New Jersey: Rowman and Allanheld (date unknown).

Griffin, Susan. *A Chorus of Stones: The Private Life of War.* New York: Doubleday, 1992.

Gruner, Elliott. *Prisoners of Culture: Representing the Vietnam POW.* New Brunswick, New Jersey, and London: Rutgers University Press, 1993.

Gutman, Roy. *Banana Diplomacy: The Making of American Policy in Nicaragua 1981–1987.* New York: Simon and Schuster, 1988.

Hagopian, Patrick. *The Social Memory of the Vietnam War.* Doctoral Dissertation. Baltimore, Maryland: Johns Hopkins University, 1994; Ann Arbor, Michigan: University Microfilms International, 1994.

Hallin, Daniel C. *The "Uncensored War": The Media and Vietnam.* New York and Oxford: Oxford University Press, 1986.

Hamilton–Merritt, Jane. *Tragic Mountains: The Hmong, the Americans, and the Secret Wars for Laos, 1942–1992.* Bloomington and Indianapolis, Indiana: Indiana University Press, 1992.

Hansen, J. T., A. Susan Owen, and Michael Patrick Madden. *Parallels: The Soldiers' Knowledge and the Oral History of Contemporary Warfare.* New York: Aldine de Gruyter, 1992.

Harding, Christopher, ed. *Wingspan: Inside the Men's Movement.* New York: St. Martin's Press, 1992.

Harris, Louis. *The Anguish of Change*. New York: W. W. Norton & Co., 1973.

―――. *Inside America*. New York: Vintage Books, 1987.

――― and Associates. *Myths and Realities: A Study of Attitudes Toward Vietnam Era Veterans*. Washington, D.C.: U.S. Government Printing Office, 1980.

Heinemann, Larry. *Close Quarters*. New York: Farrar, Straus, Giroux, 1977.

―――. *Paco's Story*. New York: Farrar, Straus, Giroux, 1979.

Hellman, John. *American Myth and the Legacy of Vietnam*. New York: Columbia University Press, 1986.

Helmer, John. *Bringing the War Home: The American Soldier in Vietnam and After*. New York: The Free Press, 1974.

Hendin, Herbert, and Ann Pollinger Haas. *Wounds of War: The Psychological Aftermath of Combat in Vietnam*. New York: Basic Books, 1984.

Herman, Judith Lewis. *Trauma and Recovery*. New York: Basic Books, 1992.

Herr, Michael. *Dispatches*. New York: Alfred A. Knopf, 1977.

Hersh, Seymour M. *My Lai 4: A Report on the Massacre and Its Aftermath*. New York: Random House, 1970.

Hild, Jack. *River of Flesh,* Vol. 7 of *SOBs*. Toronto and New York: Worldwide Library, 1985.

Horne, A. D., ed. *The Wounded Generation: America After Vietnam*. Englewood Cliffs, New Jersey: Prentice-Hall, Inc., 1981.

Horowitz, Mardi J. *Stress Response Syndromes*. New York: Aronson, 1976.

Janoff-Bulman, Ronnie. *Shattered Assumptions: Towards a New Psychology of Trauma*. New York: The Free Press, 1992.

Jason, Philip K., ed. *Fourteen Landing Zones: Approaches to Vietnam War Literature*. Iowa City, Iowa: University of Iowa Press, 1991.

Jaspers, Karl. *The Question of German Guilt*. New York: Dial Press, 1947; rpt. New York: Capricorn Books, 1961.

Jeffords, Susan. *Hard Bodies: Hollywood Masculinity in the Reagan Era*. New Brunswick, New Jersey, and London: Rutgers University Press, 1994.

―――. *The Remasculinization of America: Gender and the Vietnam War*. Bloomington and Indianapolis, Indiana: Indiana University Press, 1989.

————— and Lauren Rabinovitz, eds. *Seeing Through the Media: The Persian Gulf War*. New Brunswick, New Jersey, and London: Rutgers University Press, 1994.

Johnson, Haynes. *Sleepwalking Through History: America in the Reagan Years*. New York: W. W. Norton & Co., 1991; rpt. New York: Anchor Books, 1992.

Karnow, Stanley. *Vietnam: A History*. New York: Viking Penguin, 1983.

Keating, Susan Katz. *Prisoners of Hope: Exploiting the POW/MIA Myth in America*. New York: Random House, 1994.

Keen, Sam. *Fire in the Belly: On Being a Man*. New York: Bantam Books, 1991.

Kelly, William E. *Post-Traumatic Stress Disorder and the War Veteran Patient*. New York: Brunner/Mazel, 1985.

Kerner, Otto, Chairman. National Advisory Commission on Civil Disorders. *Report*. New York: Bantam Books, 1968.

Kerry, John, and Vietnam Veterans Against the War. *The New Soldier*. New York: Macmillan, 1971.

Ketwig, John. . . . *And A Hard Rain Fell*. New York: Macmillan, 1985.

Kimmel, Michael S., ed. *Changing Men: New Directions in Research on Men and Masculinity*. Newbury Park, California: Sage Publications, 1987.

Knappman, Edward W., Evan Drossman, and Robert Newman, eds. *Campaign '72: Press Opinion from New Hampshire to November*. New York: Facts on File, 1973.

Knoll, Erwin, and Judith Nies McFadden, eds. *War Crimes and the American Conscience*. New York: Holt, Rinehart and Winston, 1970.

Kornbluh, Peter. *Nicaragua: The Price of Intervention*. Washington, D.C.: Institute for Policy Studies, 1987.

Kovic, Ron. *Born on the Fourth of July*. New York: McGraw-Hill, 1976; rpt. New York, Pocket Books, 1977.

Krepinevich, Andrew F., Jr. *The Army and Vietnam*. Baltimore and London: Johns Hopkins University Press, 1986.

Kulka, Richard A., William E. Schlenger, John A. Fairbank, Richard L. Hough, B. Kathleen Jordan, Charles R. Marmar, and Daniel S. Weiss. *National Vietnam Veterans Readjustment Study: Tables of Findings and Technical Appendices*. New York: Brunner/Mazel, 1990.

—————. *Trauma and the Vietnam War Generation: Report of Findings from the National Vietnam Veterans Readjustment Study.* New York: Brunner/Mazel, 1990.

Lane, Mark. *Conversations with Americans.* New York: Simon and Schuster, 1970.

Lang, Daniel. *Casualties of War.* New York: McGraw-Hill, 1969.

Langer, Lawrence L. *Holocaust Testimonies: The Ruins of Memory.* New Haven, Connecticut, and London: Yale University Press, 1991.

Lansing, John. *Mau Len Death Zone,* Vol. 17 of *The Black Eagles.* New York: Zebra Books, Kensington Publishing Corp., 1988.

Lasch, Christopher. *The Culture of Narcissism: American Life in an Age of Diminishing Expectations.* New York: W. W. Norton & Co., 1978.

————. *The Minimal Self: Psychic Survival in Troubled Times.* New York: W. W. Norton & Co., 1984.

LeoGrande, William M. *Central America and the Polls.* Washington, D.C.: Washington Office on Latin America, 1984.

Lewis, Lloyd B. *The Tainted War: Culture and Identity in Vietnam War Narratives.* Westport, Connecticut, and London: Greenwood Press, 1985.

Lifton, Robert Jay. *Home from the War: Vietnam Veterans, Neither Victims Nor Executioners.* New York: Simon and Schuster, 1973.

————. *The Nazi Doctors: Medical Killing and the Psychology of Genocide.* New York: Basic Books, 1986.

Lippard, Lucy R. *A Different War: Vietnam in Art.* Seattle, Washington: The Real Comet Press, 1990.

Lopes, Sal. *The Wall: Images and Offerings from the Vietnam Veterans Memorial.* New York: Collins Publishers, 1987.

Louvre, Alf, and Jeffrey Walsh. *Tell Me Lies About Vietnam: Cultural Battles for the Meaning of the War.* Philadelphia: Open University Press, 1988.

Luttwak, Edward. *The Pentagon and the Art of War: The Question of Military Reform.* New York: Simon and Schuster, 1985.

MacPherson, Myra. *Long Time Passing: Vietnam and the Haunted Generation.* Garden City, New York: Doubleday, 1984.

Mahedy, William P. *Out of the Night: The Spiritual Journey of Vietnam Vets.* New York: Ballantine Books, 1986.

Malo, Jean-Jacques, and Tony Williams, eds. *Vietnam War Films: Over 600 Feature, Made-for-TV, Pilot, and Short Movies, 1939–1992, from* the United States, Vietnam, France, Belgium, Australia, Hong Kong, South Africa, Great Britain, and Other Countries. Jefferson, North Carolina, and London: McFarland & Company, Inc., 1994.

Mansfield, Sue. *The Gestalts of War: An Inquiry into Its Origins and Meanings as a Social Institution.* New York: Dial Press, 1982.

Marill, Alvin H. *Movies Made for Television: The Telefeature and the Mini-Series, 1964–1979.* Westport, Connecticut: Arlington House Publishers, 1980.

Marshall, Kathryn, ed. *In the Combat Zone: An Oral History of American Women in Vietnam.* Boston: Little, Brown and Company, 1987.

Mason, Bobbie Ann. *In Country.* New York: Harper & Row, 1985; rpt. New York: Perennial Library, 1986 and 1989.

Mason, Patience H. C. *Recovering from the War: A Woman's Guide to Helping Your Vietnam Vet, Your Family, and Yourself.* New York: Viking Penguin, 1990.

Mason, Robert. *Chickenhawk.* New York: Viking Penguin, 1984.

———. *Chickenhawk: Back in the World.* New York: Viking Penguin, 1993.

Maurer, Harry. *Strange Ground: Americans in Vietnam, 1945–1975, An Oral History.* New York: Henry Holt and Co., 1989.

May, Someth. *Cambodian Witness.* New York: Random House, 1986.

McCloud, Bill. *What Should We Tell Our Children About Vietnam?* Norman, Oklahoma, and London: University of Oklahoma Press, 1989.

McCullin, Don. *Unreasonable Behaviour: An Autobiography.* New York: Alfred A. Knopf, 1992.

McNamara, Robert, with Brian VanDeMark. *In Retrospect: The Tragedy and Lessons of Vietnam.* New York: Times Books, 1995.

McQuay, Mike. *The M.I.A. Ransom.* New York: Bantam Books, 1986.

Mead, Walter Russell. *Mortal Splendor: The American Empire in Transition.* Boston: Houghton Mifflin, 1987.

Meade, Michael J. *Men and the Water of Life.* San Francisco: HarperSanFrancisco, 1993.

Merritt, William E. *Where the Rivers Ran Backward.* Athens, Georgia, and London: University of Georgia Press, 1989.

Miller, Perry, and Thomas H. Johnson, eds. *The Puritans.* American Book Company, 1938; rpt. New York: Harper & Row, 1963.

Moeller, Susan D. *Shooting War: Photography and the American Experience of Combat.* New York: Basic Books, 1989.

Moore, Robert, and Douglas Gillette. *The Warrior Within: Accessing the Knight in the Male Psyche.* New York: William Morrow & Co., 1992.

Morgan, Edward P. *The Sixties Experience: Hard Lessons About Modern America.* Philadelphia: Temple University Press, 1991.

Morris, Richard, and Peter Ehrenhaus, eds. *Cultural Legacies of Vietnam: Uses of the Past in the Present.* Norwood, New Jersey: Ablex Publishing Corporation, 1990.

Mosse, George L. *Fallen Soldiers: Reshaping the Memory of the World Wars.* New York and Oxford: Oxford University Press, 1990.

Mueller, John. *Policy and Opinion in the Gulf War.* Chicago and London: University of Chicago Press, 1994.

Myers, Thomas. *Walking Point: American Narratives of Vietnam.* New York and Oxford: Oxford University Press, 1988.

Norman, Michael. *These Good Men.* New York: Crown Publishers, 1989.

Oberdorfer, Don. *TET!* Garden City, New York: Doubleday, 1978.

O'Brien, Tim. *Going After Cacciato.* New York: Delacorte Press/Seymour Lawrence, 1978.

———. *If I Die in a Combat Zone Box Me Up and Ship Me Home.* New York: Delacorte Press/Seymour Lawrence, 1973.

———. *In the Lake of the Woods.* New York: Houghton Mifflin/Seymour Lawrence, 1994.

———. *The Things They Carried.* New York: Houghton Mifflin/Seymour Lawrence, 1990; rpt. New York: Viking Penguin, 1991.

Olson, James S., ed. *Dictionary of the Vietnam War.* New York: Peter Bedrick Books, 1990.

———. *The Vietnam War: Handbook of the Literature and Research.* Westport, Connecticut, and London: Greenwood Press, 1993.

O'Neill, Eugene. *Complete Plays, 1913–1920.* New York: The Library of America, 1988.

O'Neill, William L., ed. *American Society Since 1945.* Chicago: Quadrangle Books, 1969.

Page, Tim. *Page After Page.* New York: Atheneum, 1989.

Palmer, Laura. *Shrapnel in the Heart: Letters and Remembrances from the*

Vietnam Veterans Memorial. New York: Random House, 1987; rpt. Vintage Books, 1988.

Pastor, Robert A. *Condemned to Repetition: The United States and Nicaragua.* Princeton, New Jersey: Princeton University Press, 1987.

Patterson, Oscar, III. *The Vietnam Veteran and the Media: A Comparative Content Analysis of Media Coverage of the War and the Veteran 1968– 1973.* Doctoral Dissertation. Knoxville, Tennessee: University of Tennessee, 1982.

Peers, Lt. General W. R. *The My Lai Inquiry.* New York: W. W. Norton & Co., 1979.

Pendleton, Don. *War Against the Mafia,* Vol. 1 of *The Executioner.* Los Angeles: Pinnacle Books, 1969.

Peterson, Richard E., and John A. Bilorusky. *May 1970: The Campus Aftermath of Cambodia and Kent State.* Berkeley, California: Carnegie Commission on Higher Education, 1971.

Pick, Daniel. *War Machine: The Rationalization of Slaughter in the Modern Age.* New Haven, Connecticut, and London: Yale University Press, 1993.

Pollock, J. C. *Mission M.I.A.* New York: Crown Publishers, 1982.

Polner, Murray. *No Victory Parades: The Return of the Vietnam Veteran.* New York: Holt, Rinehart and Winston, 1971.

Powers, Thomas. *The War at Home: Vietnam and the American People, 1964–1968.* New York: Grossman, 1973.

Pratt, John Clark. *Vietnam Voices.* New York: Viking Penguin, 1984.

Rabe, David. *The Vietnam Plays,* Volume 1 *(The Basic Training of Pavlo Hummel; Sticks and Bones)* and Volume 2 *(Streamers; The Orphan).* New York: Grove Press, 1993.

Raskin, Marcus G., and Bernard B. Fall, eds. *The Viet-Nam Reader: Articles and Documents on American Foreign Policy and the Viet-Nam Crisis,* Revised Edition. New York: Vintage Books, 1967.

Reagan, Ronald. *A Time for Choosing: The Speeches of Ronald Reagan 1961–1982.* Chicago: Regnery Gateway, 1983.

Rogin, Michael Paul. *Ronald Reagan, the Movie.* Berkeley, California: University of California Press, 1987.

Rowe, John Carlos, and Rick Berg, eds. *The Vietnam War and American Culture.* New York: Columbia University Press, 1991.

Safer, Morley. *Flashbacks: On Returning to Vietnam.* New York: Random House, 1990.

Salisbury, Harrison E., ed. *Vietnam Reconsidered.* New York: Harper Torchbooks, 1984.

Santoli, Al. *Everything We Had.* New York: Random House, 1981.

———. *Leading the Way: How Vietnam Veterans Rebuilt the U.S. Military, An Oral History.* New York: Ballantine Books, 1993.

Sarf, Wayne Michael. *The Little Bighorn Campaign, March–September 1876.* Conshohocken, Pennsylvania: Combined Books, Inc., 1993.

Schell, Jonathan. *The Real War: The Classic Reporting on the Vietnam War, with a New Essay.* New York: Pantheon Books, 1987.

———. *The Time of Illusion.* New York: Vintage Books, 1976.

Schlesinger, Arthur M., Jr. *The Crisis of Confidence: Ideas, Power and Violence in America.* Boston: Houghton Mifflin, 1969.

Schoenhals, Kai P., and Richard A. Melanson. *Revolution and Intervention in Grenada: The New Jewel Movement, the United States, and the Caribbean.* Boulder, Colorado, and London: Westview Press, 1985.

Schudson, Michael. *The Power of News.* Cambridge, Massachusetts, and London: Harvard University Press, 1995.

———. *Watergate in American Memory: How We Remember, Forget, and Reconstruct the Past.* New York: Basic Books, 1992.

Scruggs, Jan C., and Joel L. Swerdlow. *To Heal a Nation: The Vietnam Veterans Memorial.* New York: Harper & Row, 1985.

Searle, William J., ed. *Search and Clear: Critical Responses to Selected Literature and Films of the Vietnam War.* Bowling Green, Ohio: Bowling Green State University Press, 1988.

Shafer, Michael D. *The Legacy: The Vietnam War in the American Imagination.* Boston: Beacon Press, 1990.

Shawcross, William. *Sideshow: Kissinger, Nixon, and the Destruction of Cambodia.* New York: Simon and Schuster, 1979; Revised Edition, 1987.

Shay, Jonathan. *Achilles in Vietnam: Combat Trauma and the Undoing of Character.* New York: Atheneum, 1994.

Sheehan, Neil. *A Bright Shining Lie: John Paul Vann and America in Vietnam.* New York: Random House, 1988.

Sigoloff, Marc. *The Films of the Seventies: A Filmography of American,*

British, and Canadian Films 1970–1979. Jefferson, North Carolina, and London: McFarland & Company, 1984.

Slotkin, Richard. *Gunfighter Nation: The Myth of the Frontier in Twentieth-Century America.* New York: Atheneum, 1992.

Small, Melvin, and William D. Hoover, eds. *Give Peace a Chance: Exploring the Vietnam Antiwar Movement.* Syracuse, New York: Syracuse University Press, 1992.

Smith, Julian. *Looking Away: Hollywood and Vietnam.* New York: Charles Scribner's Sons, 1975.

Sonnenberg, Stephen M., Arthur S. Blank, Jr., and John A. Talbott, eds. *The Trauma of War: Stress and Recovery in Viet Nam Veterans.* Washington, D.C.: American Psychiatric Press, 1985.

Starr, Paul, with James F. Henry and Raymond P. Bonner. *The Discarded Army: Veterans After Vietnam; The Nader Report on Vietnam Veterans and the Veterans Administration.* New York: Charterhouse, 1973.

Stoller, Robert J. *Observing the Erotic Imagination.* New Haven, Connecticut, and London: Yale University Press, 1985.

———. *Perversion: The Erotic Form of Hatred.* Washington, D.C.: American Psychiatric Press, 1986.

Stone, Oliver, and Richard Boyle. Platoon *and* Salvador: *The Original Screenplays.* New York: Vintage Books, 1987.

Tal, Kalí Jo. *Bearing Witness: The Literature of Trauma.* Doctoral Dissertation. New Haven, Connecticut: Yale University, 1991.

———. *Worlds of Hurt: Reading the Literatures of Trauma.* New York and Cambridge, England: Cambridge University Press, 1996.

Taylor, Ella. *Prime-Time Families: Television Culture in Postwar America.* Berkeley, California: University of California Press, 1989.

Taylor, Telford. *Nuremberg and Vietnam: An American Tragedy.* New York: Quadrangle, 1970; rpt. New York: Bantam Books, 1971.

Teed, Jack Hamilton. *The Killing Zone,* Vol. 1 of *Gunships.* New York: Zebra Books, Kensington Publishing Corp., 1981.

Terr, Lenore. *Unchained Memories: True Stories of Traumatic Memories, Lost and Found.* New York: Basic Books, 1994.

Terry, Wallace. *Bloods: An Oral History of the Vietnam War by Black Veterans.* New York: Random House, 1984.

Thomas, C. David, ed. *As Seen by Both Sides: American and Vietnamese*

Artists Look at the War. Boston: Indochina Arts Project and the William Joiner Foundation, 1991.

U.S. Department of State and U.S. Department of Defense. *Grenada: A Preliminary Report*. Washington, D.C.: Department of State and Department of Defense, December 16, 1983.

U.S. Directorate for Information Operations and Reports. *U.S. Casualties in Southeast Asia*. Washington, D.C.: Government Printing Office, 1986.

Van Deburg, William L. *New Day in Babylon: The Black Power Movement and American Culture, 1965–1975*. Chicago and London: University of Chicago Press, 1992.

Van Devanter, Lynda. *Home Before Morning: The Story of an Army Nurse in Vietnam*. New York: Warner Books, 1983.

Veninga, James F., and Harry A. Wilmer, eds. *Vietnam in Remission*. College Station, Texas: Texas A&M University Press, 1985.

Vietnam Veterans Against the War. *The Winter Soldier Investigation: An Inquiry into American War Crimes*. Boston: Beacon Press, 1972.

Wakefield, Dan. *Supernation at Peace And War: Being Certain Observations, Depositions, Testimonies, and Graffiti Gathered on a One-Man Fact-and-Fantasy-Finding Tour of the Most Powerful Nation in the World*. Boston: Little, Brown and Company, 1968.

Walker, Keith, ed. *A Piece of My Heart: The Stories of Twenty-Six American Women Who Served in Vietnam*. New York: Ballantine Books, 1985.

Walker, Mark Edward. *The Representation of the Vietnam Veteran in American Narrative Film*. Doctoral Dissertation. Evanston, Illinois: Northwestern University, 1989.

Waller, Willard. *The Veteran Comes Back*. New York: Dryden Press, 1944.

Walsh, Jeffrey, and James Aulich, eds. *Vietnam Images: War and Representation*. New York: St. Martin's Press, 1989.

Walzer, Michael. *Just and Unjust Wars: A Moral Argument with Historical Illustrations,* Second Edition. New York: Basic Books, 1992.

Webb, James. *Fields of Fire*. Englewood Cliffs, New Jersey: Prentice-Hall, 1978.

Wheeler, John. *Touched with Fire*. New York: Franklin Watts, 1984.

White, Theodore H. *The Making of the President 1972*. New York: Atheneum, 1973.

Williams, Reese, ed. *Unwinding the Vietnam War: From War into Peace.* Seattle, Washington: The Real Comet Press, 1987.

Williams, William Appleman, Thomas McCormick, Lloyd Gardner, and Walter LaFeber, eds. *America in Vietnam: A Documentary History.* New York: Anchor Books, 1985.

Wilson, Jim. *The Sons of Bardstown.* New York: Crown Publishers, 1994.

Witte, Brad S. *Posttraumatic Stress Disorder and Nightmares in Combat and Non-Combat Vietnam-Era Veterans.* Doctoral Dissertation. Boston: Boston University, 1989.

Wright, Lawrence. *In the New World: Growing Up with America from the Sixties to the Eighties.* New York: Vintage Books, 1989.

Wright, Stephen. *Meditations in Green.* New York: Charles Scribner's Sons, 1983.

Wyatt, Clarence R. *Paper Soldiers: The American Press and the Vietnam War.* Chicago and London: University of Chicago Press, 1995.

Yalom, Irvin D. *The Theory and Practice of Group Psychotherapy,* Second Edition. New York: Basic Books, 1975.

Young, Marilyn B. *The Vietnam Wars 1945–1990.* New York: HarperCollins, 1991.

Zaroulis, Nancy, and Gerald Sullivan. *Who Spoke Up? American Protest Against the War in Vietnam 1963–1975.* Garden City, New York: Doubleday, 1984.

FILMOGRAPHY

This list includes many of the most important feature films related to the war and its veterans, but by no means all. It does not include documentaries, but it does include films set in other eras (such as *MASH* or *Catch-22*) that reflect Vietnam War issues. It also includes films made for television. Unless otherwise noted, all films were produced in the United States. For a more complete filmography, including films made in Vietnam, see Malo and Williams, eds., *Vietnam War Films*.

(Title. Year released. Studio, production company, or television network. Director.)

Air America. 1990. Tri-Star. Roger Spottiswoode.

Alamo Bay. 1985. Tri-Star. Louis Malle.

Alice's Restaurant. 1969. United Artists. Arthur Penn.

American Graffiti. 1973. Universal. George Lucas.

Angels from Hell. 1968. Fanfare Film Productions. Bruce Kessler.

The Angry Breed. 1969. Commonwealth United. David Commons.

Apocalypse Now. 1979. Paramount. Francis Ford Coppola.

The A Team: Mexican Slayride. 1983. NBC-TV (made for television). Rod Holcomb.

Bat-*21. 1988. Tri-Star. Peter Markle.

Big Wednesday (a.k.a. *Summer of Innocence*). 1978. Warner Bros. John Milius.

Billy Jack. 1971. Warner Bros. T. C. Frank (alias Tom Laughlin).

Billy Jack Goes to Washington. 1977. Taylor–Laughlin. T. C. Frank (alias Tom Laughlin).

Birdy. 1984. Tri-Star. Alan Parker.

Black Sunday. 1977. Paramount. John Frankenheimer.

Blue Thunder. 1983. Columbia. John Badham.

The Born Losers. 1967. American International. T. C. Frank (alias Tom Laughlin).

Born on the Fourth of July. 1989. Universal. Oliver Stone.

The Boys in Company C. 1978. Golden Harvest (Hong Kong). Sidney Furie.

Braddock: Missing in Action III. 1988. Cannon. Aaron Norris.

Captive (a.k.a. *Two*). 1974. Colmar. Charles Trieschmann.

Casualties of War. 1989. Columbia. Brian De Palma.

Catch-22. 1970. Paramount. Mike Nichols.

Cease Fire. 1984. Cineworld Enterprises. David Nutter.

Charley Varrick. 1973. Universal. Don Siegel.

China Beach. 1988. ABC-TV (made for television). Rob Holcomb.

The Choirboys. 1977. Universal. Robert Aldrich.

Choose Me. 1984. Island Alive Productions. Alan Rudolph.

Chrome and Hot Leather. 1971. American International. Lee Frost.

Combat Shock. 1984. Troma. Buddy Giovinazzo.

Coming Home. 1978. United Artists. Hal Ashby.

The Crazy World of Julius Vrooder (a.k.a. *Vrooder's Hooch*). 1974. 20th Century-Fox. Arthur Hiller.

Cutter's Way. 1981. United Artists. Ivan Passer.

Death Before Dishonor. 1987. New World. Terry J. Leonard.

The Deer Hunter. 1978. Paramount. Michael Cimino.

Die Hard. 1988. 20th Century-Fox/Gordon Company/Silver Pictures. John McTiernan.

Die Hard 2. 1990. 20th Century-Fox/Gordon Company/Silver Pictures. Renny Harlin.

Die Hard with a Vengeance. 1995. Cinergi Productions/20th Century-Fox. John McTiernan.

The Dirty Dozen. 1967. MGM. Robert Aldrich.

Dirty Harry. 1971. Warner Bros./Malpaso. Donald Siegel.

Distant Thunder. 1988. Paramount. Rick Rosenthal.

Don't Cry, It's Only Thunder. 1982. Samuel Goldwyn Co. Peter Werner.

Dr. Strangelove or: How I Learned to Stop Worrying and Love the Bomb. 1964. Columbia (Great Britain). Stanley Kubrick.

Easy Rider. 1969. Columbia. Dennis Hopper.

84 Charlie MoPic. 1989. New Century/Vista. Patrick Duncan.

Electra Glide in Blue. 1973. United Artists. James William Guercio.

The Empire Strikes Back. 1980. 20th Century-Fox/Lucasfilm, Ltd. Irvin Kershner.

The Enforcer. 1976. Warner Bros. James Fargo.

Extreme Prejudice. 1987. Tri-Star. Walter Hill.

Firefox. 1982. Warner Bros. Clint Eastwood.

First Blood. 1982. Orion. Ted Kotcheff.

Flight of the Intruder. 1991. Paramount. John Milius.

The Forgotten. 1989. USA Network (made for television). James Keach.

Friendly Fire. 1979. ABC-TV (made for television). David Greene.

Full Metal Jacket. 1987. Paramount. Stanley Kubrick.

Gardens of Stone. 1987. Columbia. Francis Ford Coppola.

Good Guys Wear Black. 1977. Action One Film Partners. Ted Post.

Good Morning, Vietnam. 1987. Touchstone. Barry Levinson.

Go Tell the Spartans. 1978. Mar Vista Films. Ted Post.

The Green Berets. 1968. Warner Bros./Seven Arts. John Wayne and Ray Kellogg.

Hamburger Hill. 1987. RKO Pictures. John Irvin.

The Hanoi Hilton. 1987. Cannon. Lionel Chetwynd.

The Hard Ride. 1971. American International. Burt Topper.

Heartbreak Ridge. 1986. Warner Bros. Clint Eastwood.

Heroes. 1977. Universal. Jeremy Paul Kagan.

House. 1985. New World. Steve Miner.

In Country. 1989. Warner Bros. Norman Jewison.

The Indian Runner. 1991. MGM/UA. Sean Penn.

Indiana Jones and the Last Crusade. 1989. UIP/Paramount/Lucasfilm. Steven Spielberg.

Indiana Jones and the Temple of Doom. 1984. Paramount/Lucasfilm. Steven Spielberg.

In Love and War. 1987. NBC-TV (made for television). Paul Aaron.

Intimate Strangers. 1985. CBS-TV (made for television). Robert Ellis Miller.

The Iron Triangle. 1989. Scotti Brothers Pictures. Eric Weston.

Jackknife. 1989. Cineplex Odeon Films. David Jones.

Jacob's Ladder. 1990. Tri–Star/Carolco. Adrian Lyne.

JFK. 1991. Warner Bros. Oliver Stone.

Joe. 1970. Cannon. John G. Avildsen.

Johnny Got His Gun. Cinemation Industries. Dalton Trumbo.

Jud. 1971. Duque Films/Maron Films. Gunther Collins.

The Killing Fields. 1984. Warner Bros. (Great Britain). Roland Joffe.

Last Flight Out. 1990. NBC-TV (made for television). Larry Elikann.

Leatherface: Texas Chainsaw Massacre III. 1989. New Line Cinema. Jeff Burr.

Lethal Weapon. 1987. Warner Bros. Richard Donner.

Lethal Weapon 2. 1989. Warner Bros./Silver Pictures. Richard Donner.

Lethal Weapon 3. 1992. Warner Bros./Silver Pictures. Richard Donner.

Let's Get Harry. 1986. Tri–Star. Alan Smithee.

Limbo (a.k.a. *Women in Limbo)*. 1973. Universal. Mark Robson.

Little Big Man. 1970. 20th Century-Fox. Arthur Penn.

The Losers. 1970. Fanfare Film Productions. Jack Starrett.

Lost Command. 1966. Columbia. Mark Robson.

Magnum Force. 1973. Warner Bros./Malpaso. Ted Post.

Magnum, P.I.: Don't Eat the Snow in Hawaii. 1980. CBS-TV (made for television). Roger Young.

MASH. 1970. 20th Century-Fox. Robert Altman.

Medium Cool. 1969. Paramount. Haskell Wexler.

Missing in Action. 1984. Cannon. Joseph Zito.

Missing in Action 2—The Beginning. 1985. Cannon. Lance Hool.

More American Graffiti. 1979. Lucasfilm/Universal. B. W. L. Norton.

Mr. Majestyk. 1974. MGM/UA. Richard Fleischer.

My Old Man's Place (a.k.a. *Glory Boy)*. 1971. Cierwan Films. Edwin Sherin.

Night Wars. 1987. Warner Bros. David A. Prior.

Norwood. 1970. Paramount. Jack Haley, Jr.

O.C. and Stiggs. 1987. MGM. Robert Altman.

Off Limits. 1988. 20th Century-Fox. Christopher Crowe.

Operation C.I.A. (a.k.a. *Last Message from Saigon)*. 1965. Allied Artists. Christian Nyby.

The Park Is Mine. 1985. Ramble (made for television). Steven Hilliard Stern.

Platoon. 1986. Hemdale. Oliver Stone.

P.O.W. The Escape. 1986. Cannon. Gideon Amir.

Predator. 1987. 20th Century-Fox. John McTiernan.

Predator 2. 1990. 20th Century Fox/Lawrence. Stephen Hopkins.

Purple Hearts. 1984. Warner Bros. Sydney Furie.

The Quiet American. 1958. United Artists. Joseph L. Mankiewicz.

Raiders of the Lost Ark. 1981. Paramount/Lucasfilm. Steven Spielberg.

Rambo: First Blood Part II. 1985. Anabasis Investments, N.V. George P. Cosmatos.

Rambo III. 1988. Tri-Star. Peter Macdonald.

The Rescue. 1988. Touchstone. Ferdinand Fairfax.

Return of the Jedi. Lucasfilm, Ltd. 1983. Richard Marquand.

RoboCop. 1987. Rank/Orion. Paul Verhoeven.

RoboCop 2. 1990. Rank/Orion. Irvin Kershner.

RoboCop 3. 1993. Orion. Fred Dekker.

Rolling Thunder. 1977. American International. John Flynn.

A Rumor of War. 1980. Stonehenge/Charles Fries Prods. (made for television). Richard T. Heffron.

Saigon Commandos. 1988. Media Home Entertainment. Clark Henderson.

Salvador. 1986. Hemdale. Oliver Stone.

Satan's Sadists. 1969. Kennis–Frazer Films, Inc./Independent–International Pictures Corp. Al Adamson.

The Siege of Firebase Gloria. 1989. Eastern Film Management. Brian Trenchard-Smith.

Slaughterhouse-Five. Universal. 1972. George Roy Hill.

Soldier Blue. 1970. Avco/Embassy. Ralph Nelson.

Some Kind of Hero. 1981. Paramount. Michael Pressman.

Star Wars. 1977. 20th Century-Fox. George Lucas.

Steele Justice. 1987. Atlantic. Robert Boris.

The Stone Killer. 1973. Columbia. Michael Winner.

The Strawberry Statement. 1970. MGM. Stuart Hagmann.

Straw Dogs. 1971. ABC and Cinerama Releasing. Sam Peckinpah.

Streamers. 1983. Robert Altman/Nick J. Mileti. Robert Altman.

Taxi Driver. 1976. Columbia. Martin Scorsese.

The Terminator. 1984. Orion/Hemdale/Pacific Western. James Cameron.

The Terminator 2: Judgment Day. 1991. Guild/Carolco/Pacific Western/ Lightstorm. James Cameron.

The Texas Chainsaw Massacre. 1974. Vortex. Tobe Hooper.

The Texas Chainsaw Massacre 2. 1986. Cannon. Tobe Hooper.

To Heal a Nation. 1988. NBC-TV (made for television). Michael Pressman.

Top Gun. 1986. Paramount. Tony Scott.

Tour of Duty. 1987. CBS-TV (made for television). Bill L. Norton.

Tour of Duty II: Bravo Company. 1987–88. CBS-TV (made for television). Bruce Gray, Bill Norton, and Stephen L. Posey.

Tour of Duty III: The Hill. 1988. CBS-TV (made for television). Bill L. Norton and Robert Iscove.

Tracks. 1976. Rainbow Pictures. Henry Jaglom.

The Trial of Billy Jack. 1974. Taylor–Laughlin. Frank Laughlin (alias Tom Laughlin).

Twilight's Last Gleaming. 1977. Allied Artists (U.S.A. and Federal Republic of Germany). Robert Aldrich.

Twinkle, Twinkle, "Killer" Kane (a.k.a. *The Ninth Configuration).* 1979. ITC. William Peter Blatty.

The Ugly American. 1963. Universal. George H. Englund.

Uncommon Valor. 1983. Paramount. Ted Kotcheff.

Universal Soldier. 1992. Tri-Star. Roland Emmerich.

Vanishing Point. 1971. 20th Century-Fox. Richard C. Sarafian.

Vietnam Texas. 1990. Epic Productions. Robert Ginty.

The Visitors. 1972. United Artists. Elia Kazan.

The Walking Dead. 1995. Savoy Pictures/Price Entertainment/Jackson–McHenry. Preston A. Whitmore II.

Welcome Home. 1989. Columbia. Franklin J. Schaffner.

Welcome Home, Johnny Bristol. 1971. Cinema Center 100 (made for television). George McCowan.

Welcome Home, Soldier Boys. 1972. 20th Century-Fox. Richard Compton.

Who'll Stop the Rain (in Great Britain, *Dog Soldiers).* 1978. United Artists. Karel Reisz.

The Wild Bunch. 1969. Warner Bros./Seven Arts. Sam Peckinpah.

Year of the Dragon. 1985. Warner Bros. Michael Cimino.

INDEX

ABOUT THE
AUTHOR

FRED TURNER HAS BEEN A FREELANCE REPORTER and critic since 1986. His features have appeared in *The Progressive,* the *Chicago Tribune Sunday Magazine,* and the *Boston Phoenix.* He has taught at Harvard University's John F. Kennedy School of Government and at the Massachusetts Institute of Technology. He lives in La Jolla, California.